Experimental Filmmaking and Punk

Experimental Filmmaking and Punk

Feminist Audio Visual Culture in the 1970s and 1980s

Rachel Garfield

BLOOMSBURY ACADEMIC
LONDON • NEW YORK • OXFORD • NEW DELHI • SYDNEY

BLOOMSBURY ACADEMIC
Bloomsbury Publishing Plc
50 Bedford Square, London, WC1B 3DP, UK
1385 Broadway, New York, NY 10018, USA
29 Earlsfort Terrace, Dublin 2, Ireland

BLOOMSBURY, BLOOMSBURY ACADEMIC and the Diana logo are trademarks
of Bloomsbury Publishing Plc

First published in Great Britain 2022

Cover design: Charlotte Daniels
Cover Image: Poly Styrene of X-Ray Spex performing at Brixton Academy,
London, 14 September 1991.
(Photo © Ian Dickson/Redferns/Getty Images)

A catalogue record for this book is available from the British Library.

Library of Congress Cataloging-in-Publication Data
Names: Garfield, Rachel, author.
Title: Experimental filmmaking and punk : feminist audio visual culture
in the 1970s and 1980s / by Rachel Garfield.
Description: London ; New York : Bloomsbury Academic, 2021. |
Includes bibliographical references and index. |
Identifiers: LCCN 2021017620 (print) | LCCN 2021017621 (ebook) |
ISBN 9781788313995 (hardback) | ISBN 9781350244443 (paperback) |
ISBN 9781350197657 (epub) | ISBN 9781350197640 (pdf)
Subjects: LCSH: Women motion picture producers and directors. |
Women in the motion picture industry. | Feminism and motion pictures.
Classification: LCC PN1995.9.W6 G37 2021 (print) | LCC PN1995.9.W6
(ebook) | DDC 791.436/522–dc23
LC record available at https://lccn.loc.gov/2021017620
LC ebook record available at https://lccn.loc.gov/2021017621

ISBN: HB: 978-1-7883-1399-5
        PB: 978-1-3502-9308-3
        ePDF: 978-1-3501-9764-0
        eBook: 978-1-3501-9765-7

Typeset by Integra Software Solutions Pvt. Ltd.
Printed and bound in Great Britain

To find out more about our authors and books visit www.bloomsbury.com
and sign up for our newsletters.

*To my mother Adrienne Barbara Garfield, whose
brave rebellions did not win her the freedoms
I have known*

Contents

Illustrations

Acknowledgements

My thanks go to Nathan Abrams, Peggy Ahwesh, Wayne Atkinson, Betzy Bromberg, Mildred Burchett-Vass, Gavin Butt, Alison Butler, Jenny Chamarette, Abigail Child, Anna Coatman, Ben Cook, Kirsten Cooke, Anna Joy David, Vivienne Dick, the late Stephen Dwoskin, Lina Džuverović, Rose Eastwood at Sadie Coles, Will Fowler, Jane Gatehouse, Roberta Gilchrist, the University of Reading (RETF fund), Sally Goldman, Bette Gordon, Veidehi Hans, James Hellings, the late Janet Hodgson, Tessa Hughes-Freeland, Melanie Jackson, Amberley Jamieson at DACS, Amelia Jones, Ajay Khandelwal, Daniel Monk, Martina Mullaney, Lucia Nagib, Virginia Nimarkoh, Ruth Novaczek, the late David and Jenny Parsons, the late Anne Pennington, Charlotte Procter at LUX, Sarah Pucill, Irene Revell, Lucy Reynolds, Anne Robinson, Syd Shelton, Pam Skelton, Susan Stein, Linder Sterling, Juliet Steyn, Leslie Thornton, Isaac Timberlake, John Timberlake, Sarah Turner, Leon Wainwright and my two anonymous reviewers.

Preface

The place which an epoch occupies in the historical process is determined more forcefully from the analysis of its insignificant superficial manifestations than from the judgements of the epoch upon itself.

– Kracauer (1995: 50)

This book has been written in part to understand the trajectory of my own aesthetic as an artist and to reflect on what it is that draws me to certain kinds of work and not others. I will be writing about artists' moving image work as an aesthetic form, not merely as a political cipher, and the critique will flow from the work to the argument rather than formulating an argument from which I look for work to analyse. What this approach constitutes is a book that may not fulfil a seamless arc but one that at times shoots in different directions within the chapters, following the multi-layered and sometimes incommensurate effects of the works themselves. The fragmented nature of the book is built into the methodology and the theorization.[1] The fragmentation also forms a fundamental part of what I argue to be a strength in the artworks that I bring into the scope of this book. Another part of what situates this book is the realization that my experiences as a punk in the 1970s, my political bias and approach to art were intrinsically interwoven and that it had brought me to enjoy work that has been largely overlooked – and to wonder why: that is, why the work has been overlooked, and why I was drawn to this kind of work.

Punk can mean many things to many people. In relation to my own life, it was an opportunity that wrenched me out of the confines of a normative and overdetermined future as a daughter of orthodox Jewish parents and propelled me towards being an artist. At that time I dimly saw that the future for me was for a 'nice Jewish husband' as the cliché goes – those three terms of course running together – and with it the expectation of children, and in the meantime, a place-holding job as a secretary. My response was to run the other way in anger and dismay. At some point I realized that my desires were more complex, more ambitious and more intellectual. So in turning towards punk, I was turning towards politics formed through the battles with Margaret Thatcher in the 1980s, second wave feminism and an aggressive 'fuck you' to any suggestion of pleasing others.

Of all that I have been certain for quite some time. How those influences became a defining feature in my predilection for montage, for lo-fi and awkwardly put-together works is the quest that fuels this book, which is not, in fact, a book about punk music as such but about a particular trajectory of women experimental filmmakers who have an approach that I am interrogating in terms of possible antecedents, contexts and interrelationships. In this book, punk is used as a paradigmatic device, not as a direct influence, nor will it chronicle artists who themselves focus on punk music itself.

My intention here is to develop an argument for a tendency within filmmaking that eschews the model of certain kinds of virtuosity of form as the key indication of a good film. Within the technology-based forms of art, technical expertise/skill is a contested site of production that goes to the heart of what the role of an artist is. The materiality of the technology has also been an important focus in avant-garde film that this book stands apart from. Instead, the work I discuss is grounded in experience and questions of provisionality: of subjectivity, of placehood and of status. The commonalities of the works documented in this book are constituted through the connections between a fragmented visuality and the absence of certainty or entitlement: this work offers its own virtuosity but one that confounds the normative signs of it. In the historical moment that I identify through the trajectory in this book, the idea of a female subjectivity emerged as a vital and valid form of practice. Without wishing to essentialize gender, there is arguably a gendered relationship to the world and these women were edging towards an idea of what that might mean – out of the formalist and minimalist paradigms of their emergence – focusing on a range of approaches and entry points for the viewer that encompasses the impact of second wave feminism or its detractions; the importance of Dada and the Weimar Republic; the development of multiculturalism; collage and the fragment within feminist art. My approach is not chronological but rather thematic, and the themes turn on specific approaches such as do-it-yourself, disintegration and hysteria. And while there is theoretical underpinning and use of interviews, the book aims to interrogate the terms it uses through the visual analysis of the art/film-video works because it is through the experience of watching the films themselves that my thesis has been formed.

Women are key to my narrative because the moments of empowerment we see in punk were so dependent on a different model of womanhood that has had a lasting impact.[2] Women noticed their subservient role within music as Poly Styrene, one of the key trailblazers said, 'There was this real aristo-rock establishment and the only way you could get in as a girl was as a groupie' (Bell 2019: 51). And they went for change. To seize an affirmative sense of being, they had to establish a womanhood through its assertive confrontational modes of presentation and representation, which itself changed the conditions of reception, the terms of cultural debate and, of course, changed the terms of art production, so what we see and what I describe is women discovering a way to speak. Many of the women in this book were part of a music scene, were in bands themselves or showed their films with bands. They were fans of punk while engaging with it as musicians and artists, thus the progression of punk and post-punk is an integral part of the art I describe; even for those artists who did not engage with punk music itself, their work was part of the fallout.

Notes

1   The book was begun in 2015 and has taken over five years to write in between acute family health issues and caring responsibilities, full-time teaching, a Head of Department role, childcare, a funded research project on the filmmaker Stephen Dwoskin and a pandemic.

2   Just as genderqueer was such a driver for the New Romantic music scene that was to follow punk. Furthermore, use of the term 'woman' follows the discourses of the period in which the focus of the book inhabits rather than the more recent and correct problematization of the male/female binary categorizations.

Introduction

The history of punk is a history of living memory and of fandom. It is a history of positioning and self-positioning, often in relation to an original moment. There are advantages to being a fan, as Catherine Grant and Kate Random Love argue: 'fandom has a fit with many artistic works and methods that embrace the excessive, the deviant, the wilful and the overblown. Importantly this approach can become a political or queered practice, one where not fitting in is taken as a starting point to imagine something or someone, somewhere else' (Grant and Love 2019: 2). In that sense this book is written by a fan about fans; however, my focus is not to do with authenticity nor an originary moment but about the fallout and its effects. Fandom, and popular music studies, including punk studies, is full of those wanting to situate themselves at the heart of the various movements. In fact, according to Greg Taylor (Taylor 1999), the film critic as a figure in the United States started as merely fans of cinema who were completely outside the mainstream of the art world. What would become film criticism was started by enthusiasts writing appreciations of films they had seen as a way of looking for an alternative modernism than that of abstract expressionism (Taylor 1999: ix). Taylor's book delineates the trajectory from the amateur critic through to the 'specialist' theorizing gatekeeper that would echo the arc in the UK from the early Film Makers Co-Op, established in 1966, and their 'anyone can show' policy borrowed from the New York Film Makers Co-Op, to the point where women left the co-op in order to set up the organizations Cinenova and Circles for the distribution of womens' films. Similarly, in the United States, Lauren Rabinovitz (1991) eloquently describes the shift from the NY Film Makers Co-Op, which was established in 1962 equally by Jonas Mekas and Shirley Clarke, to Anthology Archives, which was established in 1970 without Clarke even knowing and from whose collection her work was excluded (Rabinovitz 1991: 176).[1] So the amateur outsider and the critical gatekeeper can be two sides of the same coin, where often 'he' can put himself in the position of the one who establishes a special knowledge and becomes the trendsetter who knows the most about this obscurantist mode of production. This is often a feature of marginal forms where the enthusiast is the champion. This is not my mode of address or my aim so I don't engage with a chronological race of who did what first, but instead aim to situate these women as a loose conceptual milieu – even for those who did not know each other personally.

My own approach is also different from how popular culture often characterizes punk and post-punk – as anti-establishment, and as a sub-sector of the rock and roll lifestyle, as mostly 'bad boy' or sometimes 'bad girl', as an anti-bourgeois, anti-suburban form of representation. This more normative perspective can be found in recent books that aim to situate the term 'punk' within a film genre such as the anthology *New Punk Cinema*, edited by Nicholas Rombes (2005). I make a distinction despite some similarities to what I discuss in this book such as a DIY approach or the general tendency to handheld camera:

> what links new punk films and directors together is a do-it-yourself sensibility, an almost romantic notion that anyone can create something that matters, a troubled desire for and yet a suspicion of the authentic and the Real, an approach to film-making that foregrounds the medium of film itself, and an interest in simplicity which, ironically[,] allows for great freedom and experimentation.
>
> (Rombes 2005: 12)

However, my own book makes a very different claim: Rombes focuses his approach and intention on the ways in which punk has influenced a new auteur cinema that uses cinema distribution made more possible through digital media. My own interest is primarily looking at artists and filmmakers whom I would contextualize through the histories of experimental or underground film by artists who were often trained in art schools. Ultimately what motivates this book is the contemplation of an underrepresented group that does not cohere around a genre but rather 'the more subtle qualities of tone and mood' (Schrader in Rombes 2005: 4).[2] The artists I bring into the umbrella of punk allow me to think about work that has informed my own aesthetic through a similar convergence of punk, feminism and experimental film – all of which touched my life at formative moments of the 1970s and 1980s.

With this in mind, the book does not reflect on punk music directly and is not aiming to situate punk as a reinforcement of some notional authentic moment nor as nostalgia. The work focused on is less to do with lifestyle and more to do with film form. The ubiquitous urban grunge and edginess is often present – for the expectations of punk – but as an effect of the life lived not as the focus in itself, which is why my attention is not on No Wave film per se. The unspoken hinterland of the films I discuss is bound up with what is at stake in art practice, in different forms of art practice. It is a form that takes an experiential journey into subjectivity and takes a chance on what it finds in an open-ended kind of way.

The filmwork that I discuss in this book and particularly those that I write about in the earlier chapters and then expand upon through different frameworks are bound up with two factors: the end of the post-war contract and the deadening horizon of the bomb. From the vantage point of today, during the post-war era art was seen as an important, instrumentalizing force, and while popular culture had had a relationship with modernity and the lexicon of art practice at different points such as The Ashcan School in the United States or Pop, there was still the assumption of a transformative process that the wider public could partake in through viewing the art. This was set alongside the positioning of art within a discourse of its commodification. Film was part of an ongoing battle between the idea of art as an edifying purposeful practice in the service of social transformation or at least of social mobility – which was an idea that dominated the post-war Anglophone world – and art in the service of the bourgeoisie and the hegemony – as set out within this framework of thinking. Much of the heated warfare within film, as with much twentieth-century art, was to do with what seemed to be at stake in art as a way of expediting political change.

Duncan Reekie (2007) focuses on the distinction between the avant garde and the underground. Reekie was a key voice in the UK underground film of the 1990s and co-organized the regular and popular Exploding Cinema nights in London that saw itself as continuing a kind of punk underground. The split between avant garde and underground also characterizes debates with the art film world about the kinds of art to make, each looking in different directions with similar aims, and in some ways represents the embrace or rejection of the technological changes that Franco 'Bifo' Berardi (2017: 79) points out in complex ways to do with access to funding in order to be able to work with the latest technologies.

Technology apart, the significant and often fraught debates to do with emphasis on form and/or subject matter, in all their differences and interconnectedness, are, according to Reekie, to do with an ongoing battle of intentionality. Reekie aligns this difference with class and the ways in which class interacts with revolutionary politics and the working class or popular culture. Art production as an integral part of fomenting a radical transformation in society has been taught in art schools in a particular way since conceptualism. As Reekie explains, transformation can be multifarious and take different forms. The work of the 1970s and 1980s that I write about eschewed the minimalist interrogation of terms associated with post-conceptual practices opting for a tradition more akin with the traditions of the underground rather than the conceptualism of the avant garde. The post-conceptual moment that has dominated in lens-based work over the last few decades is in itself at odds with the work I am discussing here (Osborne 2013), and this is despite moments of support for narrative autobiographically focused work particularly by and with women (Elwes 2004: 40, Payne 2015: 132) – but this work has been elided even in recent accounts of experimental film (Payne 2015: 136). Alison Butler argues as recently as 2011 that women's cinema 'is not "at home" in any of the host cinematic or national discourses it inhabits' (2011: 22) as part of the problem producing the ongoing elisions. She has helpfully suggested an analogous 'minor cinema' similar to the minor literature as derived from Deleuze and Guattari's observations of the writer Franz Kafka. In many ways, like Tom Gunning's use, it fits very well, except that it can be too easily dismissed or misunderstood as an opposition to the 'major' cinema of men despite its *détournement*.[3]

As I have already stated, my main focus in this book is not restricted to investigate punk as a musical phenomenon, nor to define punk film as a sub-genre, but instead to analyse and situate the aesthetic and intellectual ambition of a range of women filmmakers operating during the 1970s and 1980s with punk as a contextualizing scaffold. I will argue that the kind of aspiration that musicians such as Poly Styrene and The Slits portrayed has a legacy and influence in the attitude of these women filmmakers that it is timely to address and that moments, such as the *Top of The Pops* debut of Poly Styrene, marked the emergence of a new female subjectivity that was picked up and followed through by these filmmakers. The ground had been prepared by second wave feminism but punk delivered a strident visual example of what could be possible and an alternative way forward outside the serious earnestness of the political realm. These women did not necessarily identify as feminist – certainly the punks often did not at the time (Whitman in Sebestyen 1988: 27). Nonetheless, the punk of women such as Poly Styrene, with her retro clothes of clashing colours, her shouty voice and artlessly enthusiastic dance, was an affirmative negation of the normative modes of femininity. Where femininity demanded grace and beauty, punk was a celebration of its failure. Such erstwhile versions of femininity were ditched in favour of an awkward female youth as a lived relationship with the world using an aggressive camp as cipher against middlebrow expectations of what it was to be a woman.

> There was a part of the women's movement at the time that thought, 'Oh well you can create something called the women's literature', which they still teach today: women's literature or women's studies. We were not like that. We thought it was important to take what existed in the culture and turn it around and make people see it in a different way; be subversive, if you will.
>
> (Longworth 2009)

Punk femininity was noticed and caught the attention of a generation. Arguably their visual presence – the very thing that *Top of the Pops* cameras found confusing and unsettling – was the leaven of deeper confrontations that had developed over the preceding decades around gender roles, reflected through key texts such as Betty Friedan's *The Feminine Mystique* (1963) and Shulamith Firestone's *The Dialectic of Sex* (1970). Within the space of those interceding seven years, Friedan's initial revelations around the psychological repression of housewives had been superseded by Firestone's insistence on the need to challenge the very organization of nature. The notion of being 'un-natural' was a frequent reactionary epithet thrown at punk women who rejected 'pretty' or 'alluring' in favour of a belligerence that spoke power and pride in their nonconformist body types (O'Brien in Sabin 1999: 191). Many of the filmmakers discussed here emerged at the time that a heady mix of punk and second wave feminism was taking hold. The relationship between these areas was thus constitutive.

The artists that I will be writing about and that scatter across the various chapters are Vivienne Dick, Ruth Novaczek, Bette Gordon, Peggy Ahwesh, Sandra Lahire, Sankofa, Anne Robinson, Betzy Bromberg, Leslie Thornton, Tessa Hughes Freeland, Abigail Child and Susan Stein. Very little of the work in this book has previously been written about to any extent. The reasons for this, I would argue, are firstly, patriarchy, which buries women in art historical terms, even while sometimes they are celebrated in life. Secondly, these artists have been sidelined by anterior discussions borne out of a different time, discussions bound up with expectations of avant-gardism and a focus on concerns with reductive formalism within modernism that in itself could be argued, and indeed was, to be a form of patriarchal power acting that serves to exclude women practitioners (Pollock and Parker 1981). The 'winners' in the argument have owned the dominant narrative since the 1980s, but with time, few remember what was at stake in the argument in the first place. However, the mechanisms of avant-gardism and patriarchy are connected through the policing of categories as identified by Linda Nochlin, for example, in her landmark essay *Why Have There Been No Great Women Artists* (1971), discussed in Chapter 3. Furthermore, even the tropes of patriarchy have scaffolded expectations of what artworks women make that would eschew such approaches like the excesses of the underground and its libertarian feminism. The overwhelming canonization of the minimalist approach of Mary Kelly at the expense of many other artists demonstrates that the proscription of forms other than those dominated by patriarchy is still at play. Put another way, in order to be taken seriously, women have to adopt the forms of what is deemed serious art at the time of making.

To be clear, despite the substantial popular outrage at the ICA exhibition (1976) of Kelly's *Post-Partum Document* (1973–9), because of the substance of the work in terms of subject matter, showing the more visceral side of her life (Frascina 2009: 297), Kelly's form and methodology are clearly signposted within the emerging paradigm of the time. Kelly was in a Lacanian reading group with Laura Mulvey and Yve Lomax and used a mixture of Lacanian theory, Althussarian anti-humanist structuralism and Brechtian *distanciation* as the intellectual framework for the work to deconstruct the problematic of motherhood and embargo the image of women. These theories that underpin the methodology of the artwork put it squarely within the 'canon' of conceptualism. Because Kelly's innovation is to do with subject matter rather than form, the work is more easily placed. It is in some ways subversively generative, however; as Lauren Rabinowitz puts it, 'Art is a language in these terms of representations and sign systems as well as a cultural, ideological practice. As such, it constitutes a discourse by which power relations are sustained on several cultural levels, and it reproduces those relations in language and in images' (Rabinovitz 1991: 5).

Thus the relative sidelining of art by women who use their body and their biography through their emotions rather than an obvious theoretical framework within art historical discourse is axiomatic of the proposition that conceptualist deconstructive forms are the only form of critique and the only work to be taken seriously. This idea therefore renders *Post-Partum Document* the *Ur* feminist work. *Post-Partum Document* is a significant work that deserves to be remembered as a key and influential work. However, this positioning – rather than the work itself – is at the expense of other forms within feminist practices that do not subscribe to the post-conceptual trajectory and paradigm that this work foreshadows. One example of the elision of other practices might be Faith Ringgold, who celebrated and politicized her cultural background through painting and incorporating folk narrative quilts into her art practice. Another example might be Carolee Schneemann, who made that very point about the sidelining of certain art forms succinctly with her foundational work *Interior Scroll* (1975). Famously, Schneemann, who also made experimental films, performs on a table. After reading from a book she pulls a scroll out of her vagina, on which is written a conversation stating,

I met a Happy Man/A structural filmmaker/ – but don't call me that, its something else I do – /He said/we are fond of you you are charming/but don't ask us to look at your films/we cannot/there are certain films we cannot look at: The personal clutter/the persistence of feelings/the hand-touch sensibility/the diaristic indulgence/the painterly mess/the dense gestalt/the primitive technique… He said/you can do as I do/take one clear process follow/its strictest implications intellectually/establish a system of/ permutations establish/their visual set.

(from Jones 1998: 3)

This excerpt from Schneemann's 'interior scroll' is not as well known as the performance itself but goes to the heart of the dichotomy in this book of a gendered approach to the world, exemplified through filmmaking. Furthermore the fact that the text that Schneemann cites on the scroll is not better known and discussed, in itself, speaks to the lack of understanding of the role of structuralist film in performing patriarchy.

Art that focusses on the body and subjectivity by artists such as Carolee Schneemann, Ana Mendiata, Lynn Hershman Leeson and Eleanor Antin in the United States or Alexis Hunter or The Hackney Flashers in the United Kingdom is currently going through an art historical reclamation, possibly due to the persistent championing of a few feminist art historians such as Amelia Jones, Rebecca Schneider and others as well as the new feminist turn heralded by the large survey exhibition *Wack! Art and the Feminist Revolution* (2007), at the Museum of Contemporary Art in Los Angeles. Until the last few years these artists were not much discussed, nor were they included in the big survey shows of the period to the extent that Mary Kelly was, but were set within a specific enclave of feminist art. Not to embellish the point, but the fact that Kelly's work transcended this ghettoization is due to the way her work traversed feminist subject matter with conceptualist language and its methodology of deconstructing the terms of the language of art. The artist filmmakers in this book have also similarly been elided for making work which involves, as the scroll says, 'The personal clutter/the persistence of feelings/the hand-touch sensibility/the diaristic indulgence/the painterly mess/the dense gestalt/the primitive technique' (Jones 1998: 3).

However, the discussions of the 1980s that led to the dominance of contemporary forms that exclude the 'punk films' that I write about have an even longer history in the debates between Ernst Bloch and Georg Lukács on the revolutionary or counter-revolutionary effect of expressionism or realism. The contemporary prevalence of long-look video work is bound up with the neorealism that André Bazin advocated. Bazin argued that the long shot set up a relationship with history through realism. His argument of letting the camera roll without the interference of the edit was to do with seeing more rather than having the viewer's thinking directed through the editing. In seeing more, more real life will be seen. While naturalism has a relationship with realism, it diverges through a character-driven romantic expressivity. This dialogue with naturalism goes back to the literary debates between realism and naturalism; between the so-called whimsy and essentialism of *Don Quixote* or *Ulysses* and the hard-hitting realism of Ibsen's plays such as *The Seagull*. Naturalism in this binary evolves to a mannerist whimsical essentialism as opposed to a structural materialist approach that drives the viewer towards revolution in the contingent and transformative relationship with history, or so the argument goes.

The notion of a transformative intention in art derived from Europe is intrinsically tied to Christianity, moral edification and more recently to the nineteenth-century moral crusades of those such as the influential Matthew Arnold, who saw culture as an edifying force for good (Drucker 2006: 53; Williams 1961: 19–56). The trajectory of expectations in the transformative properties of art can again be seen in the late twentieth century in second wave feminist discourses and practices of art in various ways such as The Hackney Flasher's *Who's Holding the Baby* (1978), which argued explicitly for state childcare, or Martha Rosler's *Semiotics of the Kitchen* (1975), which implicitly critiqued women's role as provider of cooking in the home. A primary development that was ubiquitous was to make art that critiqued the representation of women, and with some artists, particularly Mary Kelly, there was an advocacy for a full proscription of the image of women in art. This was, as is always the case, a contested site of discourse – however, one with persistence legacies of expectation for art production. These lineages of thinking reveal the deeper flows of approaches to art and what becomes the paradigm in any age. So while playing with the idea of popular culture, the aspirations of edification, political proselytizing and class mobility have commonly been underlying assumptions of much art practice. Political or social transformation has certainly been a focusing factor on the developing formation of contemporary art school training and art production in the late twentieth century – but not that of punk. Edification has no place in punk, at least not as an abstraction.[4] On the contrary punk revelled in its working-class and messy affinities – if not always actuality – and relationships, and it did so by committing to a do-it-yourself mode of production that I focus on in Chapter 1. The politics of punk, such as it was, was one of finding a voice in what was for these artists a disenfranchised world.

However, this is not just about class derivation either, as the class background of many punks – and filmmakers – is a moot point. Nor is it to do with whether punk was a working-class movement or not but more to do with how the presumption that punk as a working-class phenomenon freed women – and working-class people – from the expectations and mores of the middle-class world, even when it was an ersatz working-class pretension. It also freed working-class people, to some extent, from the tyranny of having to adopt a middle-class accent and conventions to progress intellectually or economically, unlike the hippy movement, which was at heart a middle-class defiance. While I do not want to overplay the wholesale escape from the effects of class conformity in the punk narrative, it certainly freed women from certain expectations that allowed the space to explore alternative forms of femininity than the beautiful wife. The proponents of punk, even in all their multifarious expectations and manifestations, were not, on the whole, interested in changing the world in a programmatic way or even working towards a specific vision. Punk, as I argue it, was more a vehicle for an experiential expression of itself – a desire for a psychic space one could call one's own that had a particular force and impetus for women. The works analysed in this book are therefore more a manifestation of immanent critique grounded in lived experience than an example of Kantian transcendence.

In the end, 1970s punk has to be seen as the last gasp of an oppositional modernism that had a long tail into the 1980s and beyond. It was a pivotal moment of transition – post-Vietnam and pre-Reagan – 'bearing both the traces of 1960s radicalism and a pre-AIDS sense of sexual liberation' (Dika 2012: xv). This was before the culture wars of the 1980s, which was a time when the instrumentalization and institutionalization of art and soft power again became normative in the art world. The art world at this time grew exponentially supported by big money that, in turn, saw a proliferation of biennales and its attendant culture with huge investment behind it both constituting and supporting the augmentation of its use in global soft power. The new biennale culture required a kind of ambition and professionalism in art that has become the normative expectation.[5]

In the UK context it was felt also – for while the Arts Council funding in the 1980s was largely still intact, the sense of an end of a period was palpable. Nonetheless these artist filmmakers who were situated in the UK in the 1970s and 1980s made their work largely outside of the art world. After leaving art school, indeed those who went to art school, they continued to operate – in terms of the narratives of history – around a few institutions such as the London Film Makers Co-Op and Anthology Film Archives in New York. Institutions set up by women such as Circles or Cinenova in London were very much in the margins of the experimental film world, which was itself dominated by the theorized position of structuralism.

Of course, these debates are over thirty years old and have developed today into something unrecognizable in the changing conditions of art practice, the political world of today and several generations of debate, yet something of these arguments remain in residual assumptions of what is at stake in art and what constitutes worthwhile art to be made, celebrated and/or supported. Certainly, the assumption that work about 'the self' is indulgent and solipsistic still persists in some quarters. Despite the latest resurgences of interest in identity politics and the demands of feminists and people of colour in the last few years, the legitimacy of the art made by feminists, the gay communities and people of colour still needs to be repeatedly argued for in the histories of art.

The wider contextualizing motif, one that weaves through this book, is to do with a social, political and existential moment of which attitudes towards class had a part to play. This was at a time when the narratives of class, which had been generally accepted as an organizing principle in the UK, were being broken down in hegemonic quarters. The assault on this way of describing society was partly because of the erosion of the concept of the working class as the driver of social change in favour of Margaret Thatcher's famous soundbite from 1987 'there is no society'. This catchy slogan was merely a front for a profound ideological shift towards a society where the expectation is that it is constituted through individuals and families wanting to make life better for themselves. This was not helped by the fashion of the time for academic breakdowns of class becoming more technocratic forecasts rather than socially engaged propositions (Savage 2016).

The 1970s was a defining decade of political transformation and pivotal in generating the world we live in today. It is often described as a decade of negation. A key example would be the strikes of 1974 as instrumental in developing Thatcher's plans towards head-on opposition of the unions in the 1980s. The 1970s was also the first decade after the Second World War where the expectation of living standards in the UK was that of collapse, and as the

1970s wore on, more and more people agreed that they were facing a sharp fall in their standard of living (Beckett 2009: 176).[6] As the 1980s came in, there was, in addition, the deadening hand of the Irish troubles in the UK and effects of the Cold War, where the fear of a future of destruction and nuclear Holocaust was ever on the horizon and infused the aesthetic of that generation. The effect this context had on much art was towards a seriousness of intent and imagery fuelled by a preponderance of politics.

Unsurprisingly the downturn in economic growth also saw a rise in racist activity. The early 1970s was a time when the National Front was battling with the Liberals for third place amongst the main parties behind Labour and the Conservatives (Worley 2013: 606–36). By contrast and of course, in a dialectical tension, it was also a decade that saw the coming of age of the post-war/post-colonial generation of immigrants who began to impact significantly on the UK and how it saw itself. Paul Gilroy identifies the drift in left activism from anti-fascism to anti-racism (Gilroy, 1991). This drift is part of a long, slow movement away from the discourses of class towards the primacy of identity politics and into the faith-based delineations that have been the focus since the attack on the World Trade Centre in 2001.

Of course, mass immigration is not new to the UK. Surveys of newspaper reportage since the 1850s would reveal a residual language that is invoked by the media at every new wave of immigration representing a continuous attack on people coming to the UK in each generation, of which the recent Brexit vote of 2016 is one such move. In the post-war era, changes in the political landscape of the world and, importantly, newly awarded independence of large parts of the world that had been colonized by the UK had resulted in relatively focused immigration in the 1950s from the Caribbean. In the early 1970s this was supplemented in part by East African Asians expelled from Uganda.[7] As was identified by Paul Gilroy and Dick Hebdige, punk music played a key role in the integration of anti-racist politics in the 1970s. As I argue in Chapter 2, just as feminism and race politics were bound together through an emancipatory outlook in the 1960s, so in the UK feminism, punk and multiculturalism also were interlinked in a way that produced new approaches to filmmaking. This is where multiculturalism can be seen as an emancipating movement, not one necessarily tied to class politics, as with classical avant-garde aspiration.

Chapters 3 and 4, like Chapter 2, develop and add nuance to a strand in punk that was identified early on. The legitimacy of punk was in some ways established by Greil Marcus in his landmark book *Lipstick Traces* (1990), which made a case for a lineage of punk. His book posited and developed the obvious historical links that went back to Dada and the Weimar period, back to artists like Hannah Höch and Claude Cahun, artists who pioneered photomontage and a heterogeneous approach to the image. I develop this thinking forwards from the Weimar period via punk to artist filmmakers like Bette Gordon, Vivienne Dick and Abigail Child. It is no accident I argue that what links punk and Dada is Siegfried Kracauer's reading of the mass ornament and the Tiller girls. The Tiller Girls were factory workers from Lancashire. Having been made redundant from the factories, they got work as part of a dance troupe who made visual effects on the stage and cinema by using their limbs in unison in such a way as they created the effect of a mechanical system of movement. In this way they were both critiquing the loss of self and the system that removed them from the workforce towards a gesture of that workforce: as a sublimation of self for the pleasure of the viewer. As I describe in Chapter 4, this moment carried analogies with post-industrial Britain during the key period of the shift from an industrial nation to a service-based nation in the 1970s and 1980s, the pivotal moment for art as described in this book.

The re-emergence of an approach from Dada identified at the time as a close precursor to punk could be seen as the same event or entity that nonetheless is transformed in a new context of a different period or epoch. Where Dada is widely accepted to be a response to the First World War, the Manhattan-based No Wave group of filmmakers, whose work was purposefully violent and lo-fi, could be seen to be articulating a response contextualized through the period of the early 1970s, of a bankrupt New York City where decrepitude and poverty were the urban norm and social care was being rolled back. In the UK, punk could equally be seen as the end of the post-war moment of expectations of economic growth and in both locations reeling from the oil crash of Autumn/Winter 1973/74 (Beckett 2009, p 129). The contingency of this specific moment of the 1970s can thus be seen in operation here as a moment of convergence of the end of modernity; the end of the post-war contract and the end of the economic expansion progressed through the political vision of the Keynesian programme in the UK. The claim from the No Wavers was that of the end of belief in the project of social mobility and its corollary of art as an edifying and transformative cipher. As we know, this claim did not mark the end of the expectations of transformation which persists. However, this new moment of disintegration and reinvention of society mores in the 1970s that erupted through punk and No Wave away from the post-war contract required new forms of visual agency from the artist that are still being played out today by artists such as Martine Syms and Arthur Jafa.

Taking the premise of Siegfried Kracauer, that '[t]he position that an epoch occupies in the historical process can be determined more strikingly from an analysis of its inconspicuous surface-level expressions than from that epoch's judgments about itself' (Kracauer 1995: 75), this book, particularly in Chapters 4 and 5, reflects through Kracauer on the ways in which the convergence of the perception of a broken-down society impacted on or produced artworks that forcefully presented the cracks in the system as a way of re-inventing the form. Kracauer's ideas are an integral part of the sediment of this book in his mix of Frankfurt school Marxism and phenomenological leanings, both of which find affinities with the kinds of imagery and concerns that are still overlooked in art more often than not. Furthermore his belief in the primacy of film as a productive source of critical ambivalence through experience and subjectivity makes his thinking a prime focus for reflection on the approach of the artists in this volume (Kracauer 1960: xi). Kracauer's argument was that popular culture holds social truths which not only reveal the operations of capitalism through their production but also give out pleasure and provide narratives through which we understand and anchor our lives and through which we re-interpret our reality. This is an approach closer to the later Foucauldian idea of power and popular culture than one which opposes popular culture as merely a doping mechanism that exerts control. It problematizes the alienation of the working classes and engages with the dirty stuff of life as lived rather than the noble aspirations of edification. The mass ornament, he argues, has more social relevance than 'artistic productions which cultivate outdated noble sentiments in obsolete forms' (Kracauer 1995: 79). This dichotomy can be seen to echo my arguments in relation to the orthodoxies of Greenbergian modernism that sought to interrogate the world through the particularities of material intrinsic to the form – that dominated, and to some extent still dominate, moving image work. Kracauer was against the instrumentalization of film because he saw it as a reductive and impoverished way of understanding film, arguing that it drew in all elements of materiality into a deeper experience for the viewer. He was the first writer to really take on the idea of reception and the importance of how the viewer took on filmwork in the viewing. Unlike Brecht and possibly Adorno, he saw popular culture as intrinsic to the epoch and a sign of the condition of the masses to be taken on board not to be judged and changed. It is a symptom not a cause. He continues to defend the importance of working with popular culture, and unlike Benjamin and Adorno, he didn't separate himself from the masses but considered himself as one of them, part of the emergent hegemony of salaried classes.

> Educated people – who are never entirely absent – have taken offence at the emergence of the Tiller Girls and the stadium images. They judge anything that entertains the crowd to be a distraction of that crowd. But despite what they think, the aesthetic pleasure gained from ornamental mass movement is legitimate. Such movements are in fact among the rare creations of the age that bestows form upon a given material. The masses organized in these movements come from offices and factories; the formal principle according to which they are moulded determines them in reality as well.
>
> (Kracauer 1995: 79)

In fact while the work arising out of the punk moment that I discuss in this volume is neither engaged in high culture nor really popular culture, it arises from a negation of both. Neither side of the high/low binary serves its interests, aiming instead to find another form in expressing, often simultaneously the negation of desire and the desiring or desired image. Desire in the films is often derived from both the virtuosity of late modernism and the pleasure of popular culture offered. If Boris Groys' proposition is true that each image is merely 'an example of the potentially infinite variety of images' that operates in the gap between what is the 'formal equality' and 'the factual inequality' of artworks (Groys 2008: 14), then the works that I look at were probably among the last works that operated in a time that saw itself as struggle for legitimacy.

In 1978 a song called *The Day the World Turned Dayglo* was aired on *Top of the Pops*. As I have described, against the political backdrop of economic downturn, nuclear threat propagated by the high point of the Cold War and the IRA – and fuelled by all these factors – was the emergence of punk rock. Punk was as much about an image as it was to do with music. In fact for most people the punk as image was the most insistent thing and propagated through the media more than the music itself which existed predominantly in small clubs and pubs around the UK. The clip of *Dayglo* was ostensibly debuting an emergent punk band led by a young female singer and was particularly notable in its excessive use of obscuring colours and shapes: yellow, purple and orange squares forming a mostly abstracted image. In the UK, this was the televisual introduction of women in punk to the mainstream via television. As the singing started, the live video faded out of distortion into the image of a woman in a green woollen hat and sky-blue silk trouser suit. This was Poly Styrene (1957–2011), dancing enthusiastically and artlessly, having fun. Poly was the lead singer who formed and led the band *X-Ray Spex*. The image quickly faded back to abstraction and distortion, pulsating in and out of this mode throughout; the sequence at times also shifted to black and white. Dynamic camerawork used crane shots zooming in and veering off at an angle, rarely remaining still long enough to offer a good look at Poly's face. Amidst this distortion and visual occlusion, only Styrene's voice, high-pitched and largely monotone, remains amid a saxophone sound that is as pulsating as the visual imagery. Even today, looking through *YouTube*, the clip shrieks youthful brash energy, but it also suggests confusion on the part of TV camera operators, producers and directors as to how to represent punk women and this new and different form of femininity.

Another example of this confusion can be seen in the camerawork of *Siouxsie and the Banshees'* first single, *Hong Kong Garden* (1978) from their performance on *Top of The Pops* in 1978. The imagery here is solarized, and while the camerawork is focused more heavily on Siouxsie herself, it is through the mask of the black-and-white effect. What is notable here is the undecidability of the camerawork. The camera, by which of course I mean the camera*man*, knows how to look at a normative female artist – that is to say, as a sex object – but does not know how to look at Poly Styrene or Siouxsie Sioux. The camera knows how to look at the desiring female subject on screen but it does not know how to look at punk women because they are not constructing nor presenting themselves as an object of desire. This is in direct contrast to the camerawork in the filming of other punk bands that consisted of men such as The Buzzcocks or The Undertones, both from the same year. The camerawork for these latter bands fulfils the normative code of focusing on the lead singer primarily with much slower zooms and pans in between fixed shots on the players and then back on the lead singer. The contrast reveals the lack of televisual lexicon for any other kind of woman than the normative desiring subject of the female singer. Thus the undecidability of the camera in the filming of the women is a testament to an emergent, unstable audio-visual subjectivity, that is, the punk woman. Even Greil Marcus, whose book *Lipstick Traces* situated punk within Dada and situationist histories, did not understand that this female persona was not 'an ugly fat woman' who could 'demand freedom' if anyone could (Marcus 2001: 147) but on the contrary: it was a complete redefinition of what a woman could be in all her manifestations. I develop an argument for a strategic undecidability of the camera of women artists in Chapter 5 that arises from the need to develop a visual language for and by women that is mainly absent previously to this moment.

Punk women seemed full of energy, flair and affirmative aggression. Their movements signalled purposefulness and stridency. As punk was a visual phenomenon as much as a musical genre, punk women were the most visually daring. Most people saw them first on TV, possibly *Top of the Pops* or interviews, famously the Bill Grundy interview when the Sex Pistols were goaded by the TV presenter into swearing on live TV. It was these instances of visibility that made punk primarily a televisual experience for most, although the furore in the tabloid press had alerted many to punk. Either way, the punk phenomenon was a visual experience for most before it was a musical experience. It can be hard now, at a time when the unkempt anarchic look of piercings and tattoos are commonplace, to recall the impact and the sheer outlying daring of the women in punk and the hostile or outright violent abuse that female punks received habitually. It is also hard to recall how few these women were and that punk was a tiny subgroup even at its apex. Viv Albertine of *The Slits*, another first generation punk band, talks of the regular attacks on them in the street as they tried to go about their business ostensibly because of their look. She describes how Ari Up, when only a teenager of fourteen, was stabbed twice in the street by strangers (Albertine 2015: 165). The contrast between these few women and the norm of its time can begin to permeate by skimming any *YouTube* episodes of *Top of the Pops* from the period 1977–9 where the majority of music was bland pub rock, prog rock or even pop, involving lots of beige and flicked-back hair. Kate Bush and

Suzi Quatro played to the camera, teasing the camera with their allure; Poly Styrene simply sings to the audience, like in any gig, ignoring the camera lens, the lens itself discombobulated. An interview from *Countdown* in 1977 shows Poly Styrene, when not performing, as monosyllabic, shy and awkward in front of the camera, completely untutored in media skills. When asked, 'Tell us a little bit about the band' her response, 'Like what?' indicated a refusal to play the established media game. Refusal to play the feminine game was part of a wider non-participation in the perceived expectations of society by punks. Not all women in punk fit within the framework delineated here. Punk was an existential crisis and the women had a range of positions within these three areas of refutation: that of normative sexiness, behaviour and musical virtuosity. As Jack Halberstam states,

> From the perspective of feminism, failure has often been a better bet than success. Where feminine success is always measured by male standards and gender failure often means being relieved of the pressure to measure up to patriarchal ideals, not succeeding at womanhood can offer unexpected pleasures.
>
> (Halberstam 2011: 4)

Conforming neither to the usual expectation of women in bands nor to the normative conventions of beauty, the expectations of musical virtuosity – even by the standards of rock and roll – were completely debunked by these women musicians – giving them licence to have fun and create their own sense of self away from the pressure of gender norms and expectations.

The mythology in punk has always been to do with the valorization of the amateur, the ignorant and the do-it-yourself bands setting up their own labels and fanzines and playing to small audiences.[8] The amateur was in direct contrast to the progressive rock model of virtuosity which modelled classically trained musicians from public schools turning their hand to popular forms of music. This was a legitimating narrative that aimed for the coming of age of rock music as the superseding form of classical music for the modern man. Soul had its own legitimating narrative of the church choir serving as the apprenticeship for stars such as Aretha Franklin, Otis Redding, Marvin Gaye and Whitney Houston amongst many others.[9] It is no accident that reggae became one of the co-inspirators for many of the musicians and the fans both in its oppositionality and its prevalence in working-class urban areas.[10]

But what of today? There has been a sharp increase in the interest and popularity of the punk movement and music. Today, with *YouTube* homemade movie stars on the one hand and the 4k intensity of cameras on the other, there is almost a fetishization of the aesthetic of the pre-digital that requires interrogation: what is the contrast between what looks like the shaky, homemade camera and the need to make under the pre-internet, lo-fi conditions of the 1980s? The use today of the poor image for example is of a different order and speaks to a different time that has yet to be seen through the lens of the earlier twentieth-century work. It also has to be noted that many of the films that I write about are still outside of the institution and not often shown in exhibition, nor written about, which attests to its ongoing challenging nature.

Notes

1 Although Clarke's work was later deposited in the NY Film Maker's co-op collection.

2 Rombes was borrowing for new punk cinema Schrader's claim that *noir* should not 'cohere around a genre' (Schrader 1972: 53). I'm borrowing here from Rombes.

3 Tom Gunning also uses the term (Winter 1989–90).

4 That is not to say that many of these artists did not want political change in the world, just that change was not the driving force of the work.

5 Although as I finesse the final stages of this book, the Covid-19 pandemic may change this all again.

6 In 1973, 13 per cent considered their position as very weak; in 1977 it was 26 per cent, when asked if they expected their standard of living to 'fall sharply' (Beckett 2009).

7 Of course, this is a crude simplification of the patterns of immigration to the UK that is describing merely broad sweeps and perceptions.

8 This is a broad sweep and I will differentiate between the women in later chapters.

9 https://www.biography.com/news/aretha-franklin-black-singers-church (Accessed: 19 August 2019).

10 Both Paul Gilroy (1992) and Dick Hebdige (1979) talked in detail about the musical allegiance between punk and reggae.

1

The last of the modern one:
Do-it-yourself and the amateur

Do it yourself has always implied a very crowded 'self'; as an ethos and as a praxis, the DIY-er has always gotten by with a lot of help from his friends.
(Everett Haynes in Hawkins 2015: 84)

Amateurism is the model by which the deflationary function of artistic incompetence in modernism and the avant-garde is embodied. It is the amateur artist – that is the artist who in some sense fails the test of professionalism and 'good' taste – that modernists and avant-gardists have looked to in order to secure what is anti-bourgeois and anti-aesthetic.
(Roberts 2001)

While Poly Styrene was in the charts in the UK and appearing on *Top of the Pops*, in New York the filmmaker Vivienne Dick was also making a groundbreaking statement, re-imagining the visual language of the depiction of women in cinema with *Guerillere Talks* (1978), a film that begins her long-standing oeuvre spanning New York, London and Ireland. Dick studied French and Archaeology in Dublin, Ireland, and found her cinematic voice in the punk and No Wave milieu in which she was involved while living in the lower east side of New York in the late 1970s.[1] Bette Gordon, another filmmaker who arrived in New York in 1979, made *Empty Suitcases* in 1980. Gordon had studied at the University of Wisconsin Madison. Both of these women are associated with the No Wave group of filmmakers, who were a loose group of people making work using super 8 cameras. They worked with no funding, with homemade props, and used each other as actors. Despite them being put together as a loose historical grouping of filmmakers, all of the artists shared a do-it-yourself ethos. While this was not a position that they would all adhere to throughout their careers, the lack of money to produce work at what was a formative time in their development as artists inevitably conditioned their aesthetic and approach.

Bette Gordon had been a structuralist-influenced filmmaker when she lived in the mid-west before settling into the downtown NY scene, where she adopted No Wave strategies in subject as well as form.[2] She later became a director with relatively large budgets and who cited Jean-Luc Godard as an influence. However, the films she made in 1980, 1981 and 1983 had a distinctive style and approach that were very close to Vivienne Dick, whose films at the time repositioned women, their interests and self-representation in a particular way that is distinct from the contribution of artists such as the 'slow camera' of Chantal Ackerman, or the auteur approach of Agnes Varda. Dick states that she started to make super 8 at Millennium Film Workshop 'but found the atmosphere there was too heavy'[3] (Dika 2012: 57). One of the constituting factors of the different approaches might well have been that Dick's films were made for music venues, to be shown between and as a backdrop to the performances of punk bands, including her own – Dick was also in a band – and eschewing the established experimental film venues. These venues would lend a very different air to the work than the serious, aforementioned, 'heavy' film venues.

To put this in concrete terms, 'Bette Gordon's 8mm film *Anybody's Woman* (1981) was made in just a week for seventy-five dollars, as an "emergency" response to the latest round of cuts to the National Endowment for the Arts' (Edmond 2016). These conditions gave rise to both form and subject matter. The lived experience of women was given a voice through these films for women: some of these filmmakers and their friends who had to work as strippers or in bars to maintain their lives as artists. To give some examples, Gordon had friends who worked as strippers, also in Vivienne Dick's *Liberty's Booty* (1980), where one of the early subjects speaking claimed the necessity of working 'on the game' as a way of paying through college; in this way the contingent factors give rise to a politics of lived relations that was separate and in opposition to the theoretical motivations of the previous generation of artists in the United States and the United Kingdom with more access to institutional jobs, equipment and production grants. I would argue that this gave rise to a deflationary aesthetic that did not adopt the strategies of the overtly theoretical approaches. What was at stake for these artists was to take a different route than the approach of films like *Riddles of The Sphinx* (1977) or *Nightcleaners* (1975). Dick and Gordon's approach to the representation of ordinary women, while alive to the theoretical questions of representation, in the films foregrounded an experiential approach of a lived relationship with their own milieu rather than one of deconstructing women as an abstracted category. This does not mean that the filmmakers that I write about had the lumpen approach to culture and thinking espoused by Johnny Rotten, the often-assumed figurehead of punk, but that they were moved by its accessibility.

> The key thing is the early [film] work responded to the energy and experimentation of punk scene and most of the people in the films were active in the scene. We were influenced by how the bands were operating – putting up our own home made Xerox posters all over lower Manhattan and screening the films in the same venues as the bands.
>
> (Dick 2020)

Many of the filmmakers read theory, as exemplified by Vivienne Dick's title *Guerillere Talks*. They operated outside of the academy/art world rather than screening their films within the established cinemas of experimental film. Artists like Gordon and Dick chose to make work through a less overtly intellectualized model of practice in contrast, say, to the Berwick Street Collective – who made work about the strike of some women nightcleaners – as indicated by the title *Nightcleaners*. The work quickly became more about the workings of a quasi-Brechtian model of *distanciation* through which the subjects would be understood. It is a testament to the power of the academe and the distribution value of cinemas like the New York and London Co-ops – and possibly to the fact that both *Riddles of the Sphinx* and *Nightcleaners* were made by women and men – and the way in which art, and film, is formed through it that the films of Mulvey and Kelly have dominion over the historical narratives of the culture of experimental film rather than the films written about here.

A venue like Max Kansas City, The Mudd Club or Club 57, where the No Wave artists played in their bands and screened their films was a kind of venue that would allow for a transgressive approach and would allow for a film to be read as transgressive, just because it was screened within that context.[4] It also exemplified the desire of the No Wave filmmakers to set out an agenda of their own making without recourse to what had gone before. Like the seemingly vacant 'I don't know' monosyllabic responses of Poly Styrene in early interviews, these filmmakers' stated aims were of a wilful ignorance of any art or previous provenance. The No Wave filmmakers claimed that they had reinvented cinema in their approach, particularly in the bringing together of art and music. As John Roberts states, 'The deflationary became a placeholder for the "democratic" or "popular" insofar as the skills of the academic professional were seen as unprepossessing signs of domination and inherited authority' (2008: 15–24). Seen in this light, proof of authenticity was not just to do with the turning away from intellectualized forms of art but also with the a complete denial of history. Putting themselves at the forefront of cinematic invention as something that eschewed *all* history was somewhat overstated[5] and chimed with the romanticism of the faux amateur that resides in art historical narratives from Monet onwards. Many of the group who had gone to art school would afford these artist filmmakers the knowledge that the lower east side, where they lived, was a neighbourhood with a vibrant history of avant garde and underground cinema. In art school they would undoubtedly have been taught about Fluxus and Andy Warhol if not earlier convergences such as Dada and surrealism even if they did not know about the specific role that the figure of 'the amateur' had played in modernism. Beth B, a prominent member of the No Wave, grew up within a highly cultured milieu as she was the daughter of painter Ida Appelbroog. By way of a further example, Eric Mitchell, another No Wave filmmaker, had made a shrine to Edie Sedgwick on his 'one-chair Lower East Side Apartment' (Hoberman in Hawkins 2015: 16). Furthermore, Dick herself worked as an assistant to Jack Smith, an underground filmmaker of a previous generation. Both of these latter examples indicated a far more knowing sense of the world than the No Wave artists' comments indicated – or that the punk moniker would suggest. The artists thus chose to adopt a 'faux amateur' position as a sign not only of the popular but their own faux proletarian credentials. However, the decision to make No Wave works was not merely one of naivety or ignorance but one of financial necessity. The anti-ideological anti-establishment imperative was itself merely a handy add-on. Undoubtedly, they all drew from previous underground sources such as Jack Smith or Kenneth Anger, who also revelled in an anti-establishment imperative, possibly through their interests in subjectivity as an expression of their non-heteronormative sexuality. So I would argue that the denial of the history of the New York scene was in part a self-positioning strategy common to many artists and should only be seen as part of a reputation-building manifesto rather than a sincere belief on their part. There was also a politics to this positioning, however flawed, that was involved with an impassioned rejection rather than a convincing denial: a declaration that mirrored the 'No Future' of punk with a 'No Past' of No Wave. Seen in this vein, the denial of history could be seen not as self-serving but another negation of a coherent lineage drawn from earlier models that critiqued the status quo. It was a message of where and how they positioned themselves in relation to the dominant modes of address and an art world that was riven with preoccupations of value rather than message or aesthetic. It was a declaration in the strongest terms that this was a radical break: that these were new circumstances that required new thinking. Ultimately it was borne out of pragmatic necessity as there was little funding for the arts and the artists did not come from backgrounds which allowed a *flâneur* approach to the world through a private income. However, this make-do requirement allowed for a self-invention of language: a freeing of the burden of discourse and the failures of history. Punk always claimed a ground-zero approach of no history, of starting again, so to feign ignorance of building on previous approaches was a convenient rhetoric to adopt. A lumpen persona was also seen as authentic and anti-bourgeois. But most of all in this case, it was a freedom from the antinomies of art and experimental film as beauty or its opposite: the assumptions of art as a transformative process that created burdensome moralizing expectations.

Vivienne Dick and Bette Gordon stand out from the No Wave group through the traces of latent humanism of the earlier underground scene and New American Cinema as reference points in their work. There are similar formal strategies and interests in working women's lives and the interaction between men and women that marks them both. By contrast, filmmakers such as Nick Zedd or Steve Nares constructed hard-hitting, brutal works which were excessively lo-fi and tackled issues like sadism, mass murderers and mind control. These films had a darker outlook than the works I am discussing here.

Spurning the humanist optimism of, say Mekas or Clarke, most of the No Wavers espoused a nihilistic vision lacking in agency or redemption in the work.

Vera Dika in her book *The (Moving) Pictures Generation* (2012) usefully explains that the cinematic approach of other women filmmakers such as 'Rainer and Ackerman presents with women in subjugation, whether implicitly or explicitly' (2012: 59). So the return to the cinematic saw the adoption of a different approach that would allow for an empowered femininity. A new empowerment of women went with the times of punk and can be seen in their strident expressive aggression. The direct address through the camera that both Vivienne Dick and Bette Gordon employ habitually that demands attention from the viewer is just one example of the way these artist filmmakers drew away from the minimalist and conceptualist approaches of structuralist film (Dika 2012: 59). Maura Edmond similarly explained how the turning away from patriarchal structuralist theories often meant a rather literal amendment to the methodologies of filmmaking rather than a complete change of mode of attention. Edmond states,

> Much of the problem of mainstream narrative cinema was understood in terms of formal structure and so the solution – the counter cinema that was advocated – was conceived along similar lines. If the 'rules of thumb' that govern mainstream narrative cinema are irrevocably patriarchal, then a successful counter cinema must invent a new rulebook that inverts the logic of the old one. This approach was often realised in the most formally literal ways: if classical cinema's camera 'penetrates' the frame, moving from long shots to close ups, a feminist counter-cinema must stay wide and move horizontally; if classical cinema is shot from the perspective and spatial experience of a (presumed) male protagonist and male cinematographer, then a successful feminist counter-cinema must frame its shots lower, from the relative height of a woman, and so on. In sharp contrast, No Wave women exhibited a fervent, punk-fueled commitment to the creation of an oppositional and often nihilistic anti-aesthetic.
>
> (2016)

It is the refusal to 'take care' of the quality of the material or technology that differentiates the filmmakers in this chapter and book from structuralism that highlighted the material and technology as the carrier of meaning par excellence – through critiquing the negation of true meaning as a medium of alienated subjectivity – as well as the refusal to theorize and counter-theorize. Particularly it is a refusal of these artists, despite their focus on human relations, to offer a vision of transformation in their films, that differentiates punk film from its closest ally of the earlier New American Cinema (NAC), given the lo-fi and communitarian approach of NAC as they declared: 'We don't want false, polished, slick films – we prefer them rough, unpolished but alive; we don't want rosy films – we want them the colour of blood' (Everleth quoted in Hawkins 2015: 7).

Despite attempts here at claiming affinities with the NAC, most of the No Wavers' films, including Dick and Gordon's work, did not demonstrate much interest in a poetic transformation of the everyday that was the orthodoxy of the New American Cinema. Nor were these artists interested in the formalist claims for transformation of the classic avant garde. These filmmakers had no time for the lofty declarations of any of the previous generation with their post-war optimism. These artists were also not particularly aiming for a resistance to pop culture or narrative through the endgame-ism of structuralist film. In fact there was open disdain and hostility to structuralist film amongst many of these artists (Edmond 2016). Their endgame was of a different order that rejected the seeming subtlety of a critique of society through theoretical formulations. The conceptualist imperative of interrogating the material was an irrelevance to the crushing reality of the world around them. With no belief in the future, this was a social and political endgame and required other strategies.

No Wave, like punk, can be seen as constitutive of part of the long-standing debate based on the binary position of avant garde versus the underground. While Greil Marcus has positioned punk as a latter-day oppositional force in a redemptive manoeuvre in his manifesto that articulated a lineage back to Dada and the situationists, I would argue that while there are some political motivations for some of the work some of the time, as a whole punk could not even be bothered to be oppositional. It did not see itself as avant garde but its stridency was scattergun, an angry rant rather than a formal activism. It did not proffer a singular focus or intention but was heterogeneous and somewhat vague in its overall aims. Despite the popularity of the negative epithet 'sell-out' bandied about at the time, punk represented a negation of the redemptive agency that accompanied the avant garde in its endeavour to bring art into the service of the transformation of society – even Dada, with its energy and declarative force. It gave the impression of a deep malaise that had no faith in action. The punk notion of 'sell-out' was not to do with an active opposition. Ambition in the guise of rewards from the institution in the form of money or contracts was an act of agency that was the negation of stasis. That level of inaction is unsustainable, however, and just as Bette Gordon ended up making a film for 1 million dollars, most punk bands who were able succumbed to the lure of the big label, despite the cries of 'sell-out'. Punk, as an attitude and lived experience, has to be heterogeneous with immanent lived contradiction. Any movement to sign up to the mainstream record companies was a denial of the authentic moment of facing the reality of 'no hope'. The contradiction implicit in this stance is just that when opportunity comes knocking, you take it. No hope then gives rise to hope. Punk film is, like punk music itself, unsustainable as a long-term position except as an ongoing renewable entity, regenerating through the generations as post-punk. Most of the artists that I write about in this chapter and the book as a whole have since developed finesse and artistry in their work, with longer forms and cleaner transitions between ideas and passages in their films – but this was not what concerned them in their youth.

Although Vivienne Dick made her early films in New York, Ireland, the country of her childhood – and where she now lives again – was often woven into the films, as part of the politicizing strategies. By the same token, some punk bands were overtly political in their message such as the Irish band Stiff Little Fingers (politicized by living through the Irish Troubles). The thrust of the music in general was more in line with the kind of politics of the underground. In film terms then, punk and No Wave had as much in common with the underground as the more stated politically motivated situationism. Although they were anti-bourgeois in their motivation, it was more libertarian than revolutionary, as was the oppositional attitude of the underground. What differentiated punk was that it was ostensibly concerned with the concrete and everyday conditions of living and against what it saw as the excesses of hippies and rock music that derived from a relative state of privilege compared to the punks. For some it was not even that worked out but represented an urgent immediacy that could not even imagine the excesses of the previous generation. Mainstream music was also scorned as purely commercial, lacking in the ability to understand the grittiness of urban 1970s difficulties. Despite superficial connections in intention, there were thus some profound contingent differences between the underground moment of the earlier generations of the late 1950s and early 1960s and this 1970s moment, as I will discuss later in this chapter through readings of the films Robert Frank's *Pull My Daisy* (1959), Andy Warhol's *Chelsea Girls* (1966) that I compare with Vivienne Dick's *Guerillere Talks* (1978) and Peggy Ahwesh's *From Romance to Ritual* (1985). Maura Edmond puts the context succinctly, through the words of Johnny Rotten at the time:

> The central aesthetic and ideological premise that underpinned punk (music in the first instance and then the culture broadly) was its 'clear the decks' and 'back to basics' agenda. Punk was simultaneously a violent canonical rejection of the popular music of the day and an open-armed invitation to (youthful) amateurs that bordered on proselytism. 'It was easy, it was cheap; go and do it!' and at the same time 'I hate shit. I hate hippies and what they stand for. I hate long hair. I hate pub bands'.
>
> (Edmond 2016)

The approach I am discussing here is then essentially a philistine approach. The adoption of popular culture, porn, violence and the seedy was an attack on the ways in which artists were expected to adopt certain markers of knowingness even within the destabilization of the previously held norms of form. What John Roberts rightly argues in *Photography and Its Violations* (2014) is that the use of the snapshot in recent contemporary art is a realignment of older expectation of the snapshot as non-art borrowed from the 1920s and 1930s while also trying to 'deflate' the expectations of finesse that dogs the museum-based 'post-conceptual work': this is what the punk filmmakers stood for in an earlier time. Roberts makes this claim for art production in the 1990s and 2000s, but I would argue that this is also the case in the late 1970s and early 1980s of the punk moment. The realignment with the 1920s and 1930s will be dealt with in a later chapter, but what is important here is the way in which these artists operated and critiqued through the logics of deflation via a do-it-yourself amateurism.

John Roberts articulates the ways in which the amateur is a performed figure in modern art, and how the snapshot – or within my argument, the super 8 camera[6] – and its 'intimacy with the banal the contingent and the "ordinary"' challenges both the hierarchy of artistic skill and which artistic subjects are held to constitute legitimate aesthetic experience'. He continues, 'the snapshot has been a highly efficient means not only of stripping down the inflated artisanal skills of the traditional artist, but of questioning the academic and professional aggrandizement of modern art' (2014: 78). Roberts is thinking through those issues as categories with effects and implications; however, I would suggest that as well as the critical potential implicit in these categories of shifting the understanding of what the artist was from a skilled artisan towards intellectual labour was also a choice by artists in order to critique. What the artists often do not take into account is that critiquing the aim is to assert a new paradigm that ultimately has the effect merely to usurp the previous order within the art world hierarchy. However, Roberts's argument assumes a level starting point that women would not have experienced in the 1970s and 1980s. Indeed, there is no indication that artists such as Gordon and Dick were strategizing at this point and used super 8 because that was what they could get their hands on. There was, of course, an element of performing as they had knowledge if not money and were not the naïfs their work might suggest. I would posit that the negation of the imperative to finesse a refined femininity was mirrored in the intention to remove normative refinements in film.

DIY is not new, however, and there are many precursors who would make claims to the bohemian milieu, anti-bourgeois 'lo-fi' aesthetic. Bette Gordon and Vivienne Dick's work bears some relationship with their forbears, which lends some depth despite the disruptive and iconoclastic formalism. So, in addition to the economic necessity, there was an existential imperative to relearn and reinvent a female self through DIY that required a more 'root and branch' approach than many of their predecessor feminist artists. This new form, however, had a particularity at the end of the modern moment.

Jim Hoberman, one of Dick's early supporters (Connolly 2004), described her work as 'scuzzy lyricism' (1979). Compared to the schlock brutality of some of the other No Wave films and filmmakers, Dick's work is and was even then more humane, focused more on empathy than shock, but only in content and narrative which is in sharp contrast to the structure and composition of the works. It is through the disjointed narrative and lack of any redemptive finesse that these early Dick films, as part of the DIY mode of production, demonstrate an affinity with the brutality of the deprivation and the basic living conditions. In the early works such as *Guerillere Talks* (1978) and *She Had Her Gun All Ready* (1978), there is a deliberate avoidance of overarching intellectual schema within the film's structure and the rhythms of editing that signal cinematic virtuosity even in experimental film. Both films are disjointed and celebrate their amateurish presentations in, say, *Beauty Becomes the Beast* (1979), offering a montage that, while using a narrative drive of some sort, eschews any pretensions to dialectical instrumentalism – although there are other ways of reading the dialectic that make Dick an exemplar. One example might be through the exposure of the lived contradictions of women's lives in her works – more immanent critique than dialectical editing. Even the overwrought Lydia Lunch seems to be 'queering' the term *avant la lettre* in the way she deflates her hysteria through schlock sarcasm.

Guerillere Talks (1978) is an episodic series of visual interviews of her friends, all women. The visual simplicity and insistent do-it-yourself nature of the work that embodies a general 'scuzziness' in its *mise-en-scène*, however, belies a conceptual sophistication that is at odds with the film itself. The relationship, or rather the collision, of on the one hand, a literary reference and, on the other, a philistine visual handling signals a deliberate turning away from virtuosity towards the idea of creating a new female language, much like the approach to music of, say, The Slits and later The Raincoats, who invented an approach to music from the ground up. The title of the film is inspired by the science fiction novel *Les Guérillères* of the French feminist Monique Wittig. The novel *Les Guérillères* imagines a complete destruction of patriarchy and a concomitant reinvention of language for and by women. In terms of invention Dick is clearly searching in these early films for an approach of community rather than of the individualized eloquence of the auteur.

Les Guérillères was published in the United States just five years earlier in 1973, amid great interest from the second wave feminist movement. The use of Wittig in the early film foregrounds not only the central place feminism plays in Dick's oeuvre but also the kind of feminism to which Dick subscribed that is closer, as a broad brush approach, to the theoretical feminism that developed out of French philosophy of, say, Luce Irigaray than Anglo-American feminism, which seemed to arise more out of political activism.[7] Wittig, who saw feminism through the issues of difference and societal constructions of heteronormative patriarchal thought as much as through the concrete issues of equal rights, was at odds with much American second wave feminism. Wittig used the lesbian experience to think through a radical break with phallocentric institutions, language and thinking, denying difference between women and men and advocating instead for an embodied celebration of womanhood. The portraits in Dick's film clearly aim to think through the implications of *Les Guérillères* for a cinematic language.

The novel is visceral both in its sensuousness and in its depiction of violence. In the beginning of the novel women are living a fantasy of natural womanhood in the jungle, which is then interrupted by violence. A bloody war ensues between men and women, with women being victorious. The violence and lyrical poetry in the novel are the emotions that aim to underpin the mood of the film. The novel is episodic, written in poetic prose of short disconnected paragraphs that give little contextual information. These paragraphs are interspersed with women's names in an unknown language. Nothing is contextualized beyond the time and place of the events. There are no temporal shifts nor theorization: the writing is elliptical. The writing is in the moment: the focus is experiential.

Although the mood set in the novel cannot be compared with the film, there are other features that would directly link the writing form of Wittig's *Les Guérillères* and the construction of the film *Guerillere Talks*. The film by Dick, similarly, features only women. It is episodic and celebratory, but true to the formation of punk that Dick was expressing at the time, it replaces sensuousness with deadpan and violence with grunge: violence would come in a metaphorical sense with subsequent films such as *Beauty Becomes the Beast* (1979). Like the novel *Les Guérillères* (1969), the film *Guerillere Talks* (1978) is elliptical in form and experiential in cinematography and narrative. Each reel of super 8 shows a different friend in a different part of her everyday world. The *mise-en-scène* is in the moment in the way in which it is shot and structured with in-camera editing, no establishing shots or cutaways and each vignette consisting of a stand-alone reel that has its own distinct flavour in collaboration with the subject of the section. In fact, the film opens with no contextualizing device at all and jumps from subject to subject, straight into the moment with no links established visually or discursively. Formally *Guerillere Talks* constitutes a radical shift in filmmaking: compare for example the earlier Frederick Wiseman's *High School* (1968), which, while claiming the experiential directness of his fly-on-the-wall documentary – and of course the political importance of this – still conforms to the conventions of establishing shots such as a long pan of the streets describing the neighbourhood of the school throughout the opening credits. In Dick's *Guerillere Talks*, made a decade later, the opening is sudden. The super 8 lead-in which is part of the film – much like the way the lead-in is used by Shirley Clarke in the earlier *Portrait of Jason* (1967) – takes us straight into a loud grinding noise that continues throughout the first reel and a sideways shot of a woman's face and back playing pinball, with accompanying noises of the machines and incidental out of shot voices. In direct contrast to *Portrait of Jason* or, say, Warhol's *Screen Shots*, the protagonists are completely indifferent to the camera.

The subject in the first section of *Guerillere Talks* is one of Dick's friends, a woman sporting a short haircut and studded leather jacket: already in this first image the ideal of normative femininity is rendered irrelevant in a number of ways. The construction of the shot takes a novel position in relation to

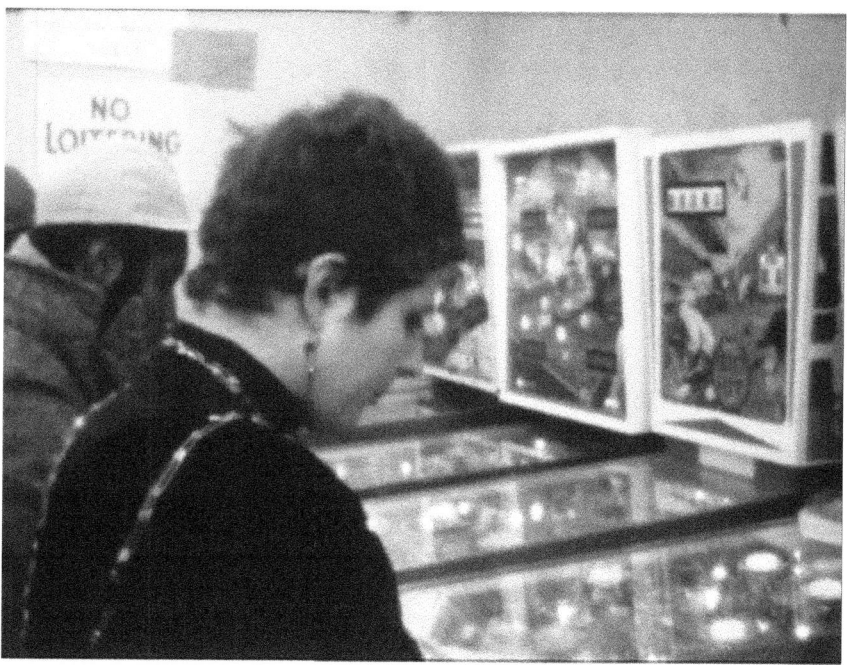

Figure 1. Still from *Guerillere Talks* (1978, Vivienne Dick). Courtesy of the artist.

the filming of women. The camera is shooting the woman from behind, and to the side, slightly angled behind the woman who is self-absorbed playing pinball, not in itself a normative feminine pastime. The woman is not aiming to please the viewer and is ignoring the camera. In cinematic terms, she is not in love with being filmed nor is the camera eliciting desire in the filming of her as subject. The leather jacket that she is wearing and the cigarette that she is smoking, as with the setting of the amusement arcade, denote her as a motorcycle rebel – but not in an edgy, glamorous way. This reel, like the others, relies on the in-situ lighting. The camera is handheld and awkwardly posed. It is an intense image, with no distance and the claustrophobia ramped up by the noise of what sounds like a pneumatic drill off camera. The back of the figure looms large. There is nothing here that is alluring to a viewer, and the general message is of not caring for the audience at all. An incidental profile of a man in a hat, who is playing on the next pinball machine along, bobs in and out from behind the silhouette, looking up a little to see what is going on, only momentarily distracted from his playing, serving merely to interrupt the concentration on the woman and interfering with any notion of composition or performance from the filmmaker, lending even more of an amateurish air. At one point a boy's head and then hand appear from the bottom of the screen, wanting to be part of the image. The boy talks to someone, but the noise of the games arcade makes his voice hard to hear. The camera closes in even more, focusing on the woman's hands working the flippers. It moves around the machine but with no seeming overarching intent, except to show the Evel Knievel facing of the pinball game, yet another rebel reference that links the film into a history of the romance with rock and roll that filmmaker Kenneth Anger played with. The noise of the pneumatic drill continues alongside the close-ups of the pinball until the end of the reel, when it all ends abruptly. In its love of the incidental and documentary the film is reminiscent of the UK's Free Cinema, except this work of Dick eschews the professionalism in sound and the love of beautiful composition that was the hallmark of filmmakers such as Lindsay Anderson, and savours awkwardness instead.

Other diverse vignettes follow. Each reel of *Guerillere Talks* has neither narrative drive nor structural design: just one continuous take. In this way it is reminiscent of Andy Warhol's shorts. The second bears no relation to the first and features different women. This reel takes place in the private space of an apartment. It is possibly night time and it seems that only a table lamp lights the room. There is no evidence of cinematic lighting. The dark shadow the table lamp casts gives drama through contrast. The camera finds its opening focus on a white telephone. The camera then pans in jerky movements to the wall. There is a distracted quality to the camera movements as if it is looking for the person and finally finds them almost by chance. The objects here act as establishing shots of sorts. The subject is the musician Pat Place, who is also a friend of Vivienne Dick, whom we finally see, when the camera 'finds' her, knocking a nail into the wall, then intently knocking with her hammer onto the metal of the storage heater and then appearing to nail her head as a comic gesture to insanity. We do not see the whole room, nor the whole person. The camera shows a limb here, a head there. We are aware of the camera at all times trying to keep up with the small movements of Pat Place. It is thus a fragmentary appearance from a fragment of the piece that is itself fragmented.

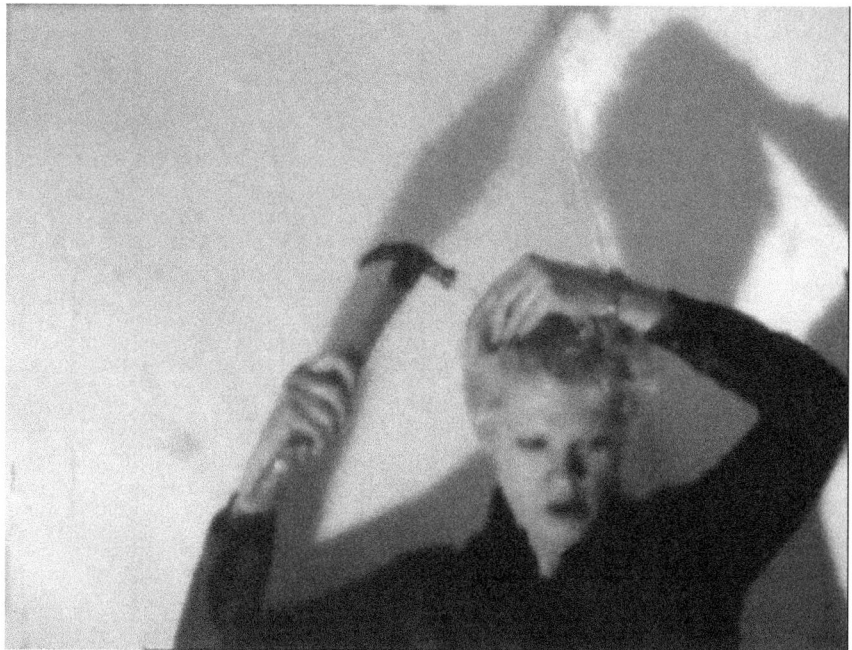

Figure 2. Pat Place in *Guerillere Talks* (1978, Vivienne Dick), screen grab. Courtesy of the artist.

In this portion of *Guerillere Talks*, there is some talk but it is unremarkable as the camera continues to hover around, unable to be still, catching the storage heater, general detritus such as light bulbs and bits of paper, and again the wall on its way, before an in-camera edit and a pan that encounters Pat sitting on a bed reading out loud. As with the lighting, the sound is incidental here too. The camera follows the line of Pat's head moving up to the ceiling as if the wall is as important as the subject. 'You asked about my 45s?' She reads a letter from her parents,

> thinking of selling them? If I were you I'd hang on to them, those Beatles records will be worth a lot more than they are today. I'd be happy to sell them for you if you want me to. I'm not sure about the tranquilizers Pat. They are a controlled medication and it really isn't safe for you to take them indiscriminately. They are especially dangerous with any form of liquor. The doctor warned me last week. Why do you think you need them?

The camera finally stops at Pat's head as she puts down the letter, picks up a toy gun and, looking down, shoots it off into the air, with the radio talking in the background. And so it goes on for another minute until the end of that reel, the randomness of the dialogue echoing the seeming randomness of the camera.

In this vignette Pat Place exposes herself as a kind of faux pioneering cowboy tough guy, in contrast to the Evel Knievel reference in the previous episode or vignette. In her reading of the letter there is a self-reflexive nod towards comparisons with an historical avant garde. The long association of the art scene and drugs is knowingly played out here and forms part of the foundations of a do-it-yourself culture. Pat Place's reading of the letter in this scene also reminds us that 'rock and roll' is not value-free, nor outside of any system. This kind of scene, established through the underground that is exemplified by earlier films such as Andy Warhol's *Chelsea Girls* (1966) or Nick Roeg's *Performance* (1970), is offered by Dick as a differentiating device in this sequence of an innocent ersatz experience of the 'is that what we are meant to do?' kind seen in *Guerillere Talks*. In the even lower-fi replication and faux innocence of parental concern through the reading of the letter, this film is both an homage to Warhol at the same time as critiquing his pretensions and his somewhat cynical use of other people's pain. It is almost like a double bluff in its exposure of the way that the system feeds off people's inadequacies while at the same time referencing Warhol's own faux cynicism. However, differently to Dick, whose work is about the everyday and the immediacy of the moment and the making of her community, Warhol separates himself out to create a goldfish bowl that exposes the inadequacies and vulnerabilities of his associates. I am thinking here particularly of the scenes in *Chelsea Girls* in which the artist Brigid Berlin displays her addictions and the last scene featuring Ondine. In this scene, in black and white, Ondine, acts as pope and confessor drawing out the fantasies of the women he is in conversation with. At one point his interlocutor at that moment, Ingrid Superstar, calls him a phoney and he turns on her, throwing wine in her face, hitting her and calling her a phoney. He repeatedly calls her 'a bitch', 'a dumb bitch', 'cunt' and 'whore'. In losing his temper, he exposes his sexism and egomania. She tries to defend herself, tells him to leave her alone and leaves the set. He follows her and continues, offscreen shouting at her, how she spoiled the whole scene, 'May god forgive you my dear because you don't know what love is'. Later he tries to defend his actions, obviously realising he has exposed himself. All the while this is going on, in colour, in the left-hand screen of a diptych movie, Nico is the subject. The filming of Nico is silent, intensely lit in reds, then pinks and yellows, blues and greens. The camera zooms in and out at times, is fixed at times, intent on observation of the subject, all creating a kaleidoscopic, iconic visuality. Later Ondine is heard talking off-screen about drugs to what sounds like a young woman. The unseen young woman giggles hysterically while Ondine holds up a syringe. The film ends abruptly. *Chelsea Girls* is an epic *tour de force*, deeply ambiguous as the actors are acting and not acting concurrently. Sound, lighting and the split screen are used to create atmosphere and distance, filled with both bathos and pathos. It is thrilling while also leaving a lingering sense of distaste at the abjection of the characters. The film is highly skilful in its appearance of de-skilling. This is a clear example of what John Roberts would develop as the relationship of the artist to the amateur (2008: 15–25). While there is often an assumption of authenticity in relation to the idea of the amateur approach to art, Roberts unpacks this position, stating that amateurism was a nascent and ambiguous identification with the limits of a professional academicism, and therefore, more properly, identifiable with an intra-professional deflation of the signs of academically or heteronomously imposed skills. Thus there was an emergent sense that, by skirting the bounds of technical 'incompetence,' or by withholding a professionally imposed facility the artist would secure a greater vivacity and authenticity to the act of painting that would be in keeping with the artist's displaced or marginalized standing.

(2008: 22)

While in modernity, the artist as producer and proletarian technician became the new amateur, well-positioned to present the authenticity of culture from below. However, what Roberts claims of Warhol is that,

if high culture was derogated here, there was no celebration and defence of the amateur as a potentially transformative cultural figure. On the contrary, particularly with Warhol, there was an almost nihilistic stress on the indistinguishability between the amateur's skills and the professional artist's skills. Both were seen as equally delimited, so the question of the amateur's cultural exclusion as a reflection of the work's place in the intellectual division of labor didn't come up.

(2008: 20)

I would argue that in *Chelsea Girls* Warhol's positioning of the protagonists in the film put him very much in the role of the expert who uses the subjects to reassure the viewer that they are exactly where they are meant to be: the bourgeois viewing public, safe in their homes and completely unlike the subjects they are looking at. By contrast in *Guerillere Talks*, the protagonists are not shown addled by drugs, parading their inadequacies and doubts in an abject way to a film team set up to observe and record. In Dick's film, the protagonists film themselves, in so doing, performing themselves. As such there is an empowering sense of agency, despite the surrounding detritus. A few vignettes later in *Guerillere Talks*, Lydia Lunch stands located outside the tenement block. The scene begins with a pan of the rubble outside. Moving along we catch the glint of the sun and the shadow of the filmmaker walking towards Lydia Lunch, with the microphone that comes into the shot. The camerawork is the same as the other vignettes, handheld with mainly diagonal

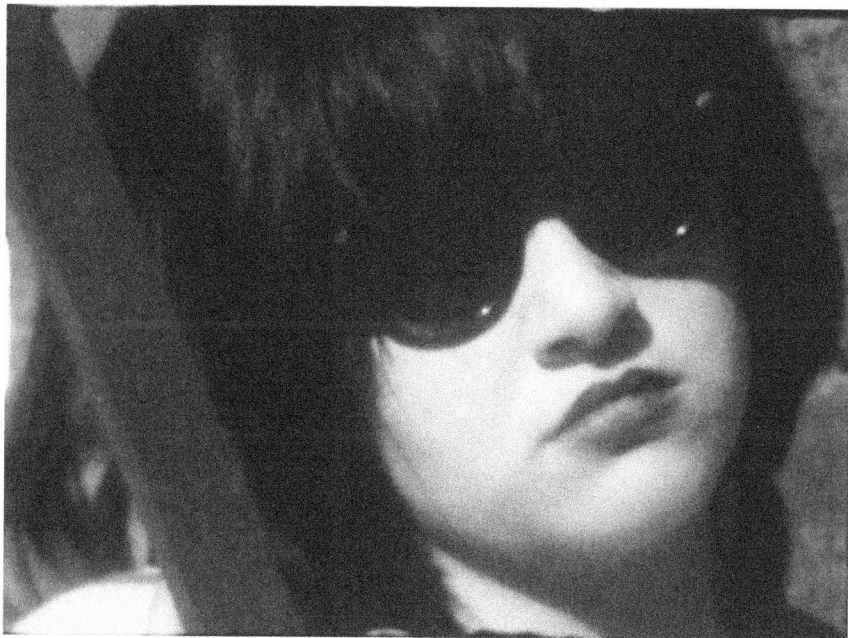

Figure 3. Lydia Lunch in *Guerillere Talks* (1978, Vivienne Dick). Courtesy of the artist.

shots. The lack of white balance by now lends a visual richness of its own as if each scene seems tinted differently. Lunch, another performer in the nascent punk music scene and friend of Vivienne Dick, is the main focus, with heavy black sunglasses, PVC mini-skirt and emphatic red lipstick. She is hugging the fire exit, ranting at the camera, modelling a television reporter, about the destruction and violence around them, that the only toys they get is what others throw away. 'What else is there but violence and destruction and anger when you have nothing better to do than run around burnt playgrounds. You know I wish I had a regular swing set like other kids but no I gotta hang out in a fire escape.' This is Lunch at her best, in a farcical hysterical parody of a child pretending to be a news reporter, or perhaps it is the other way around. Overall the camerawork, like the subject matter, is from the ground up, finding its way in a gesture of naiveté that has its own history in the underground, so different from what Vera Dika calls the 'objective camera' of Warhol.

Authenticity was a key marker of the new American cinema and this is another way in which Dick differentiates her cinema. There is some superficial resemblance between Dick and Jonas Mekas. Mekas is the filmmaker popularly associated with the New American Cinema[8] in his use of autobiography and his diaristic camera work. Both of them use the handheld and their everyday milieu to capture just what happens to be going on around them. However, the habitual 'god voice' through the narration from his viewpoint, of observation and reflection on the world that brings portent to the everyday in Mekas's films, becomes in Dick's work a 'talking back' via a series of female protagonists. Dick is not availing the viewer of the benefit of her knowledge gained through life via a voiceover. Instead in many of the vignettes of *Guerillere Talks*, Dick is using the device of the direct address to ask the protagonists to reach out to the viewer by telling the viewer what they *feel* directly, even more so through the construction of the film, where the women each had a collaborative relationship to the way in which they were filmed, framed and portrayed. They do not play with the desiring camera in a knowing game of cat and mouse, as does the performer Jason Holliday, the star of *Portrait of Jason*; instead, they deliver themselves through a different kind of raw defiance. In this way, of 'talking back', the voice of the filmmaker demonstrates her humility to the world around rather than an overt manipulation of it. The effect is a lack of judgement that does not announce its vision as a modern positivist evocation that assumes of the world a certainty. At best it offers a deeply contingent ambivalence about the world of women who are having to make do: disenfranchisement finding its voice.

The women in Dick's films are not presented as glamorous. In any case they do not care for the viewer's judgement: it is a vision of a modernity that has failed to deliver its own promises. The women being filmed perform an angry stubbornness that creates its own dynamic and power that is not set up to be alluring for the viewer but that has its own allure over the viewer in their passion for the real. The dereliction as well as bankruptcy of New York is palpably conveyed in the aimlessness and unharnessed anger of the protagonists in these empty, impoverished, dirty rooms as well as the performed paucity of technical virtuosity in the filmwork.

In Dick's early films, exemplified through *Guerillere Talks*, there is a sense of aftermath that is distinct from earlier comparative films. In some ways this is an inversion of the *Chelsea Girls* film, where the protagonists were generally from affluent backgrounds – living in the Chelsea Hotel – but dogged by an internal poverty that is derived from a sense of inadequacy and distress; in Dick's film the protagonists are poor – living in run-down lower east side tenements – but the poverty and distress are external. The characters in *Guerillere Talks* are rightly angry but not self-destructive. Instead of the viewer watching the characters combust as in *Chelsea Girls*, we are watching the characters express their reality.

Guerillere Talks is also an impatient piece compared to the longer *Chelsea Girls*. While both films are episodic, in the former film each vignette is three minutes, the length of the super 8 cartridge, whereas in *Chelsea Girls* each passage is approximately thirty minutes. *Guerillere Talks* is made up of handheld shots, while *Chelsea Girls* consists of mainly tripod shots and is screened as a split screen playing overlapping episodes composed to be disruptive. What I mean here is that the former film does not unfold in a way that a longer piece would. The contemporary assumption of virtuosity of the long look shot is a useful analogy to musical choices in relation to the brevity of most punk songs that would last three minutes in comparison to the length of the prog rock or jazz equivalent as a supposed testament to its musical virtuosity.

The title of each film also signals a stark contrast: the affirmative *Guérillères* of Witting's book title transported into the film using a similar title refers to strong women fighting for autonomy in a brutally sexist world. In contrast, the women presented in the Warhol film through the title as 'Girls' are, through that title, positioned as nonautonomous, immature subjects to be looked at. Thus the (male) viewer is outside of the narrative, reinforced by the camerawork. He is looking in, at a 'purgatorial voyage through the lives of the New York bohemians' (Granath 2007: 00:12). Warhol was pointing his camera at a self-styled bohemian entourage, and while it, famously, was *his* entourage, the approach to the shooting told a different story: that of estrangement and separation.

Despite the rawness of the emotions and experiences depicted, such as the ubiquitous heroin addiction and the role-playing of emotional breakdowns, the formal choices add a decadence to *Chelsea Girls* in its knowingness. This is enhanced by the decision to make it a split screen, which distances the viewer through the excess of the slippage between each screen, preventing the viewer from fully engaging with the subjectivity of the protagonists it portrays. In sum, the composition and the cinematography position the viewer as voyeur to this fly-on-the-wall film, entreating the viewer to take pleasure in the excess on the screen. To return to *Guerillere Talks*, the protagonists in the Dick film form the film through collaboration. They are portrayed in a way that is less worldly and with seemingly lower expectations of life, hanging out in the backyards full of rubble and detritus, in the penny arcades or the walk-ups in the lower east side or the east village of New York. This distinction is in some ways slight but is reinforced by the formal differences in the filming and its presentation. Instead of the rock and roll of heroin and the excess of hurt, there is banality and anger in the poverty-stricken neighbourhoods, if anything a parody of the suffering of the 1960s generation and their heroin chic. So an opposition forms between bohemian decadence and the urban alienation of poverty through these two films, which in some ways re-inscribes the popular conceptions of the differences between the 1960s and the 1970s broadly. The glamour of Warhol's drug-fuelled grunge has given way to the grunge of poverty.[9]

Although I would not like to make any simplistic definitions in temporal terms, the *weltanschaung* that this represents is one that marks the shift from hippie to punk: the post-war optimism giving way to the despair and cynicism of the end of the century. In *Guerillere Talks*, the viewer is brought into the world of the protagonists by the seeming artlessness of both the filmmaker's camerawork and the subject.

I would like here to introduce the filmmaker Shirley Clarke as a further contextualizing precursor. Her film *The Cool World* (1963) is an example that can be seen in relation to Vivienne Dick's *Liberty's Booty* (1979), in that it fuses fiction and street documentary. However, Clarke's later film, *Portrait of Jason* (1967), is more apposite to discuss here as it is in some ways more closely comparable to a discussion of *Guerillere Talks* as both use the direct mode of address, focusing on the portrait and the relationship between the protagonist and filmmaker through the cinematic gaze.[10] In *Portrait of Jason*, Clarke films Jason Holliday speaking to camera for twelve hours in her rooms in the Chelsea Hotel, telling the camera about himself in a feature-length portrait. Some of the devices suggest a close comparison, such as the visible focus pull that is part of the film, and so constitutes a particular meaning: the amateur subject and their portrayed relationship to the filmmaker in the film – a comparison with the image of the filmmaker in Dick's film. However, while *Jason* has the intimacy and claustrophobia of *Guerillere Talks*, Dick's work is less formally concerned with the structures of its making as *Jason* appears. Dick's work does not appear to be interested in critiques of the form as interrogated by *Screen* magazine and others and is less concerned with the medium itself as form. It eschewed the way that the structuralist filmmakers used Brecht to forge a politics of the experimental film and more about how the form and self-reflexivity give rise to an experiential reading.[11] Furthermore although both are concerned with the effects of their immediacy and the affective gaze, the two films cannot be compared through what they were trying to achieve. The disparity in location between the Chelsea Hotel shabby chic dilapidation and the lower east side dereliction gives rise to the difference in aim that is still akin to the contrast that I have identified between *Chelsea Girls* and *Guerillere Talks*. Like *Chelsea Girls* the camera is gazing at the exotic subject, but in this film, the exoticization is both class and race. Jason is a Black hustler, brought to the hotel to parade by Clarke's then-boyfriend who knew Jason, but is interrogated through the camera by Clarke, an outsider of sorts, bifurcated in her Jewishness but economically privileged, therefore just as much an outsider to the milieu she filmed as Warhol, unlike Vivienne Dick, who had no outside income and was economically part of the scene she filmed.

In contrast the women in *Guerillere Talks* are naturalized and embedded in their own milieu; wherever they were from originally, they are living together in this milieu. In many ways through the filmic devices Dick intimates her own incorporation into the society she films. The 'actors' here have agency both in form and substance. In *Portrait of Jason*, Jason Holliday is performing for the camera, albeit performing himself. Over a long period of time he is subjected to the fixed gaze of the camera, and of the presumed white audience, performing his difference. He plays with the camera and keeps us guessing regarding who is using whom. He is working with the language of the oppressed, that is through the language of sublimation and fantasy – although *Guerillere* is arguably more contrived through Dick's direction of the subjects and their acting. The ambiguity in this film is what gives it its enduring power and is compelling viewing, yet the need for ambiguity belies the oppression of the subject who has lived, by his own admission, as well as his performance, a chameleon-like life of hiding in order to survive. Although talking back to the camera, Jason is talking back as one who is subject to the camera and as one who is living his life as a subject of prejudice. He plays as someone who knows that his power is precarious and lacking in agency through his increasing inebriation and the fixed lens directed at him, while he performs for us. He is performing as a performer, playing his selves in a game of smoke and mirrors.

In Dick's film the camera develops its way of looking through the filming and is clearly set up in conversation with the subjects. *Guerillere Talks* seems to be shot in relation to the responses to the subject in an ongoing negotiation contingent on the context and conditions – so for example, in an episode filmed inside an apartment of a woman confessing her feelings of inadequacy, the reel is shot propped up on some makeshift platform – the image is not quite still enough for a real tripod – while in another reel, Dick, camera in hand, walks around a photographer friend who is pointing her 35-mm camera at her/us while Dick is filming her. Yet another follows the figure and shoots around the space inhabited by the subject. The importance of these decisions is that each vignette, formed through the camerawork, is not just filming of the subject but feeling the relationship between the filmmaker and the subjects through its filming. The action and activity of the camera, relating in movement to the subject, energize the camera and also the viewer. Jim Hoberman spoke of Dick stating, 'Her camera is a kind of third character throughout' (1979). I would argue that its character becomes the bridge to the viewer, engaging the viewer. The subjects become 'one of us' not 'one of them' through her camerawork. For all the self-reflexive devices of the filmwork in *Portrait of Jason* and the shocking subjects of some of the figures in *Chelsea Girls, Guerillere Talks*, while building on these predecessors, gives the viewer more sense of the filmmaker's relationship with the subject than either of the other films discussed here. In this way it is more reminiscent of Jonas Mekas and his polemic of the liberation of the self: 'art as an action and not as a status quo', and the development of his camerawork through time in *Lost, Lost, Lost* (1976) (Mekas 1960: 2–12). In a similar way to Mekas, through the camerawork, Dick is actively finding her way in relation to the situation she finds herself in rather than the theatre of action unrolling in front of the tripod that is the position in *Chelsea Girls* and *Portrait of Jason*. These protagonists know they are being filmed and are playing up to the camera and following direction. Without a production team in *Guerillere Talks*, there is an intimacy to the filming enhanced by the amateur acting but mostly through the demonstration of an ongoing relationship between the protagonists and filmmaker. *Chelsea Girls* and *Portrait of Jason* also have an 'in-the-real-moment' address, but in the latter two, it is one of a knowing contract between the filmmaker and the potential viewing subject, where any equality of the subjects is hard won. This points to another example of the difference between *Chelsea Girls* and *Guerillere Talks*. In one of the scenes of *Chelsea Girls*, in the famous hotel that hot-housed bohemian intellectual talent, a female becomes increasingly overwrought towards the end of the particular scene and confesses her neuroses to her companion in the scene, who appears to be a therapist, or at least acts as one. Despite the content and the lack of other Hollywood attributes to the *mise-en-scène*, the viewer here is subject to a more usual Hollywood dynamic of watching the male and female protagonists interact in a gendered dynamic that the viewer is a merely silent and invisible witness to, invited to identify with the male and judge the female but from the safe distance of cinema observer: the man is looking at the woman, questioning her and passing his diagnosis. This is a male gaze. By contrast in *Guerillere Talks,* a young woman, sitting against a wall by a window, confesses her feelings of inadequacy to the camera, while talking about making the film together until they get it right, involving the viewer in a more direct relationship that fuses with the filmmaker, and brings the viewer into the room, sharing the vulnerability of the woman, living in the rundown walk-up in the lower east side, at a time when New York was bankrupt. What I am suggesting here is the differentiation between the portrayal and dissemination of a specific kind of anti-establishment, bohemian bourgeois subject as in the Warhol piece, and its contrasting *Guerillere Girls*, which operates from the point of view of a disenfranchised milieu filmed from the inside.[12]

In addition to the comparison of Warhol, another obvious juxtaposition as identified by Jim Hoberman in his landmark review of No Wave, *No Wavelength: The Para-Punk Underground* (1979) is that of the earlier film directed by Robert Frank and Alfred Leslie, *Pull My Daisy* (1959). I would suggest that *Pull My Daisy* as a film had a sense of discovery and optimism about it formed through an attitude of *cool*, distinct again from *Chelsea Girls*, which was self-consciously abstracted through its dual-screen mode and presentation of characters inside an established scene. These films by Vivienne Dick, *Guerillere Talks, Beauty Becomes the Beast,* and the earlier films of Frank and Warhol, *Pull My Daisy* and *Chelsea Girls* respectively, all have profound similarities in their desire to critique bourgeois norms and expectations. However, there are also subtle but key differences between these films that point to the divergent conditions and temporal location of their making that are worth exploring to identify the distinctiveness of the 1970s and the aesthetic that I'm delineating here.[13]

The film *Pull my Daisy* (1959) by Robert Frank and Alfred Leslie would have a different relationship to the works of Vivienne Dick than *Chelsea Girls* but to consider *Daisy* would illuminate what was new in Dick's approach. This was a film that defined the Beat generation and the slacker attitude of defying bourgeois mores by hanging out, drinking, talking and playing music instead of having a job. The most important feature of the slacker was to not work a 9–5 job, thereby refusing the pressure of the accumulation of consumer goods and property. It was a way of aligning with 'the truth' of life rather than the signs and images of mass culture. However, it was also a way of tasting the *frisson* of danger, of breaking the rules without having to live its effects, safe in the knowledge deep down that you can return to your class norms, a 'badge of dissatisfaction' if you like, of consumerist culture and capitalist greed. Following Andrew Ross in his classic text *No Respect: Intellectuals and Popular Culture*, I would like to posit a dialectical relationship that sees 'popular culture as a site of contestation in itself, rather than view it as an objective tool with which to raise or improve political consciousness' (1989: 11), and in some ways these earlier underground films have a clearer relationship to the kind of work that the punk films do.

The narrator and author of the screenplay is Jack Kerouac and it stars Larry Rivers, Allen Ginsberg and Alice Neel amongst others, all part of an artistic milieu. Thus it is also a portrayal of an insider's milieu, and one that, like *Guerillere Talks*, poses a nonconformist, alternative lifestyle in downtown New York (Hoberman 1979).[14] In many ways this is a more direct comparison with *Guerillere Talks* than *Chelsea Girls*; however, the work has to be read through its context that was on the brink of the 1960s, at an earlier moment in an age of prosperity and growth. It portrays the artists, writers and poets as cool through a belief in the bohemian artist as epitomized by Jack Kerouac. There is a long history of counter-culture existence but the importance of this generation was its rise as a paradigm because of the increase of national wealth: leisure was at this time no longer open merely to the upper classes.

In this short feature a group of guys come into a NY loft where a family live. The casual manner in which they enter and engage indicates that they are frequent visitors. The family consists of a woman who is a painter and her husband, a poet, who also works for the railway, and they have a young daughter. It is only parenthood that requires full-time work and a home. The guests drink, play music and engage in lively discussion. There is a sense created in the film of the invention of a new better life of art and culture away from the trappings of middlebrow aspirational existence that requires the sacrifice of a safe salary. The implication is also one of choice. By the end of the film, however, the husband and wife have rowed and the tensions between the expectations of freedom from conformity for the artist and the needs of family life burst open. The bohemian idyll is shattered, here portrayed by the wife urging the husband to be sensible and to stay home.[15]

Compare this to the narrative in *Beauty Becomes the Beast* (1979). Here, there is a scene where a man is sitting on a park bench with a dog describing how he has had to fill out long application forms for 'shitty low paid jobs' and how he walked twenty blocks on Broadway to find work only to come out of it still with no job. In a moment of bathos, he later tries to mug Lydia Lunch

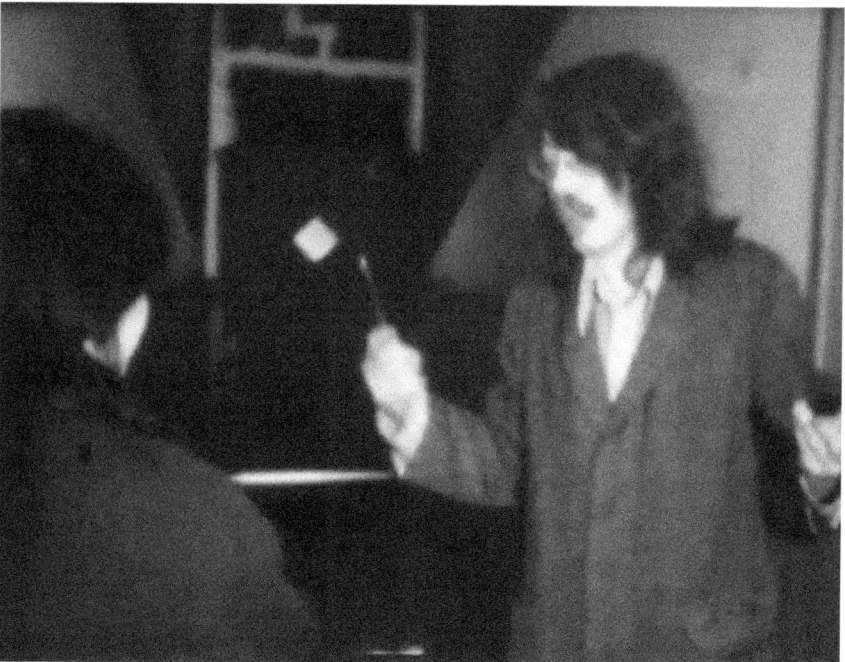

Figure 4. Mark Mood and Lydia Lunch in a still from *Beauty Becomes the Beast* (1979, Vivienne Dick). Courtesy of the artist.

by following her into the apartment building with a knife. He is pathetic and easily yields the knife to her, then has an argument and leaves in disgust. In *Pull My Daisy* (1959), a classic of downtown New York bohemia and one that is compared to Dick by Jim Hoberman, the choice is whether to be boho or a square. Should the 'guy' get a job to look after his 'kid' like his wife wants him to, or should he remain the bohemian he wants to be and hang out with his artist mates? There are two issues that mark this film as a point of differentiation here. The first is of a masculinity intact as represented in the earlier film by Frank and Leslie. That is, that the man has choices, unlike his counterpart in the Vivienne Dick film. The main problem here, according to this patriarchal narrative, is that he is held back by the woman who has trapped him into bourgeois normativity rather than being held back by the wider system itself. The other pertinent issue is of the assumption of choice that is denied in the later 1970s depiction of masculinity. In order to have choice one must have direction: the character in *Pull My Daisy* has this. In Dick's film there is no sense of purposefully 'slumming it', but of having to make a life out of having no options and with no future to invest in. So any message regarding an 'authentic' life that popular culture might proffer in this earlier film is largely undercut by the lack of benefit in the latter-day image of the man on the margins of society. There is no woman holding him back, pulling him into bourgeois norms. It is the woman living on the edge while he barely lives at all. In contrast to the representation in *Pull My Daisy* of the woman wanting the man to have a job so that he can look after his family, in *Beauty Becomes the Beast*, the man wants a job to sustain himself but is unable to obtain even this level of stability.

The portrayal in the Dick film is of a milieu formed through lack of hope rather than one drawn of hope: the choice is of conformism or nothing, rather than conformism and a new world. Here the nonconformism of living on the margins is not portrayed as desire but as desperation. In fact there is not even a family in this world of extended adolescence and no gender differentiation; all are equally lacking in direction, if anything a normative gender inversion. There is not the same level of camaraderie in the portrayal, merely a shared sense of exclusion, or at least the camaraderie is shown through the temporary joy and liberation of the Motown dance scenes rather than the timelessness and duty of the expectations of a family home represented in *Pull My Daisy*. The warmth of the home – a reference to a *heim* remade, with all the connotations of heritage and tradition – portrayed in *Pull My Daisy* gives way in *Guerillere Talks* to blank walls in fragments of rooms and urban alienation outside. Here there is no conviviality except through the camera. Dick is filming in the rubble of the previous generations of filmmakers and their expectations of modernity: to protest you need to have a stake and the *néant* here is one of no stake. Central to the loose genealogy I am building here is the shift in vision, not merely one of class but from that of the male viewpoint to that of the woman. This is exemplified in the juxtaposition between the woman, played by Delphine Seyrig, and her husband, played by Larry Rivers, in *Pull My Daisy*. Seyrig in the film is at best a peripheral player. She represents the conservative forces pulling him back from the progress of the male bohemian figure in modernity, or it could be said the infantilism of boys' playtime, as they hang out smoking, bantering and playing their musical instruments. In *Guerillere Talks* and *Beauty Becomes the Beast*, it is the women that hold the vision of the zeitgeist. This new time of punk that I exemplify as the last modern gesture through the Vivienne Dick film is a time where women can invent themselves from ambivalence towards a new commanding vision constituting themselves central to this new modernity being built out of the rubble.

Reconfiguring the representation of women not just as central to the films but as sexual beings was integral to the punk aesthetic that I am delineating here and a long way from the womanhood depicted in *Pull My Daisy*. Just as the matter of fact clashing clothes and braces of Poly Styrene and monkey boots was a sign of anti-femininity, the figure of Jordan or Siouxsie Sioux posed the inversion femininity stripped of its innocent façade to the hypersexual – both wore costumes subversively of leatherette or of stockings, garters and torn tights visible as the top garments rather than hidden as undergarments. Both the desexualizing and the parody of hypersexualizing were as important as each other for the rebuilding of the sense of self as emerging out of patriarchy to a new womanhood. What is particular about the punk approach in this regard is, as with other subject matter that the punk filmmakers choose to work with, both the deflationary approach and the lack of judgement of their subjects, in this case sex work. The representation of sexuality is an extension of the approach of working within their own milieu rather than the representation of others. What stands out in their approach is the way in which the women artists identify with the sex workers as exemplified through the interchangeability of actors, artists and sex workers in these films. This approach is partly generated by the experience of some of the artists working in the bars and cinemas and of those who were living 'cheek by jowl' in the neighbourhoods that supported the sex industry: so this was the lived reality of the artists' lives.

Baby Doll (1982) by Tessa Hughes Freeland discusses the realities of sex explicitly as a way of expressing the reality of women's sexual lives from their own point of view. It is close in form and content to others in this book, such as Bette Gordon's *Anybody's Woman* (1981), to be discussed next;[16] Vivienne Dick's *Liberty's Booty* (1980), discussed in Chapter 5; and Lizzie Borden's *Working Girls* (1986). Betty Gordon describes of the attitude of this milieu in her making of *Variety*: 'I was interested in investigating what it would mean to use pornography – and I came out of a kind of very strong anti-porn movement that had sort of existed before me that was really pressuring women to regard pornography as oppressive and victimizing, and I rejected all of that' (Longworth 2009).

Baby Doll (1982) is approximately three minutes long. It is filmed on 16 mm in black and white and describes the feelings of women who work as Go-Go Girls in the now-defunct Baby Doll Lounge on lower Manhattan. Opening the film is a commentary on the judgement on women and its contradictions. The woman opines that if you work as a professional dancer in one of the establishments such as that depicted in the film, you are considered as 'selling your honour', yet the sheer number of establishments that use women as professional escorts and dancers for the delectation of men, she continues, is such that it reflects the overall misogyny of men towards all women. Meanwhile the visuals are of the kind of neighbourhood corner bar that the woman describes. A second woman speaks and the visuals shift from the universal to the particular; this is another example of the ways in which many of the films in this book move between the particular of their milieu and the universal as they see it and back again to talk about women's lives. In the film, two women are walking up some stairs and start dancing in front of a mirror. They talk about how dancing used to be an art. There is not much space in this room, more of a landing at the top of the stairs, and the camera is close to the women who are putting on make-up and dancing in their petticoats with low-heeled sandals. The voiceovers are of women talking about men, and the visual footage is of two everyday women dancing, cavorting, putting make-up on, sexily but without pretensions to glamour or sophistication. Doing it for themselves. The depiction is of a very particular 1980s woman, strong, playful and sexy in their own terms. This device, of using women from their cultural milieu overlaid with the voices of women in the sex industry, is a common one in these films, and this device aims to collapse the notional dichotomy of the good and bad woman or the Whore versus the Virgin Mary/wife and is used as an equalizing force within the film, stating categorically that we are all sisters together.[17]

Anybody's Woman (1981), by Bette Gordon, begins with a pan from a car of the downtown New York porn shops, X-rated movie theatres and strip clubs. We are soon introduced to a young woman in pink tights, ankle boots and a mini skirt outside a porn theatre called 'Variety'. The next shot is of the same woman in her loft apartment. She puts on a record and there is an insistent telephone ring in the background rather like the tension built by the phone ringing in the earlier mainstream film *Klute* (1971), which was about a sex worker whose life was under threat by an ex-client stalker, which adds to the

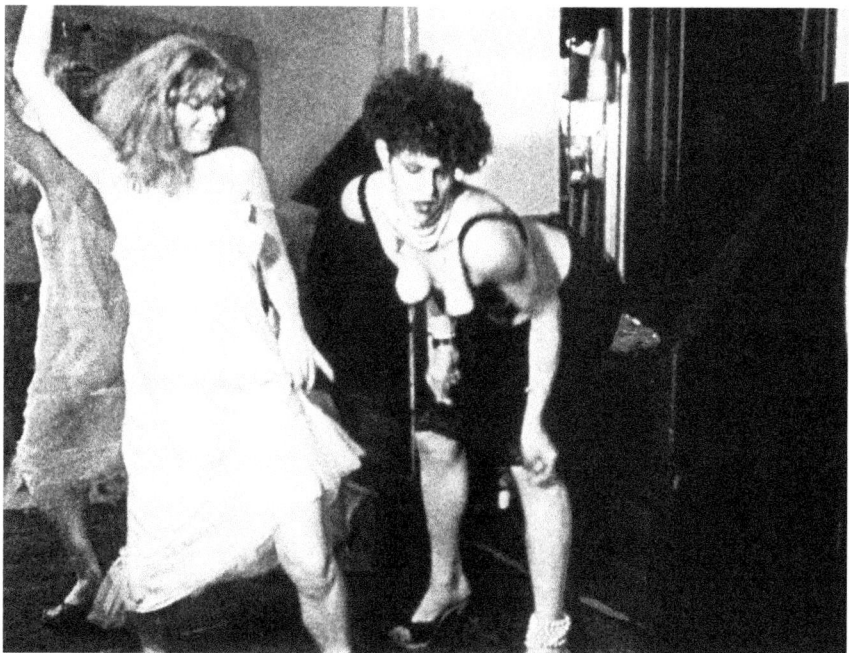

Figure 5. Ferne and Irene in *Baby Doll* (1982, Tessa Hughes-Freeland). Courtesy of the artist.

sense of threat in the Gordon film. In *Anybody's Woman* the young woman picks up the phone and hears a man stating obscenities down the phone. Here, unlike in *Klute*, the protagonist does not react and there is no build-up of tension afterwards. Unlike the Jane Fonda character in Klute, this woman is not afraid, merely exasperated. The woman then sits at a desk and flicks through press photographs of movie stars and pornography while a voiceover narrates a commentary on a film plot by Dorothy Arzner, one of the few women Hollywood directors of the 1920s–1940s (Everleth 2018). Gordon's film is, in fact, titled as an homage to the earlier Arzner film of the same name from 1930 (Hawkins and Gordon 2015: 141). The film then shoots a range of street shots of porn 'dives' and posters. Several scenes ensue, each with the narration of explicit sexual fantasies and the sounds of sex: one in a cafe, another of the sounds of a woman's climaxing and finally a man (Spalding Gray) recounting a sexually explicit scene in a porn movie. Each of these explicit scenes are put together in a deflationary way, with the heightened language of sexually explicit fantasies or pornographic content narrated in a deadpan way, with her friends' amateur acting and with no reaction from the listener on screen. The sound of the woman climaxing for example is accompanied by the visuals of the main protagonist (Nancy Reilly) pacing about an empty cinema lobby bored – both highlighting the sexual nature of the scene and inflating its effects through the non-reaction, or deflation, of the protagonist. Like many films of this milieu there is no denouement and Gordon herself recalls that there seemed to be more consternation at the abrupt end to another similar film, than the use of explicit sexual material.[18] There is no consternation or anger just a telling as if part of everyday experience like any other.

Peggy Ahwesh in *From Romance to Ritual* (1985) makes use of the narration of friends to relate their sexual experiences to build up a picture of the gamut of heterosexual relationships and their failures. She makes the case for an archaeological understanding of the development of patriarchy and its effects, both literally and metaphorically. Unlike Dick and Gordon, as well as a departure from her slightly earlier approach that owes more to Warhol such as *The Pittsburgh Trilogy* (1983) and *The Fragments Project* (1980s), which arguably are more punk, this film, *From Ritual to Romance*, contextualizes the portrait elements with a contextualizing history. The history of patriarchy is bound in this narrative to the ways in which women deal with their sexual relationships. She does this, however, like the others in this chapter, through a deflationary, grungy and punk DIY aesthetic 'my work has an underachiever, self-deprecating quality' (MacDonald 2006: 126), that gives a direct and strident power to the work. Like Vivienne Dick, Ahwesh was a fan of Jack Smith and Andy Warhol. She was also closely aligned with the punk scene, although in Pittsburgh where she lived at the time, and like other artists in the punk scene, she showed her films in venues where punk bands played (MacDonald 2006: 118).

From Romance to Ritual (1985) approaches relations often through the direct address of women. Unlike Freeland and Dick's approach, this is thoroughly encased in the film within a set of vignettes that situates the current lived relations, within wider contextualizing issues, more akin to Sandra Lahire or Susan Stein, both discussed later in the book. The interplay of punk and feminism is very clear here. The film questions the normativity of patriarchy through a brutal testimony of a violent heterosexual, interracial relationship, a failed marriage and single parenthood, which is contrasted with

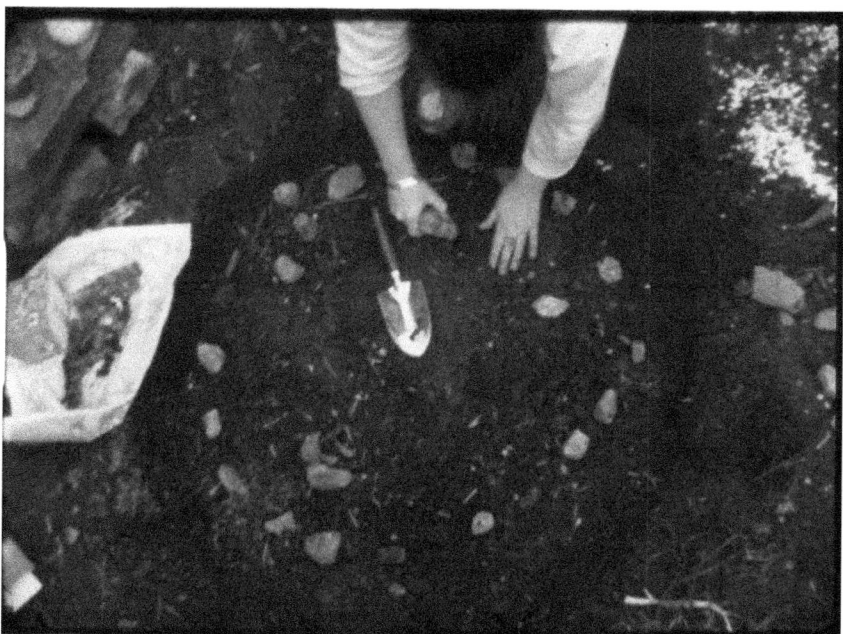

Figure 6. *From Romance to Ritual* (1985, Peggy Ahwesh): frame enlargement from the Super 8 images. Courtesy of the artist.

the description of a prehistoric matriarchal society and is a subversion of the anthropological book of the same name from the 1920s, which sets a trajectory from the pagan to the Christian. Through the reference Ahwesh is questioning the naturalization of patriarchy through history.

The film opens with the meeting of the contemporary and pre-history through an image of the ancient stones at Avebury in England. The camera is handheld, like most here, filming in the manner of home movies. Three elderly people with working-class southern English accents discuss that they know these stones are as old as Stonehenge even though they cannot remember the dates. One of the elderly men goes on to explain the stones as being for rituals and how the stones looked originally and how it was used as a temple. Cut here to a woman, Peggy's downstairs neighbour, talking about her experiences with this 'crazy Black guy'. She recounts in incredulity her eight-year relationship with a violent man, laughing at herself, talking loudly over some cascading synth music by the post-punk band Devo playing in the background. Although the woman begins by sitting, most of the reminiscence is told while the woman talks walking around the room, in her run-down flat, typical of this era and milieu, smoking. The camera is following her around as she walks around the room, moving from foot to foot, putting her beer in the fridge, smoking. For much of this we can only see her torso, sometimes her head and shoulders. She is shouting over the music, which makes her sound slightly hysterical and adds to the drama of the tale. She finally ends the monologue saying, 'the last time I saw him I really had the creeps'. As she says this, there is a jump cut to several seconds of a building being demolished by explosion and then to another longer sequence of a woman, Margie Strosser, also in *Pittsburgh Trilogy*, telling the story of Avebury, using the earth and toy props to explain the development through history. As with the other motifs, this is returned to. It is shot from above, but just a little above in a wry subversion of the 'god shot', the woman is sitting in the dirt. She makes a circle with a trowel and moves the stones around it, digging haphazardly as illustration of her narrative as she speaks. For example, she describes the journey to the maypole from its beginnings as a penis stone, how roads got built and so forth. She tells it hurriedly and loudly, moving the pebbles and dirt around with her hands and trowel, owning the narrative but in an impatient way. The narrative is interrupted and split into two by two further vignettes. One is of two adult women playing in a

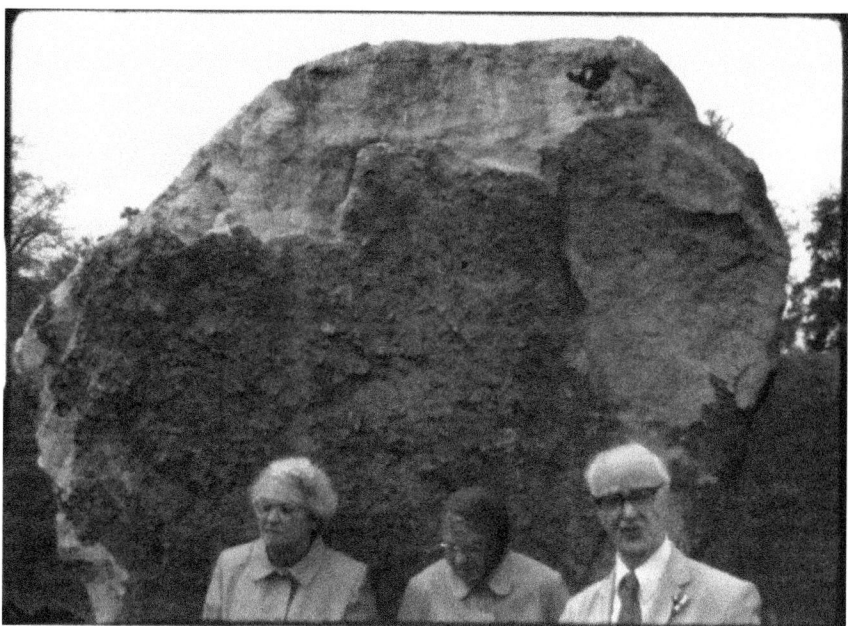

Figure 7. *From Romance to Ritual* (1985, Peggy Ahwesh): frame enlargement from the Super 8 images. Courtesy of the artist.

mocking way with Barbie and Ken dolls, constructing an ironic narrative of courtship, laughing all the while. The other is a young girl of ten or eleven, being tested on her spelling by her mother in the bedroom while she dances and does acrobatics to music.

Unlike the Gordon and Dick films, this is an angry film and one that puts men at the heart of blame. It is a story of survival, of transformation through from abuse to power, from matriarchy to patriarchy and back again. There really are no men in this film except as seen by women, as either old and slightly doddery or through footage of men, dressed up, humorously parading at a carnival, with vastly elongated penises and horns, as tricksters in their own stereotyping just as the women are 'playing' with the Barbie dolls in a humorous and critical retelling of the heteronormative mating game. The women foreground their own experience in all its rawness. They describe history and show their relationships with each other and their children in this film – and all in a new way. There is nothing demure or staged about the camerawork, the editing, the *mise-en-scène* or the narratives. Any staging that is attempted is acknowledged freely, such as talking out of narrative, not hiding the lapel microphone and breaking the fourth wall. All is shot in a deliberate rough-and-ready way, with abrupt jump cuts and sudden endings, replicating the life-as-lived desire for authenticity that many of the films in this book espouse using similar strategies. The convergences and disparities between class and race as well as gender are laid bare through the descriptions of the interracial relationships, the run-down housing, the contrast between the carnival men and the women performers. The film is about desire, the desire of women for men and the subsequent disappointment. It is also drawing equivalences in the desire of the women for the 'other' of men and blackness and its impossibilities due to the asymmetry. This is despite the empathy and desire for equality in its drawing together the experiences of the oppression of women and Black popular culture as represented by the carnival.

Punk was a moment of cultural explosion that marked the end of the line: if there were no more jobs, then there would be no more graciousness, no more trying to please or appease. Everything was up for grabs. In his book *No Respect*, Andrew Ross claims that there is a profound relationship between the immigrant experience and popular culture (1989). Popular culture in the United States has a role as an Americanizing agent and through ambivalence, another unstable state. He argues that the immigrant is promised much – in the United States – and achieves much. However, he is expected always to be grateful. I would argue parallels in relation to class and gender. In the Peggy Ahwesh film the women are fed up with being grateful and are instead disappointed. In *Anybody's Woman* and *Beauty Becomes the Beast* there are no expectations of anyone and certainly not of the state. It is a hermetic world of contempt for those in power. The Bill Grundy moment in the UK was one in which young working-class men demonstrated their lack of faith, in fact paraded their contempt, in that world order particularly, and the commanding generation who set out to belittle them in the eyes of the public.[19] That generation had not provided the stable jobs that they had had access to; the goodies were no longer coming. For women, this took its own turn in relation to gender norms – women need not be gracious to men either. The expectation of delectation and servicing the needs of men portrayed, even in its bohemian mores, in *Pull My Daisy*, was over. As I described in the films by the women in this chapter, women were at the centre of their cultural and concrete world that heralds a different reality to the earlier generation. No longer is it an exception; it is now portrayed as the norm. The dual impact of sexual and domestic insubordination produced its own form in these new films.

Johanna Drucker in *Sweet Dreams* draws the argument in relation to slacker art. She states that there is a relationship between labour and value through fine art, and that slacker art arises at a time when labour markets are devalued. Although the Dick, Ahwesh and Freeland films were made at a time shortly after the collapse of oil prices in 1974 and punk is tied to a period of hardship and upheaval when the threat of nuclear annihilation was still a part of the cultural lexicon, *Pull my Daisy* and *Chelsea Girls*, both slacker films, were made in a time of relative and increasing prosperity. The combination of prosperity and fear of a nuclear ending had a different effect to the nuclear fear of the 1970s that coincided with an economic contraction. So, what was at stake between the 1950s and the 1980s was contingent on these extant factors despite an obvious genealogy to support the development of the films through the post–Second World War generations. Where there is a link it is between the ability to refuse the middlebrow and its expectation of suburban affluence and the ability to live within alternative communities that is tied to the making of art and its aesthetics. So just as Johnny Rotten in a BBC Radio 4 interview from 2014 claimed that punk was 'a direct assault on mediocrity' so Parker Tyler in an earlier period posited cult film as a B movie that was integral to an anti-bourgeois expression (Drucker 2006: 96).

The idea of the B Movie as anti-bourgeois expression can be seen as a possible lineage of a deflationary aesthetic that forms a cache out of necessity. Greg Taylor (1999) argues that Matthew Arnold's edifying tendency has been an overriding driver of form and intention in art in the United States in the nineteenth and twentieth centuries. He makes a forceful argument that the cinema critic has been instrumental in developing a different voice and focus in art that is counter to the purifying and reductive tendencies in the post-war American avant garde. This move against the virtuosity of material that the B movie represented, Taylor argues, arose out of the expansion of the middle classes and the protection of the authority of art and aesthetics for the buying classes in the mid-twentieth century to whom, through a bowdlerized version of Clement Greenberg's theories of the purity of medium specificity, adept handling and formal finesse had become the narrative for abstract painting.

There have been many instances of alterity critiquing some of the legacies of Greenbergian modernism. Many of these, such as T J Clark in *Pollock and After* (1985: 21–88), discuss the problems with Greenberg's modernism through his assertions of the importance of negation of the medium. For Clark, negation is the moment of the breaking down of the medium, the awkwardness of the aesthetic or form and its relationship to the disintegration of the bourgeoisie at the time of writing. Postmodernism also celebrated a 'mash up' approach to medium or style. According to Greg Taylor film criticism evolved over the last half of the twentieth century into an art form in itself. Taylor argues that the development of the importance of film, in the United States at least, represented a flight from the bourgeois taste-makers and painting-buying conformists as well as a way to negotiate the self-positioning of the intellectual in post-war US culture. Kitsch was part of that flight, as was schlock – literally, in Yiddish meaning damaged goods – and camp. Taylor identifies two important thrusts away from the middlebrow: that of the cult and the camp, important in the early film critics' analysis of film culture. Cult was in essence an engagement with the obscure and the forgotten in such a way as it elevated the critic as expert or taste-maker supreme. Camp was to do with a re-reading – a queering – of normative mainstream codes. The punk aesthetic that I would identify here is an interweaving of these two forms, which in either case represents a counter-tendency against the overriding *doxa* of neo-minimalist formalism as the defining criteria of good taste, and therefore good art. There is also the sense – qua Clark – that punk remains a key moment of modernist gesture, and I will examine this conception further in relation to punk film in the following chapters (Taylor 1999).[20] First, however, I will explore in Chapter 2 the constitution of self that embraces a cosmopolitan modernity. This was crucial to the impact of punk and central to many of the artists in this book.

Notes

1   It was later, after New York, when living in London in the 1990s that Dick studied for an MA in film and video.

2   '[N]ot totally, all my films, even the short ones, engage with narrative, non-traditional narrative, but there are characters and a kind of subject – for example, Michigan Avenue has a beginning, middle and end of a loose love story' (Gordon email, 15 February 2021).

3   'That's funny I used the term "heavy" for Millennium Film workshop! Did I really say that? Anyway maybe "serious" or "reverent" is what I meant. I would have been thinking of Anthology Archives at the time – where I saw a lot of American Independent Cinema for the first time – many of the films screened were silent and there was an air of reverence in the cinema. The seating was hard and the atmosphere was "arty"' (Dick email, 16 August 2020).

4   The films had sound and would play in their own right between bands so they had their own screening conditions but did not have the reverence that, say, Anthology would have, where the total focus would have been on the film (Dick email, 16 August 2020).

5   This is pointed out also in Hawkins (2015: 321), where she notes that Beth B claimed that the crossover of music, cinema and art was new. Beth B, having gone to art school and having grown up within an art milieu, would have known about the earlier generation of artists such as Fluxus, who broke down category divisions between art forms.

6   It is no accident that Roberts names Nan Goldin as a proponent of the use of the snapshot, a close ally of Dick and Gordon.

7   This historic division and its critique are explained in Gambaudo 2007.

8   The New American Cinema was established in a statement by Jonas Mekas. It stated that cinema is a personal expression: that it is anti-censorship, avoiding the myth of the requirement of a big budget; establishing new funding systems and small budgets as an ethical position; and establishing their own distribution centre, film fund and festival (quoted from Everleth: 20 September 2007).

9   *Pull My Daisy* explores the gendered tension between the need for stability in bourgeois terms – the mother wanting it for the child – and the desire for the men to follow their drunken whims, oblivious to the needs of others.

10   I will be comparing this to Dick's *Liberty's Booty* in a subsequent chapter.

11   Of course concern with form is unavoidable within the rectangular construction of the lens, and in any case, Clarke was not a structuralist filmmaker at all, believing herself in the power of the experiential lens.

12   See Gavin Butt's work on *Portrait of Jason* in Mercer (2007).

13   Hoberman (1979) identified the films *Chelsea Girls* and *Pull My Daisy* as possible precursors to Vivienne Dick.

14 Hoberman also makes the first link between punk and camp here.

15 There is also a gender bias in this film towards the men being the inventors, taking chances with the women pulling them back to safety and domesticity.

16 Many in this book also incorporate women's sexuality or attitude towards sex explicitly such as Dick's *Liberty's Booty* (1980), Bette Gordon's *Variety* (1983) and *Anybody's Woman* (1981).

17 Such as *Liberty's Booty* (Dick 1980) and *Anybody's Woman* (Gordon 1981).

18 'Anybody's woman was more like an essay film, and exploration of ideas that served as a notebook and sketch for what would later become VARIETY' (Gordon, email 15 February 2021).

19 https://www.theguardian.com/theguardian/1976/dec/03/greatinterviews (Accessed: 5 April 2019).

20 Manny Farber was also a painter but turned to film criticism as he saw abstract expressionism become a sell-out.

2

The last of the modern two: Visualizing women, otherness and the cosmopolitan punk

The process in which anti-fascist and anti-racist activism became a movement rather than an aggregate of uneven and disparate local groups significantly had its origins outside the realm of politics. It relied for its development on networks of culture and communication in which the voice of the left was scarcely discernible and it drew its momentum from the informal and organic relationship between black and white youth which sprung up in the shadow of 1970s' youth culture

(Gilroy 1991: 155).

The Slits had their first single in 1979. They were an all-women early punk band in London who formed in 1976. *Typical Girls* was on the A side of the single and *I Heard It Through the Grapevine* was on the B side. Both songs borrowed in different ways from Black musical roots. *I Heard It Through the Grapevine* was a punk remake of a Marvin Gaye soul classic with a subverted, scratchy reggae off-beat, and a gender swap. While *Typical Girls* is an original composition, the song itself references a range of markers from African-Caribbean culture.

In the first instance this song was a manifesto where the women aimed to differentiate themselves decisively from everything that might invoke normative femininity. The song cited examples of normative femininity that erodes a women's sense of self, such as feeling bad about themselves because of worrying about their looks, their weight, their smell. These *Typical Girls* are thus overly susceptible to others' views. The song becomes, in its own way, a powerful critique against the patriarchal media that punishes women for non-conformity.

In the video made to accompany *Typical Girls*, the women play on a bandstand in Regent's Park, dancing in a new and quirky way more akin to Emile Nolde's *Dance around the Golden Calf* (1910) with limbs springing out at awkward angles, than the usual swinging hips allure of disco dancing of the time. The Slits also wear clothing considered 'non-feminine' at the time: work boots, leggings, men's shirts. Now, forty years later, this kind of clothing and dancing have been subsumed into the portfolio of feminine acceptability. At the time it had not been seen before and this is exemplified by the focus in the film that begins with the women walking in the park towards the bandstand. The camera follows behind two of the women, Ari Up and Palm Olive. Ari hands Palm a handkerchief and she blows her nose loudly while chewing gum – both a flouting of femininity. The camera catches her smiling self-consciously before jumping to a shot of a middle-aged, balding, overweight man in his shirtsleeves walking towards the camera. The camera lingers on his changing expression from blank stare to befuddlement and finally quizzical disapproval. This man is us, Joe Public, walking through the park noticing strange characters gathering. The camera jumps between the man and the punks, interlacing and positioning the two constituents as living in two very different worlds – the normative white male world and the new other world of alien women. The heightened sound of the birds tweeting serves to juxtapose the song in its violence and posit the punks as opposite 'the natural'. It is filmed using documentary strategies, and the sequence implies that it is the appearance of these women in their strangeness, walking along the path, that causes a stir. So before they even get to the place of performing their music, they are already a spectacle, performing their contempt for 'typical girls', inciting silent derision from the public. They know, as women, they are judged for their look and they use it against itself. The shot of the man highlights the lack of response from the public, who do not act, but pass by the women in silence. This silence, the unspeakability of their transgression of femininity, as with Poly Styrene, is to be contrasted with the mobbing of the Sex Pistols in the street or even the mobbing of the Beatles, an earlier generation of female transgression. Possibly the only transgression seen to be allowed by women was this overriding image in popular culture of female fans overwhelmed to hysteria as a form of abjection, offering her body to the male pop star.

The Slits perform their song on a bandstand in the park. The audience is incidental, neither fans nor punters, but people eating their sandwiches, indifferent also to the performing Slits. The absence of response – unlike the anger at the Bill Grundy interview – is as something that is not symbolized and cannot be assimilated. However, it is not merely their visual personas that are unreadable but the discordant valances of their unique and new musical hybridity worked through heavy dub reggae rather than the more usual soul or blues.

That The Slits marked their offensive against normative femininity in musical terms, that is through a reggae off-beat, speaks through the decades of the twentieth century of exoticization of the African-Caribbean that goes to the very heart of popular culture and its relationship with cool as an identification with a critique of the status quo. Ross suggests that the common experience of outsiderness between intellectuals and Black culture was a common link but was without symmetry. However, I will argue here that while the lack of symmetry and ambivalence is, of course, a continuing problem that has its own urgency – and while beyond the scope of this book is a discourse to which I have contributed to elsewhere[1] – for the purposes of this chapter I will put forward the position that in the excess of the naïve and misguided intentions of whiteness, the practice of assimilating Black vernacular forms has allowed some positive effects to emerge nonetheless. These contributions to the changing of attitudes towards the Caribbean population as a whole have endured. Today, since 9/11, the race debates have given way to faith debates and the focus on migrants is as much to do with Eastern Europeans as those from the post-colonial nation states. Racism still occupies the narrative of Britishness, and the force of Black Lives Matter and the ongoing Windrush scandal both demonstrate the distance still to be travelled towards equality in the UK. Nonetheless, African-Caribbeans now occupy a different space in the UK than in the 1980s and while also being subject to institutional – and overt – racism, black and brown communities are unarguably at the heart of Britishness. Not to underplay the continued racism that drives British institutional life, there is a confidence and an expectation of belonging to Britishness to which previous generations of African-Caribbeans aspired: punk, while a minor cultural force, was one of the tipping points of that transition.

'Punk Rock', stated Poly Styrene, inspired by an early Sex Pistols gig, 'gave me a platform to put a band together and do it my way' (quoted in Letts 2005). Poly Styrene, the lead in the band X-Ray Spex, was a Black woman. Rhoda Dakar in the 2019 book on Poly Styrene contextualizes her attraction to punk in relation to their identity. 'Now it is completely common to be biracial, but back then it was fairly unusual. In a way we were embraced by Punk, because it was full of people nobody wanted' (Bell and Howe 2019: 27). As described in the introduction, Poly Styrene was a punk icon from very early in punk history. The impact of X-Ray Spex was swift and by 1978 she was on national TV with a second single.[2] Her mother was a Scots-Irish woman and her father Somalian. The pressures on Poly Styrene would have been different to other punk icons such as Ari Up, Laura Logic or Siouxsie Sioux. As a mixed-race woman with northeast African heritage, her position as an outsider would have been manifold at the time: as a Black woman, Styrene would have had to put up with both racism and sexism, and as a woman of mixed Somali/British heritage, she felt an outsider to the largely Caribbean Black community, which may go some way to explain Styrene's musical proclivities:

> I was born Marianne Elliot-Said, to a white mother and a Somali father. It was Bromley, 1957. My mum was really open-minded, or maybe just colour blind, as she couldn't foresee how hard it would really be for my dad to live with us. After a few years, we moved to Brixton but it still didn't work. Brixton was a West Indian neighbourhood and dad's skin was really light. Everyone thought he was of a lighter caste and so they maligned him along with the white folks. My mum ended up on her own with mixed race kids, and it was hard, especially when I decided to leave school at 15.
>
> (Styrene 2005)

This music that trumpeted the emptiness of contemporary life effected such a transformation that in the following decade, the terms of reference were to have changed completely. Possibly because of her non-normative blackness within the context of London in the 1960s, where she grew up, Poly Styrene changed both the form – through punk – the content and the expectations of whiteness in certain musical forms in the UK. Her presence pre-empted a normalization of blackness in the public sphere, without the burden of representation. In other words, Poly was a Black woman doing it 'her way' by not talking about blackness. This wasn't assimilation. It was a transformation both within music and beyond.[3]

The arguments that could be marshalled to think through her relationship to Black cultural forms are similar to those argued out in the 1980s in relation to the film collectives Sankofa and Black Audio Film Collective at the time of production (Mercer 1987). Reading the texts from that period, common debates around that work were reflecting on what makes a Black vernacular form, what influences are legitimate to use, whom to speak to and what constitutes a Black voice. While in some senses Styrene was modelling a deracinated reinvention, Sankofa and Black Audio Film Collective were ostensibly proffering an inverse proposition more akin to Ové's: that of a rooted visibility. That is a simplistic reading, however, as the Sankofa films that I will look at take a position that is rooted but complex. They offer, through formal means, a possibility of a progressive contemporary multivalent idea of subjectivity, one that is provisional and contingent, through the language of film as well as subject matter, just as Poly Styrene was offering contingent and precarious subjectivity through form and subject matter in her own way through punk. Both were aiming for visibility on their own terms through the differences of a new vernacular that they were themselves forming out of their lived experience.

The music X-Ray Spex played was unique and did not conform to already existing genres that are associated with Black-identified music, for example soul, nor the now more punk-associated reggae.[4] Nonetheless, this is an interesting contrast to the bands of white punk musicians who played reggae-inflected music, such as The Clash or The Slits. Poly Styrene herself did not talk at the time about her blackness; however, she was one of the first to offer to perform at the first Rock Against Racism gig. There is no reason that she should conform to any notions of a 'Black musician', but it is clear that punk gave her a space to act without the pressure or expectation of 'community', save what she invented for herself, while borrowing from a heterogeneous range of references. Her lyrics were prescient, about consumerism, global warming and other issues that were to do with her existential alienation rather than a direct expression of her Blackness, which, given her stated difficulty of fitting in to any community of her childhood, is not surprising. This is not just to do with lyrics as to do with the combination of those lyrics being embedded within a musical vernacular that did not 'speak community'. Poly Styrene's vocal control was veiled behind a lack of conformity in its use that sounded out of control to many. Punk in the 1970s was a liberation from the expected conventions of craftsmanship and narrative seamlessness. Its modus operandi was the inverse: to not care about audience, and also to argue – or sing – for a form that questioned social mores. It was a new expressionism that was not focused on rationalist critique nor instrumentalizing art. It modelled a new culture for a new moment. The high-pitched shriek of Styrene marked the death rattle of modernity.

So Styrene sang without recourse to a Black community. She inserted herself into the wider limelight through inventing her own way of songwriting and performing that did not belong to a known preconceived form, that was in itself being inventive and casting off previously held assumptions regarding behaviour, mores and the visual languages of both. Her position, as the lead of a white male band rather than just as the singer fronting them, was part of a wider cultural shift that, I suggest, may have helped to make the space for the next generation of Black visual artists such as Keith Piper, Eddie Chambers and Claudette Johnson to imagine and demand visibility on their own terms in the early 1980s. It may have helped to imagine a different visual address as British citizens of a wider world further exemplified by the late 1980s British musicians of *Soul II Soul*. The ostensible trajectory from Rock Against Racism through to the Blk Art Group set up by Chambers, Piper et al., is a parallel trajectory to that of the trajectory that led to Black Audio Film Collective, Sankofa and Ceddo, and was a moment before the merging of independent film with the art world. The shift that Poly Styrene's band X-Ray Spex represented as a role model was the move from a singular, differentiated community proposed as an interior whole which can be exemplified through the film *Pressure* (1976) towards a visible and complex representation of self as explored through Poly Styrene. And this transformative move was a mere two years after *Pressure* (1976), the first Black-directed feature film in the UK, by Horace Ové.

Pressure was a pioneering film in its own way. In terms of professional structures in the British film world, it was groundbreaking for a Black man to be directing a feature film despite a rich sector of independent films. This was a unique opportunity to give visibility and voice to the Caribbean community resident in the Notting Hill area. Notting Hill was a pressure cooker, and the film came out the same year as the Notting Hill riots in 1976 which started on the evening of the last day of the carnival, so a film that aimed to discuss and make visible the pressures of the community from the inside was important. The device of neorealism of bringing bystanders into the frame or of dropping actors into a documentary scene was axiomatic for those who wanted cinema to be in the service of the social and political sphere. These devices can be seen in the next generation such as Sankofa, which I discuss here, or Black Audio Film Collective but is more connected to the lineage that produces filmmakers like Ken Loach, for example. The form of Ové's film drew from cinematic roots such as neorealism and the Free Cinema. However, the impact of setting up the internal contradiction within the film as a form of immanent critique, a mode of address that was largely taught at art school, is absent in *Pressure*. Neither were there the defining features of political modernism of Brechtian distanciation that defined counter cinema (Rodowick 1994). It was later in the 1980s that art school approaches to the moving image emerged as a Black cinematic voice through those such as Black Audio Film Collective and Sankofa, and even later still, in the 1990s that artists of colour began to be supported in a consistent way towards major prizes and blue chip gallery engagement. The conditions had not yet arisen to make the equivalent of Poly Styrene in art possible, let alone a critical Black vernacular form. The lineage of Black artists from Ové to Sankofa, to, say, Steve McQueen, within the context of the UK, is one from neorealist to modernist conventions towards a postcolonial vernacular, in a way that foregrounds an emergent embedding and confidence in the UK's Black communities within only a few decades.[5]

There are many factors that precipitated these shifts, some social and some to do with precursors and exemplars, but the access to funding in film production is a critical side to development that is often overlooked in the discourses of art. Furthermore, the films made under these conditions were until recently considered a different category of production. Within independent film, the video workshops offered an unprecedented boost to a generation of people of colour. It brought funding to people without access to the art world on the one side and without access to the film or TV industry on the other – the so-called independent sector. The video workshops had been campaigned for and negotiated by the Independent Filmmakers Association and resulted in the ACTT workshop declaration of 1981. However, the intention of the ACTT workshop declaration had, through the Scarman Report, focused the aims towards an inclusivity that had not previously been a priority. The Scarman Report had been commissioned in direct response to the riots across the country – and again in Notting Hill – in April 1981. The report had a long-term impact in changing the law and in shaping the approach of the police – and other institutions – to the BAME communities for several decades to come; arguably it shaped the mores and expectations of a generation in the late twentieth century. The ACTT Video Workshop Declaration in 1981 thus helped the coalescence of Black film collectives, such as Sankofa, Ceddo Film Collective and Black Audio Film Collective, through localized and national funding from the Greater London Council (GLC) and Channel 4, organizations that were committed by then to 'encourage diversity' as was the workshop declaration itself. Importantly it gave a salary to those funded through the workshops.[6]

Two strands are running through this chapter that are interlinked. Each is moving in opposite directions characterized by The Slits running towards a frisson of black otherness as an offering of a more authentic existence – as Ari Up would have perceived it – and Poly Styrene working through punk as an equalizing factor that allows her to negotiate her subjectivity away from 'community' expectations.[7] Both journeys represent a form of escape from normativity that speaks to the constraints on women of all cultures. Punk enabled them to find both a home and a freedom in music. In the same way punk allowed women a freedom from the double burden of the constraints of cinematic convention and to question the constraints and boundaries of any community, be it white or black.

In describing these somewhat parallel and contrasting flows, I will be reflecting on specific films: *The Passion of Remembrance* (1986) by Sankofa, *Rootless Cosmopolitans* (1990) and *Tea Leaf* (1986) by Ruth Novaczek, and *Liberty's Booty* (1980) and *London Suite* (*Getting Sucked In*) (1990) by Vivienne Dick. These films are by artists from a range of diasporic positions. Notably there are distinctions between the European-derived diasporic artists such as Dick and Novaczek, who were Irish and Jewish, respectively, and the artists from the African or Asian diasporas such as Sankofa or Alia Syed. I will also be looking at Anne Robinson's film *Real Woman* (1984) as well as Lizzie Borden's *Born in Flames* (1983) as examples of the new normativity of multiculturalism by white artists, all of whom were part of the decisive turn towards a new language of exploring cultural identity in film in the UK. My intention is not to conflate the different diasporic experiences of the members of Sankofa (African-Caribbean), Ruth Novaczek (Jewish) and Vivienne Dick (Irish) nor to overplay equivalences. My aim is to reflect on these disparate films through the times they are in, as a turning point in race relations and the importance of the wider cultural influences in this moment. However, before discussing these specific filmmakers, I would like to introduce an earlier film from the United States, *The Cool World* (1963) by Shirley Clarke, by way of differentiation both from the later British films and from a British site of production. In order to open up the discussion on later films, I will at first focus on Horace Ové's film *Pressure* (1976).

Pressure (1976) can be usefully contrasted with Poly Styrene as she rode the crest of the wave of punk and is a testament to the miasmic change that her presence and persona within music delivered. Styrene can also be marshalled to speculate on the tensions between the desire to represent and the burden of representation as well as the opposite directional flow of these two forms of expression. *Pressure* is a narrative-led slice of life feature film which shows the stresses under which a young Black man and his milieu lived in west London over a period of several days. The pressure described is both macro and micro: on the one hand the backdrop of the film is the politics of institutional racism, the activism of the British Black Power movement and the role of the church within the Black community and of Christianity within the protection of institutional racism.[8] On a micro-level is the pressure Tony feels to find a job, to conform to his parents' and community's expectations in stark contrast to the expectations – or rather assumptions – of him by the white community by whom he is trying to get hired. Tony is also dealing with his brother's expectations of him to become 'politicized' and the pressure by his less fortunate mates to hang out in a squat with them and live their life. Disconnected and disappointed by his inability to get work, and indifferent to the separatism represented by his brother's pan-African political position, he hangs out with his seemingly ne'er-do-well friends who did not work as hard as him at school and who are just getting by. What is to be noted about this film is twofold: firstly, the way in which Horace Ové used the language of realism to produce a coherence that is part of the fiction of race politics, despite the different positions of Christian or pan-Africanist representations; to some extent this was an intergenerational discussion. In this coherence the film's narrative aims to show a coherent representation of a community in west London that can be owned: owned by him. Even the disjuncture of the dream sequence serves to explain the possibility of a singular Black narrative of revenge. Secondly, and important for my argument, is that this representation is devoid of credible women characters or characterizations. The Black experience is envisioned and explained as a world that is for and about men.

Introducing this comparison between Ové and Poly Styrene is not to undermine the strengths of *Pressure*, nor the difficulties the director would have had to overcome in order that the film be made, which was an achievement in itself. *Pressure*, as a sensitive and sophisticated portrait of a particular and common but marginalized experience of young British men, fulfils the traditions that Kobena Mercer identifies in *Black Film, British Cinema* (1987) as important for his generation, and important in activist circles: transparency, immediacy, authority and authenticity. These characteristics offered the promise of neutrality, a mirror to the community's experience, and, given the racism at the time prevalent in the representation of the Black communities in the media, an important corrective both for the communities and for the wider public. The film aims to reveal the real story of young Black men to offer visibility to the white community and invite their empathy through the difficulties of racism and its concomitant stereotyping that they encounter on a daily basis. However, the film also falls into the trap of what we can now see as the burden of representation: a singular narrative that emphasizes the same kind of cohesion in structural terms that it is trying to refute from the white community – in its stereotyping – by in effect stating, 'No, you have got it wrong, this is the Black community really'. Within the scenario of the film, a character like Poly Styrene could not exist. Despite these criticisms from the vantage point of today, as an early film about 'the community' within a narrative of influx, danger and turmoil this film was also an important statement of presence for the west London Black British community. It spoke of the wider concerns of the perception of young Black men in west London as a counter to the racist narratives of stereotypes that prevailed. Stuart Hall discussed this in his landmark text that outlined the ways in which capitalist society had created a moral panic around Black youth through a mugging narrative as a scapegoat for the economic and hegemonic collapse in the early 1970s (Hall et al. 1978).

The comparison with *Pressure* is somewhat awkward, but the contrast is drawn with the intention of highlighting the radical break for Black women that Poly Styrene represented. It took another decade for there to be as strong a Black voice in art, particularly in film, supported by both the aforementioned Workshop Declaration and a landmark Arts Council for England report by Naseem Khan, 'The arts Britain ignores: The arts of ethnic minorities in Britain' (1975), that called for funding to be given to ethnic minority communities in the UK.

What today might be seen as a Black vernacular form in contemporary video art did not emerge so much through this trajectory in Britain. The later artists such as Zarina Bhimji (b. 1963), Janaan Al-Ani (b. 1966), Zineb Sedira (b. 1963) or Alia Syed (b. 1964), who have been celebrated in the last few decades, were all educated in fine art departments rather than in film departments, following in the footsteps of Mona Hatoum (b. 1954), who was a pioneer of sorts. The art school trajectory is to some extent different to that of political documentary that belies what Kobena Mercer suggested as 'a preponderance of a realist aesthetic' (1994: 56).

So the early 1980s was a period where filmmakers forged new languages that gave voice to the exploration of a range of counter-hegemonic identities in the UK. This was an era of an emergent multiculturalism, which had yet to undergo the critiques of its limits – characterized through newspaper articles claiming its failure in the late 1980s and 1990s.

The post–Second World War British press and the public imaginary of the 1970s and 1980s foregrounded narratives of an erstwhile homogeneity coupled with negative stereotypes of immigrants and their effect on the status quo. There is an influential body of scholarship arisen out of the Birmingham Centre for Cultural Studies as one prominent example that has served to disprove that misguided narrative, exposing it for the fiction that it is. While racisms are ongoing in British popular culture and on the rise again, as represented in the recent scandalous and shameful deportations of the children of Windrush migrants as just one example, it lacks quite the pervasive consensus that it had in the 1970s and the early 1980s. This period, in fact, defined the framework for the future steps that have been taken as a model of inclusivity.

The decade of the emergence of punk, that is the 1970s, saw the unravelling of this consensus of assimilation in the UK. The aims of assimilation of so-called minority communities for the next generations, who grew up born and educated in England itself, gave way to the demand and expectation of multiculturalism and visibility (Bauman 1988; Steyn 2000). The assimilation discourse itself was a middle-class project. The aims were to fit in and be accepted by the so-called host community. Assimilation as an idea actively maintained the antimonies of host and visitor: that of an 'us' and 'them' and of class assumptions of the incomers. Within those binary oppositions, a false homogeneity of each antimony was also presumed. This can be seen in class terms as the normativity of 'host' and migrant that was in itself a misnomer that presumed certain ways of life. This presumed way of life conformed to a very few: that of white – read here Church of England – middle class. There was a tacit assumption that schools would teach those values to make the immigrant children acceptably English. In other words, the aspiration to be accepted was tantamount to the aspiration to be middle class. And for the purposes of my argument here, middle-class status and whiteness were equivalences.[9]

Punk rejected the middle-class project *tout court,* identifying instead with working-class subjectivity. At that time Black culture was positioned as working class. On the one hand this idea brings to mind the fetishization of working people and of blackness that is common in the predominantly white middle-class make-up of the art world and the cultural milieu at large. Popular culture as fetish has been characterized by Andrew Ross in *No Respect,* where Ross analyses the appropriation of class, race and sexuality into mainstream hegemonic American culture. By contrast, Mica Nava, a sociologist in the UK, in her book *Visceral Cosmopolitanism* (2007), posits a more optimistic addition to the discussion of the false narrative of homogenous Englishness by framing it through the prevalence of liaisons between white working-class women and Black men as an identification along class lines on the one hand and also through their alliance as commonly discriminated individuals. In Nava's view, experiences across sexism and racism occasioned an opportunity for the bonding of these couples in the post–Second World War era. Her work sets a corroborating context for reggae and punk that is central to my argument. 'Reggae not as authenticity but as a signifier for a group of victimised, disenfranchised youth who didn't belong in the establishment' (Hebdige 1979: 64).

Mica Nava's position is marginal within the climate of current race discourse that has once more given rise to the debates regarding who can speak for whom. While there are considerable gains in the visibility and stridency of the re-engagement with feminism, trans and 'race' debates, what has been lost, with the current resuscitation of identitarian political discourse, is the generosity of equivalences that can bring solidarity across different forms of oppression through class discourses – slavery happened to me and the Holocaust happened to you, patriarchy happens to us all: all are atrocities. This has given rise to hierarchies of victimhood that pits one type of oppression against another and assumes bounded communities that are in competition rather than the more real entangled, performative relationships to community (Garfield 2001: 63–70).

With the Americanization of race politics, the framing of identification or alliance-building has entered discourse as a symptom of exoticization. While legitimate in some ways, it is yet another factor that undermines possibilities for alliance or fealty between differentiated communities. In its differentiations and divisions it also renders invisible people's multiple identities. For example, Anna Everett's citation of *The Crying Game* (1992), which criticizes its use of the Black trans woman as a cipher for white privilege. This is an apposite example of how a nuanced point of the film was missed in Everett's hegemonic worldview from the United States: Ireland through her eyes is not seen as a country which has also suffered under colonial rule and has a complex history in relation to England. She states, 'And just when my exasperation prompts me to ask; "Why don't they just leave blacks out of it?" I realise that in our racialized culture over-privileged whiteness requires underprivileged blackness' (Everett 1995: 37). What Anna Everett did not see in her subject position was the intersectionality of gender and race through the place that those from the Republic of Ireland played as 'other' in the British imaginary because of their own relationship to the UK. In order to develop the reductive position she holds, Everett needs to gloss over the very complex narrative of a Northern Irish Catholic who had allegiances with the IRA into the simplistic issue of skin colour. Ireland's history is one of colonization, forced famine and atrocity by the British. In her reading, Everett, albeit unwittingly, erases not only the historic discrimination but also the ongoing discrimination and abuse such a person would have had in England during the Troubles. The equivalence set up through the simple black/white binary does not work here.

This kind of ethnic insiderism is as much a problem today in the twenty-first century as it was in the 1980s, when Werner Sollors coined the phrase, and is a way of foreclosing on alliances in an invidious race to the bottom that can nonetheless be heard in arguments of who can play whom in a film. In other words, questions still emerge regarding whether a straight actor can play a lesbian or if you have to have Jewish ancestry to make a film about the Holocaust. A recent painful controversy revolved around a painting in the Whitney Biennial in 2018 regarding whether a white artist can paint a Black victim of race hatred. Hannah Black, Coco Fusco – both themselves black – and others had an intense debate about whether Dana Schutz's painting of Emmet Till could be exhibited or even allowed to exist. In this way multiculturalist discourse becomes a discourse of exclusions and visibility.

Back in the 1970s it all seemed less complex, although it never really is. Levels of xenophobia and racism were being ramped up by the political climate of fear and the media, on the one hand, and on the other, political unrest and fight-back in predominantly Black areas of cities in Toxteth, Notting Hill and Handsworth raised awareness of the issues of the Black communities that went beyond them into the wider communities. The result was one of a political consciousness and a climate of action against state oppression that many punks identified with.

If the inclusion of the Irish into the lexicon or at least the link with multiculturalism is to be questioned here – as with Anna Everett's elision – it must be remembered that at the time IRA activity as well as rhetoric of a war against oppression was a visible and dominant part of the landscape of the Irish in the UK. The SUS laws that structurally embedded racist activity in the police force, combined with the Troubles, gave a sense of urgency to the resentment against what was considered 'police oppression' – a byword for many young people who identified as alternative or oppositional.[10] Stiff Little Fingers, a popular Ulster punk band, is an obvious example of the ways in which politics and music often shared a platform through consciousness-raising within punk in the content of the music as well as coming together as in Rock Against Racism, so much so that bands such as the Angelic Upstarts, their name trading on their white working-class provenance, used *Police Oppression* as a title of their double A side single – The *Murder of Liddle Towers* being the other A side – in 1978 and The Clash put a cover of Junior Murvin and Lee 'Scratch' Perry's *Police and Thieves* on their first album, released in 1977.

This shared lexicon and existential camaraderie for a range of differently colonized urban youth who were made to feel, by the state, that they did not belong drew these two seemingly unlikely disenfranchised groups together – of a self-declared white working-class group of people and Black urban working-class young people – if only in musical terms. Paul Gilroy describes some of the links and overlaps of language and the way in which the forces of youth culture in punk drew out an alliance that changed the climate in the UK in relation to race and culture. He suggests that 'the dread notion of "Babylon System" allowed disparate and apparently contradictory expressions of the national crises to be seen as a complex, interrelated whole, a coherent structure of which racism was a primary characteristic' (1991: 123). Dick Hebdige, in his book *Subcultures* (1979), also comments on the relationship between reggae and punk, identifying this alliance at the heart of punk: 'punk includes reggae as a "present absence" – a black hole around which punk composes itself' (1979: 68).

It was this informal alliance between reggae and punk which helped bring into being, which had its inception in 1976, and alongside Campaign for Nuclear Disarmament (CND) became a motivating force for politicizing a generation. It was an alliance as much against an older generation of rockers as it was an alliance of younger disenfranchised people. The apocryphal narrative is that Red Saunders, a documentary photographer, wrote a letter to the music press in protest at the racist and anti-immigration comments by Eric Clapton at a gig in Birmingham. The letter asked for anyone wanting to join a rank-and-file protest to write. He received over 300 letters and subsequently organized several gigs, firstly in a pub in Forest Gate, East London, then at the Royal College of Art. The third gig was to be after an anti-racist march in Victoria Park, also in east London (Huddle in Huddle and Saunders 2016: 13–14).

The first open air gig in 1978 attracted 80,000 people (Huddle in Huddle and Saunders 2016: 16), with the line-up being overwhelmingly punk and reggae. Punk was thus an important pivotal moment for the integration of Black culture within the UK. According to Billy Bragg, 'when punk came along, which was a bringing together of white culture punk and Black culture reggae, I was already primed for that so Rock Against Racism was the first activism I was ever involved in … going to see The Clash at the first Anti Nazi League rally'.[11] There are different accounts of who brought whom on board, whether the Socialist Workers' Party (SWP), who were some key organizers, galvanized punk in favour of anti-racism or whether punk musicians were already making those moves. This disagreement over origin is a distraction. What actually matters is the mobilization of music and its wider impact on young people who regarded equality as the future within one of the first mass normalizations of what was later called multiculturalism in the UK. Even seemingly unpoliticized young punks such as Jordan, the famous punk shop assistant of the punk fashion outlets Sex and Seditionaries, were being brought into this rubric as with Billy Bragg, who has had a lifelong commitment to political activism and anti-racism. 'As early as May 1977 Jordan was expressing a preference for reggae over "new wave" on the pages of NME (7 May 1977): "It's the only music we [i.e. Jordan and J. Rotten] dance to"' (Hebdige 1979: 28). The normalization of a Black presence through the alliance of music and politics, in turn, had an impact on the arts for those coming of age as filmmakers and artists following on in the 1980s and the way in which they represented the people around them as I discuss later in the chapter.

The 1970s is often characterized as an era of racism, of neo-Nazi skinheads, and the 'rivers of blood' speech given by Enoch Powell, who was the MP for Wolverhampton in 1968, but I would suggest that a different picture emerges in contextualizing this assumption through the comparison with Rock Against Racism and Rock Against Communism. Rock Against Communism is sometimes cited as proof that punk could go either way politically and was not 'naturally' a liberal or left community of fans.[12] With a backdrop of a heightened politicized culture in the UK, it is not surprising that political activists saw punk as a battle for heart and minds, and in this we can see the early encroachment of marketization on youth culture. Rock Against Communism organized its first gig at the Conway Hall and is discussed in various ways by some historians to suggest that punk had no specific leanings and was open for business by anyone willing to canvass and recruit (Sabin 1999; Worley and Copsey 2016). However, the comparison between the audiences for Rock Against Communism and Rock Against Racism need only to be compared for this so-called even-handed argument to be demolished: the Rock Against Communism gig attracted an extremely small audience that would not sustain a movement. It also had no backing within the music industry itself; for example, Rough Trade, Screwdriver's punk record company, on the day of the Rock Against Communism gig, was so disgusted by its alliance with racists that they smashed all remaining records by that band in its warehouse (Worley and Copsey 2016: 2).

There are also those who point to the use of the swastika – notably by Siouxsie Sioux and Sid Vicious – as shock tactics that were used in punk, particularly in the early days, and is often used as a justification for the view that punks had neo-fascist tendencies. I would argue that the use of the swastika was marginal, not sustained, and most often quickly repudiated. There is also the interesting argument put forward by Jon Stratton that punk was a manifestation of the trauma of the Holocaust, and the use of the swastika could also be seen as part of the residual backdrop of the times, a symptom of the wider trauma by the next generation (2008: 195). I would argue this was a reflection of the abjection of the early punk persona, an identification with the most reviled in society. Of course it had the added bonus of not only shocking the establishment but everyone!

The overwhelming support for Rock Against Racism, 100,000 people who came to the first Victoria Park rally, puts Rock Against Communism firmly into the outside edge of the peripheral sector of politics. It is also notable that unlike Rock Against Racism, there were hardly any women present in the Rock Against Communism venture. So while there was some actual fascist activity and organizing through punk channels, there was no actual appetite for fascism. All the enthusiasm was pulling in the opposite direction. Furthermore, at this first Rock Against Racism rally the bands that performed on that day set the agenda for the decade, in musical terms – also unlike the Rock Against Communism rally, which had no impact. Thus the mixture of punk and reggae bands was prescient as was the use of reggae within punk songs and – albeit often watered down and softened – later used commonly in mainstream pop or new wave. To understand how radical this inclusive approach was, it should be seen in direct contrast to the later Live Aid, where ASWAD volunteered themselves to perform but were seen by the organizer and figurehead, Bob Geldof, to be too obscure or amateur a band to include.

ASWAD were refused the opportunity to take part, which exemplifies the way that Live Aid was a corporate simulation of activism and a continuation of the asymmetry of charity as opposed to the generosity and inclusiveness of the earlier Rock Against Racism.[13]

Dick Hebdige claims that punk got its language of alienation from reggae and the milieu around it. As he says, 'Reggae was not as authenticity but as a signifier for a group of victimised, disenfranchised youth who didn't belong in the establishment' (1979: 64). Conversely Paul Gilroy argues that anti-racism emerged in the way it did and particularly galvanized as a movement through the 1980s because of the contribution of punk to the anti-racist narrative and particularly to Rock Against Racism. In *Subcultures*, Hebdige's position on the relationship between punk and reggae was that in its stance of alienation from mainstream white society punk drew its sense of itself from the alienation of the young Black men and women that gave its expression to reggae. Notting Hill, then a run-down part of London, also the location for *Pressure*, was a well-known hangout for west London punks, who went to Portobello Market to buy mohair jumpers and meet up – Camden Market and Brick Lane being the north and east London equivalents. The area was in the heart of the west London African-Caribbean community, with dub and lovers' sound systems continually playing in the street on market days.

This was evidenced by the very early incorporation of reggae at venues such as The Roxy Club to the exclusion of any other music: one of the legendary venues of early British punk, 'Heavy reggae had occupied a privileged position inside the subculture as the only tolerated alternative to punk' (Hebdige 1979: 67).[14] The pervasiveness of reggae, not just as a music but as an expression of an integral part of inner city life – as witnessed in the markets of London – was the key element of this turn towards multiculturalism and the acceptance of its normativity. There has been a long-standing white engagement with Black music. The difference in this instance has less to do with the modes of appropriation and more to do with the far-reaching impact in the UK.

The equivalences of these two music styles, punk and reggae, did have some appropriative traction when bands such as The Clash used it in their own work: *White Riot*, a response to their own involvement in the 1976 Notting Hill riot, and *Police and Thieves*, a cover version of the popular Junior Mervyn version. Ari Up of The Slits went further: she was possibly one of the first to have dreadlocks and her German accent became a hybrid Caribbean accent, although Bo Derek famously wore cornrows only a few years later in the film *10* in 1979. However, for Ari it was not just a case of appropriation as the punk and reggae cultures were more deeply intertwined; for example, the first album *Cut* (1979) was produced by Dennis Bovell, with whom The Slits had a long-standing musical partnership. Don Letts was also deeply involved in the punk scene. By the early 1980s The Slits were using reggae and funk as their core source material. Soon after The Slits broke up, Ari Up formed The New Age Steppers, which included Neneh Cherry – daughter of Don Cherry, also close to punk – in its line-up. Eventually Ari Up moved to Jamaica, where she lived until her untimely death from cancer in 2010. Thus, as according to Paul Gilroy quoting Dick Hebdige, the drawing together of music and politics in Rock Against Racism meant that 'hitherto coded and unacknowledged relationship between black and white styles became an open and inescapable fact' (Gilroy 1991: 122). It was the ways in which the punk bands established a new hybrid that was taken and established through the widespread success of Rock Against Racism that established a new expectation of equality for so many young people in the UK.

The instances of multicultural accord are not linear progression, however, and there are earlier comparisons to be made of cultural characters as well as the ordinary people cited by Mica Nava, as described earlier. Ari Up can be compared in some ways to the earlier Harlem Renaissance character of Mezz Mezrow, who so identified with Black culture that he actually saw himself as Black despite being Jewish of Ashkenazi origin.[15] Cultural appropriation is a complex subject with much at stake as it is closely bound up with power relations and zones of influence. In this instance, however, and at that earlier time, it would have been offered by Mezz Mezrow as a critique of the privilege of whiteness rather than what would be seen today – as a misappropriation of that privilege and an over-identification as fetishization. In the earlier period of the 1950s Mezrow would have averred that 'Jewish American Culture, by assimilating upward, was abdicating the special role of critique available to social outsiders' (Damon 1997: 155), and therefore identifying with African Americans was for him a form of solidarity, as I argue with the working classes and the Irish in 1970s Britain. Ari Up, I would also suggest, would have taken this view. Now, of course, as well as – at its worst – cultural theft, it would be seen as a display of faux authenticity of the most dubious kind; with the development of the identity politics debates the privilege of whiteness is known to be too powerful and pervasive to overcome and too overwhelming to abdicate from in such an easy way. The strength of feeling against Dana Schutz's work is a testament to the current militancy. Justifiable resentment by people of colour at those who can access white privilege has since undermined any appropriation of cultural forms, despite the contributions of writers such as Zadie Smith or Hannah Black, who both work out of hybrid ethnic forms – or provenance – in different ways.[16]

What this chapter is arguing here is that punk was a moment in British cultural history that created a space for the white communities that would give licence to the acceptance and normalization of a postcolonial Britain. In the urban centres for Rock Against Racism generation, the message was that to be black *is* to be British in the UK. History is an image: an impression that lingers long after the detail has submerged and been forgotten. The impressionistic image of young people doing it together, enjoying themselves and celebrating in a mode where your colour, origin or ethnicity is irrelevant, is a powerful, sustained image. A decade later Paul Gilroy was by then able to identify that the networks, language and communities of punk made a 'qualitative shift in racial politics' (1991: 151) and was instrumental in changing the emphasis from anti-fascism – organized vanguard left politics – to anti-racism – Rock Against Racism and mass mobilization of single-issue politics. Against those who claim that the impetus behind the mass movement was the Socialist Workers Party, Gilroy is very clear that although the initial impetus may well have been political activists, it was networks outside of politics, namely people and communities who coalesced around music, that created anti-racism as a mass movement, so the link made between punk and anti-racism was instrumental in galvanizing anti-racism and the normalization of multiculturalism within the younger generation. This I would further suggest is evidenced by the general shift in language from anti-fascism – language of class – towards the anti-racism – language of identity politics – and particularly evidenced in the inability of Trotskyist groups to recruit more than 15,000 ever in the UK, a fraction of those who went to the Victoria Park gig in east London.

While I agree with Gilroy's assessment of the music sweeping along an embrace of otherness and embedding anti-racism into a generational discourse, it also, unwittingly, began a movement away from the joined-up politics of collective class action towards the culture of single-issue politics that gave with one hand and has taken away with the other, so that while women and Black people derived some semblance of equality the lack of opportunity for working-class people disproportionately affects Black people which becomes racism by another guise. The young punks were willing to buy into a collective voice that coalesced around music but were much less willing to commit to more radical change and eschewed left wing vanguard politics in favour of a libertarian emancipatory expression of politics. Furthermore, despite the 'doing it together' narrative the punk phenomenon was still overwhelmingly a white boys' club: women were a minority in punk and non-white figures like Poly Styrene – and the ordinary Black punks not in the limelight – were game-changing pioneers who eschewed the authenticity that might have been found elsewhere. I would suggest furthermore that what Poly Styrene represented was directly to do with the way in which the expectations of women within a minority community can be doubly restrictive, as a woman and as a Black woman and subject not only to racism and patriarchy but to the expectations of one's own community. Therefore, the incentive to move out of one's community might be one of freedom from those restrictions, of the particular way patriarchy envelopes the lives of women from all communities. In this way feminism was constituted for all women through the emancipation that punk offered.

The songs these women wrote were all songs of emancipation from the normative femininity: *Typical Girls* (The Slits), *Germ Free Adolescents* (X-Ray Spex), *Old Tart's Song* (Poison Girls). In a similar vein, the link formed with reggae, the equivalences and syncretism between the white punks and these other forms of music were not to do with cool or authenticity – except maybe as a dialectical inversion of cool through its opposite of expressionist grunge – but to do with a shared sense of disenfranchisement and lack of opportunity coupled with an aggressive anti-establishment cynicism born of this disenfranchisement. Despite ostensible cynicism of the punk persona, there was much room for optimism, and the new equality of gender, colour and sexuality was a cause for celebration that can be seen in some of the film works that I will now turn to.

Real Woman (1984) by Wildtrax Collective[17] is a case in point to my argument of normalization of blackness by white filmmakers set against mainstream cinema – even independent – by white filmmakers: the inclusion of Black actors is often at their own expense. Anne Robinson is an artist who graduated from St Martin's in 1987 and who had been into punk. Her film is a celebration of the camaraderie of women of all classes and colours in contrast to the later 1990s view that Anna Everett exemplifies. In Everett's analysis, the Black actors offer a kind of 'fort/da' process, whereby the raison d'être is to be a counterpoint to the white actors who are the players. This could be said to be somewhat analogous to the way in which women are the counterpoint to male actors. The concluding epiphany to her text is worth repeating: 'and just when my exasperation prompts me to ask; "Why don't they just leave blacks out of it?" I realize that in our racialized culture over-privileged whiteness requires underprivileged blackness' (1995: 38).

Real Woman is not this kind of film. The underprivileged, as it is described in the terms of Everett, could be translated into class terms in the British context and in this film where the women are marked as working class and therefore equal to each other. Thus, in this instance class overrides race. In the UK, where interracial marriage is very common – and was even in the 1970s – the racialization of all discourses offers a skewed understanding of the power relations where class-based discourse was the marker of left-wing politics, that gave way to identity politics in the 1990s, broadly speaking.

Robinson's film is a fun short of four minutes that is not much more than a song promo for a punk band. It features The Poison Girls in a back garden playing the song. One of the women is pretending to iron. After the song intro, she throws the clothes and iron into the grass and the film cuts to them getting on a bus for what turns out to be a trip to the seaside with their friends. The film is clearly made on a very small budget, and while the band itself is made up of mostly women, all white, the friends gathering on the bus and playing in the sand include several Black women as part of the group all cavorting. All the women eat together, play together in a fairground, laugh together and sing together in the coach back home. A vignette of a hand-drawn kitchen with a man and woman interacting resulting in the woman smashing the plates on the floor is intercut with a further shot of a woman setting fire to washing on a line in the garden. Both these scenes interrupt the main flow of women having fun on their day trip. The narrative is minimal: women enjoying themselves, having a laugh at the seaside, and the film is edited in jump cuts throughout.

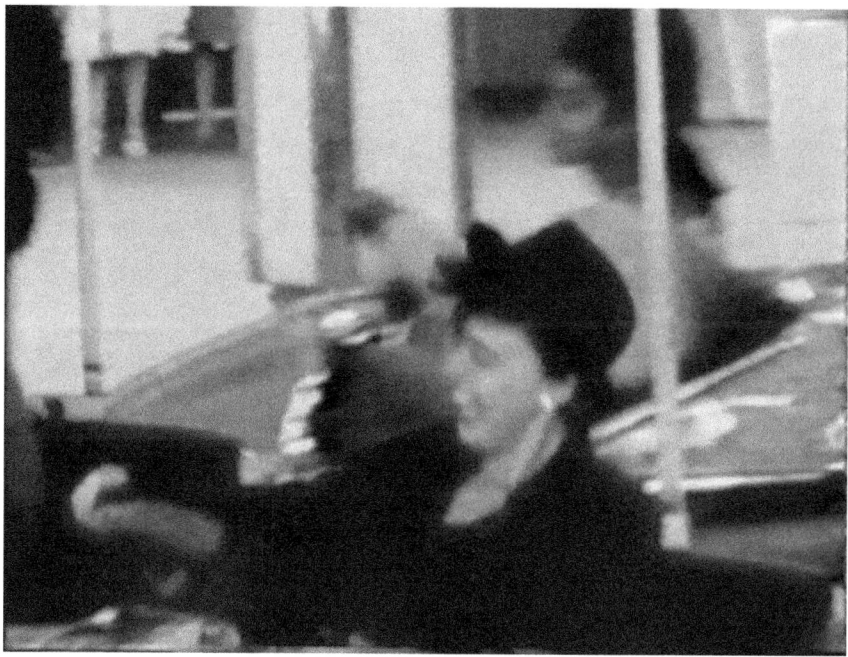

Figure 8. *Real Woman* (1984 Wildtrax Anne Robinson, Caroline Sheldon, Claire Glassman and Jeanette Iljon). Courtesy of the artist.

What is significant, and needs remarking upon, is the way in which blackness is completely unremarkable. These women aren't 'being Black'; they are not ciphers or symbolizing anything. They are not exploring Black consciousness: they are representative of a feminist impulse towards solidarity that was sadly fractured and short-lived. This impulse of feminist solidarity ties this work together with Novaczek and Dick, who were all widening the chain of equivalences between Black artists and artists from non-black and non-hegemonic groups.

The interventions of Robinson, also Novaczek and Dick to be discussed later in the chapter, require contextualization through former attempts to incorporate or work with Black subjects by white people in film in order to understand the full scope of the shift in consciousness in my exemplars. These earlier attempts have become undermined as lacking in legitimacy through the debates around exoticization and fetishization of the Black subject by white people. While there is an obvious truth to that not to be ignored, earlier generations of artists arguably, in certain contexts, need to be seen from within their time. The argument of Andrew Ross and Maria Damon in relation to Mezz Mezzrow is apposite here, that those who chose to live within the sphere of rock and roll in the mid-1950s and earlier were living de facto within a prescient multicultural microcosm, which was at the time marginalized and delegitimized. Like punk it was a tiny milieu that was to cast a long shadow. Within the United States particularly, to live within the multicultural milieu exemplified an active political identification specific to the history of segregation in the United States, one that was a direct critique to the racism in American society in the most profound way and particularly at a time when actual segregation was still a fact below the Mason-Dixey line.

So just as the humanist versus anti-humanist debates of the 1990s are now in the early 2020s obsolete due to the prevalent acceptance of the anthropocene, the artists Maya Deren and Alexander Hammid (*Meshes of the Afternoon*), Shirley Clarke (*A Cool World*), Stephen Dwoskin (*Ballet Black*) and Kenneth Macpherson (*Borderline*) need also to be looked at with an understanding of the thinking of the time in addition to the critiques from the position of today's context.[18] These are all groundbreaking films that aimed to capture what at the time would have been called the Black experience each in their own way, even while that was not the direct focus. However, it is important to look at examples of these post-war films in order to see the breakthroughs that the films of Dick, Robinson and Novaczek made in the 1980s to the understanding of multiculturalism.

Maya Deren (1917–61) is often cited as the godmother of women filmmaking.[19] Her most famous film, *Meshes of the Afternoon* (1943), made in collaboration with Alexander Hammid, demonstrates a famously surrealist-infused exoticized idea of femininity that aligns it with African subjectivity through the music, corporeality and magic. Her long-standing interest in Africa and magic – she went to live in Haiti in the last years of her life – was part of a wider European obsession with what they saw as an authenticity of a pre-industrialized society. This flawed assumption runs through modern art. Shirley Clarke (1919–97), although of the same generation, twenty years later in the 1960s made a series of films that dealt with the urban Black communities.

Shirley Clarke had immersed herself in the filming of the Harlem African American community with her partner Carl Lee, who was African American and himself came from Harlem. The result was a series of films that could be seen as a trilogy of American Black culture: *The Connection* (1961), *The Cool World* (1963) and *Portrait of Jason* (1967). These films are both progressive and problematic in that they focus on the problems and effects of racism rather than on solutions.[20] From today's perspective this would be seen to be stereotyping Black people as troubled and 'street', while authenticating their credentials as cool from the point of view of the bohemian drug-taking artists of the 1960s. From Clarke's point of view, as a stated communist, that is a humanist and universalist, she was concerned with authenticity of representation and framing the issues, particularly the effects of racism, as a symptom of the capitalist system. Her long-standing engagement with the street life in New York, nonetheless, can be seen as part of a dialogue that serves as part of a lineage of both visual activism through documentary and revealing the attitudes of different generations towards depicting blackness in film and their relationship to this other community of otherness.

This can be seen most clearly in *The Cool World*, and the opening scenes that frame the piece, of the preacher disclaiming the white devil. It can also be seen in the many ways that the film diverges from the original play (Nogués 2015: 140–3). In terms of storyline, this film shares some similar concerns to the Ové film, such as a focus on the pressures on Black men specifically and how their lives are shaped by racism, so often forced into petty crime or a naturalized expectation of crime as the only fulfilment of Black masculinity. These films are in stark contrast to the later films of the 1980s that describe and situate Black activism and turns away from the representation of Black subject as victim.

The final of the three films representing African American life was *Portrait of Jason* (1967) discussed in Chapter 1. It is a direct-address documentary of a Black man whom Clarke knew through her boyfriend Carl Lee. The focus on Jason, featured as a direct-address monograph feature film, was ambivalent: it is only the recuperation of Holliday's performative play that lends a lasting legacy beyond a colonial gaze.[21] Shirley Clarke was a wealthy Jewish woman, but in terms of gender and her status as a filmmaker, she felt very much an outsider. She claimed to identify with African Americans as fellow outsiders and worked closely with her boyfriend Carl Lee who grew up in the Harlem that was the subject of Clarke's film, *The Cool World* (1963) (Nogués 2015: 143).

Clarke's ethnicity as a Jew may also have had a bearing on her interest in the Black experience drawing on an extensive pool of inter-ethnic collaboration between African Americans and Jews in the arts. Despite her claims, the lack of symmetry between them is underlined by knowing that, in her apartment at the Chelsea Hotel, Clarke plied Jason Holliday all night with alcohol and marijuana in order to help him tell his story in a lively way. However that – and her wealthy background aside – the ambivalence can be seen, not only in the way Jason plays with the expectations of the camera as described earlier but also in the way that Holliday identified with the Jewish immigrant 'made good' narrative of Fanny Brice, an earlier comedienne from a poor Jewish Brooklyn, who became a Ziegfeld girl and was represented loosely in the blockbuster film starring Barbra Streisand, *Funny Girl* (1968). Holliday declared he wanted to play Brice in his cabaret act so whatever the economic reality of inequality, the fantasy was a projection on both sides.

While *Portrait of Jason* troubles the notions of insider and outsider it is still, however, an example of the cultural tourism to be set against a culture from below that defines the punk work that I am delineating, germane to this chapter, in relation to 'race'. Unlike *Pressure*, discussed earlier, and other films by Clarke, *Portrait of Jason* has implicit claims to the avant garde and its lineage. This film was legendary but rarely viewed until it became a DVD in 2008. Therefore, in the 1970s and 1980s it would probably not have been screened or may be known by the contemporary filmmakers I will be analysing here. *Portrait of Jason* is nonetheless important as a landmark film where the Black protagonist spoke back.

The importance of these precursors is not just because of their focus on race but also to do with the self-reflexivity that questions the veracity of the camera through a number of devices that lays claim to an avant-gardiste approach *that had the subject at its centre*. The distrust of the camera and its indexical claims are clearly seen in the later generation of filmmakers that I describe. The importance of this distrust for artists dealing with ideas to do with ethnicity and 'race' is to do with the way in which film and other media have been used to prop up racist stereotypes through lens-based representation in journalism as well as in cinema. Stuart Hall particularly has been instrumental in revealing the ways in which racist beliefs are perpetuated and produced through the visual in the media through the convergence of thinking in anti-humanist

Marxist theory that focused on ideology and alienation in tandem with the part that cinema plays in the capitalist machinery. A key strategy for video and filmmakers has been to dissect the engineering of visual representation even more so for Black artists who have embraced lens-based work en masse for this very opportunity.

This issue would not have been on Clarke's mind in this way. Her modernist spur to question the material is beholden to an earlier iteration of the debates that reveal the force of cinema and its role in framing ideological constructions of reality from the classic avant garde that Hall would have built on. There are several ways in which the construction of Clarke's films are revealing this distrust of the lens: the lo-fi approach, the handheld camera in all the films, the references to the filmmaker within the film – breaking the fourth wall – in both *Portrait of Jason* and *The Connection* – and the direct references to the materiality of the film in *Portrait of Jason*. In *The Cool World* we have a montage of found footage and filmed footage, professional acting and amateur, a voiceover that distantiates – all these devices are used by the later artists I focus on. Famously popularized in the New American Cinema and in fly-on-the-wall documentary, both forms that Clarke has been duly involved in forming, handheld camera has been a sign of authenticity for many filmmakers to the point of ubiquity.[22] However, these films of Shirley Clarke's could also be characterized by the more recent proliferaton of mock documentary.

The mock documentary is generally attributed to Jim McBride's *David Holzman's Diary* (1967) but Shirley Clarke's *The Connection* (1961) and *The Cool World* (1963) predate McBride's film by several years.[23] The manoeuvre of this kind of work, of self-reflexivity that shows how much the documentary itself is a fiction, was a way of developing a language that eschews the subscription to authenticity and transparency usually ascribed to documentary. Each of these films find ways in which the filmmaker reveals the operations of the documentary to be fiction through their own presence. This productive form proliferated in the 1980s and the 1990s through the popularization of postmodern theories of the abandonment of what were called grand narratives and the assumptions of a singular take on the world. The breaking down of grand narratives had been in part constituted through the postcolonial struggles, theorists and a concomitant growing awareness of the rights of others by white intellectuals. Mock documentary has become a particularly popular trope as understood in its most recent incarnation through the idea of constructed histories that in turn question the idea of truth and what might be at stake in history – work such as the Atlas Group or the Otolith Group – from the late 1990s onwards. According to Peter Osborne, it is this self-conscious narrativizing of history that marks the contemporary moment (Osborne 2013: 28).

There is rarely an originary moment. We could, for example, go back to Vertov's *Man with a Movie Camera* (1929) as an example of a classic mock documentary if we take the incorporation of a cinema, camera and camera operator into the otherwise documentary film. In each generation a particular version is rehearsed due to the questions and conditions of that moment, and Shirley Clarke should also be seen as an important part of this trajectory of revealing the artifice in documentary, although Jim McBride is often credited with its initial emergence. What is significant is the moment in which increased interest developed in the mock documentary was precisely a time when the values and mores of the so-called establishment were being questioned and bitterly fought over regarding the assumed core values on a mass scale in the 1960s and then again in the 1980s. It was also another strategy that arose out of what was seen as the failure of direct cinema to bring change. The development of the questioning of the documentary form and the proliferation of the mock documentary in its current form of withering and witty indictment that developed in the 1980s and 1990s are a further testament to the breakdown in belief in a singular truth as characterized through the postmodernist debates of that period. This was also a period in which the core assumption of the documentary mode of production was also questioned, specifically the belief by the revolutionary vanguard that art and culture could change the world and that revealing an atrocity will in itself produce change. There was distrust of the documentary image and activist art, both considered too didactic. As the United Kingdom and the United States bought more deeply into the political moment of Thatcher and Bush senior, the culture wars fuelled a further turn in the art world, away from dealing directly with political issues towards the playful irony of the 1990s characterized, in the UK at least, by the yBa's, the young British artists. 'In many ways, part of the dominant text of the 1990s was an expression of happy release from the dreary preoccupations of the 1980s' (Piper 2005: 35). Mock documentary within this context can be seen as a way to narrativize politics.

For people of colour there is even more at stake in the critique of the dominant political narratives. Living within a state of double consciousness in a white world is living within a state of critique. If you have to be aware not only of your own being in the world but also at the same time of how others see you, and that doubleness informing your sense of self, this state of seeing yourself from inside and out at the same time may in itself explain the alacrity with which artists of colour embraced a creative practice of narrativizing politics as a critique of dominant discourse on history.

So mock documentary, handheld camera, montage and direct address are devices that have recently become commonplace but in the 1970s and 1980s were developed in a particularly awkward way that drove towards a different effect than the notion of the existentialist-driven notion of authenticity which was paramount for the artists of the 1950s and 1960s. The new commonality of disjunction had to do with heterogeneity: an acknowledgement of the impossibility of a singular experience of community.[24]

The distrust in recent decades of the documentary form as a carrier of truth afforded the work of future generations who transformed the mock documentary as a way of talking about experiences. All the films I focus on in the second half of the chapter use a kind of mock documentary in various ways for a range of different reasons that will be discussed. However, a lack of trust in authority was clearly emerging in culture which would concur with increasing interest in a way of making films that deflated established norms of representation. We can see this deflation in films such as *Born in Flames* (1983), *The Passion of Remembrance* (1986), *Liberty's Booty* (1980) and *London Suite (Getting Sucked In)* (1990).

The films of Sankofa, Black Audio Film Collective and Ceddo formed part of a renewed and expanded Black activism and aspiration towards visibility in the UK that emerged in the 1980s. These films by a younger generation find other solutions than those that can be seen in the intergenerational tensions arising out of frustration, anger and neglect of their rights, that are described in Ové's earlier British film of the 1970s, *Pressure*, which arose from a previous generation of assimilation. The Scarman Report that brought legislative change was a prime factor in the development of focus on the Black communities. There was also the incremental effect of ongoing anti-racist activism as well as a push-back against police containment. The context of this activity saw the emergence of Black film collectives that were supported by the establishment of the ACTT Video Workshop Declaration in 1982 through GLC and Channel 4 funding, each committed to 'encourage diversity'. The Workshop Declaration offered a revenue funding stream that Black filmmakers embraced with alacrity enabling a renaissance of production and distribution of Black filmworks. Sankofa was constituted through this funding. Sankofa was a film collective founded by Isaac Julien, Martina Attille, Maureen Blackwood, Nadine Marsh-Edwards and Robert Crusz in 1983. The first film by Sankofa was *Territories* (1984), which was Isaac Julien's degree show film at St Martin's School of Art. Sankofa went on to make six films before their break-up in 1992.

The relationship between politics, culture and art is always connected and can be seen in an early example of the link between anti-racist activism and the development of the proliferation of art funding and dissemination to ethnic minorities as it was outlined by Naseem Khan. According to Khan, Robert Hutchinson and John Bustin, two officers in the Arts Council, were aware of the changing nature of the British community, possibly, she thinks, through left-wing anti-racist activism and in turn the need for change in response. These two young white men commissioned Naseem Khan to research on the cultural needs of ethnic minorities. Despite their good faith, the funding officers themselves were naïve in their expectations of the scale of the issue: what was envisaged by them as a part-time six-month project for one person took four people eighteen months to produce.[25]

So the report 'The arts Britain ignores: The arts of ethnic minorities in Britain' was published by Khan for the Arts Council in 1976, co-incidentally in the same year that Rock Against Racism began. The report argued for the need to fund, foster and support the arts produced by ethnic minorities in Britain (Khan 2005: 117). The report had a slow but increasingly expansive effect on funding patterns as it became apparent to metropolitan and local authorities that the arts produced by the so-called minority communities in the UK needed funding (Khan 2005: 119). Without doubt this relationship between the cultural expression of expectations of multiculturalism was supported in practical terms by funding policy that created a groundswell of activity. The tensions between the effects of the report and the aims of Rock Against Racism have much to do with, in the British context, the aspiration to be an equal partner in cultural production and the expectation of celebrating a distinct heritage for the community. In retrospect the response to the Khan report was often also naïve. As Eddie Chambers states, '"Ethnic Arts" tended to define and regard the arts and cultured expressions of Black (or more specifically, non-white) people in somewhat fixed terms. "Culture" was regarded as something of a fixed self-referencing entity that the darker peoples of the world carried with them for all time, as part of a historic continuum' (Chambers 2014: 44). To some extent, however, a construct of managerialism, while instrumentalizing and confining, also in some ways worked to fulfil the requirement to expand the reach of art practice beyond the so-called white world. I would argue that it was the interplay of both the Khan report and Rock Against Racism that produced younger contemporary artists who consciously drew from a range of sources to make work that broke out of the burden of representation towards producing a language on its own terms; this was a developing process that went through various generational iterations, and indeed the Khan report was itself a responsive document arising out of the needs and activities of community organizations. The wider cultural shifts events and the multivalent evolutionary meanderings of art practice do not generally have a direct and clean relationship. It is difficult, therefore, to say what exactly had the greatest impact or influence, but certainly Rock Against Racism was a very public entity that formed a significant part of the move towards the widespread acceptance and celebration of a diverse and complex community. It helped produce the confidence to manifest and challenge a new subjectivity which ran alongside the local government funding of multicultural celebrations of the type that Chambers critiques. Even despite the critiques, many of which are justified, art got made in response, in defiance of or against the well-meaning but sometimes crude offerings. What the focus on 'ethnic minorities' gave most of all was access to funds whereby art could get made and exhibitions hung. It has to be said also that it was not until the 1990s that there was a critical mass of artists, enough for Kobena Mercer to note that the 1990s was an era of 'multicultural normalisation', which in itself, in his view, brings its own problems and issues to do with globalization, fetishism and commodification in a neoliberal world which art embraced with alacrity at the time (Mercer 1999–2000: 51–2).

So while Black consciousness was changing towards more visible activism, white punk was moving towards embracing the values, preoccupations and concerns that would effectively force them outside the bounds of normative acceptability of the time. The condition of being outside normative acceptability was an everyday experience of young Black people – and, of course, older Black men and women also – at the time.[26] The aspiration of young people as a whole towards working-class culture both Black and white I would argue reached its most widespread zenith at this juncture of punk – only to be outstripped in the 1990s by hip hop and rap – and was to leave an ongoing legacy characterized through mockney and later worked through the hip hop surge into a Black street argot that is now normative amongst white working-class millennials: each wave – from jazz through to hip hop – has increased the critical mass of Black cultural vernacular in white consciousness. Thus, as Paul Gilroy pointed out in his game-changing book from 1987 *There Ain't No Black in The Union Jack*, the very definition of Britishness was changing through the presence of the Black communities in the UK.[27]

Punk music, and the social mores that developed out of this, as I have been arguing, was the last gasp of modernity where universalism as a coherent and radical rallying cry was being re-negotiated towards a new era of overdetermination through the identity politics that has now become a recognizable mode within the art world today. While much focus and discussion on Black arts have been on the artists who were included – or sometimes excluded – in Rasheed Araeen's landmark exhibition, The Other Story (1989) or the Black Art Group (1982–4) and that trajectory, there was a parallel development of film and video work through Sankofa and Black Audio Film Collective that has not had the same level of attention within the debates on Black art in the 1980s, possibly because it arose directly out of the funding stream of the video workshops.[28]

The films looked at here offer a loose trajectory of sorts of art that address the issue of this 'new' subjectivity. The so-called new subjectivity was expressed in a number of ways that arose out of these contexts.[29] A new syncretism emerged, I would argue, from the intersection of punk and its correlative Black communities that gave rise to transgressive forms of filmmaking and the latest remake of Black culture. Key to this remake was Sankofa.

I have described a running towards – exoticization – and a moving away – embracing wider frameworks – in music and in film, from the burden or desire to represent that confined Shabazz and Ové. I would describe the work of Sankofa as looking in both directions. It is difficult to see Sankofa as a bridge towards contemporary work by Black artists because they were short-lived and heavily criticized at the time. This kind of work, overtly political and dense, was elided in favour of the more formally led long-look work that has become the main form amongst successful moving image work. I am thinking here specifically of artists such as Zarina Bhimji or Zineb Sedira.[30] For Sankofa, when the workshop money ran out, they found it more difficult to make work and the films they did make after that point became more formally conservative (Wheeler 1995: 131–43).

Sankofa came from a mixed disciplinary background of fine art film, cultural studies and media. That they came together as a collective of lesbian and gay artists may have been important in the iconoclastic nature of their work as well as the way in which women were of equal interest in the films. The work of Sankofa was work that addressed community – like the film *Pressure* – but at the same time, as an analogue to Poly Styrene, worked through languages that freed them from realist constraints and afforded an invention of visual reflexivity and expression.

Kobena Mercer in *Welcome to the Jungle* (1994) posits the newness of Black British film and discusses its production and reception.[31] He describes some of the key players in establishing a new aesthetic. This was a period of emergence, where strategic positioning was a requirement in order to establish even an idea of a Black artist's visibility and what that might mean. Certainly the 1980s generation – differently to Horace Ové and Menelik Shabazz – included artist filmmakers that were to change the expectations of the diasporic cinematic voice. Mercer argues that the films of these collectives constituted a new Black vernacular in opposition to the forms of the so-called neutrality that embody realist narrative films that had pervaded the previous generation. Arguing against the assumption that the sources of Black Audio Film Collective and Sankofa were Godard or other such Eurocentric influences, these films were posited as speaking from the community for the community. Although Judith Williamson, another key commentator in the 1980s, points out quite the opposite in a way, that these particular film collectives were focused on by Black artists and critics precisely because they used experimental film strategies to explore themes of Black subjectivity rather than more conservative documentary or realist tendencies. In some ways this argument demonstrates the novelty of this kind of work, that a conference was dominated by the arguments that wanted to situate the work. Furthermore, that the only way it seemed at the time to contextualize the work was to think about inside or outside the community and to reflect on provenance through that dichotomy of where the work might have come from. These arguments over the burden of representation have recently re-emerged under a different guise of cultural appropriation such as the aforementioned recent anger and debate over the Dana Schutz painting of Emmet Till in the 2017 Whitney Bienniale and whether such a brutal event can be used for aesthetic pleasure in paint.[32] Nonetheless, now, after several decades of many Black artists making a range of work, there is no longer a discussion that comprises legitimacy of sources for Black artists but a tacit understanding of the heterodox nature of 'community'. If indeed 'community' is even a concern in the work.

Thirty years after Sankofa disbanded, there is currently a proliferation of successful women artists of colour who use the lens. In the 1980s this was not the case. In fact, there were very few Black women practitioners. It is interesting to note the lack of intersectionality: that at a time when feminist discourse was at its height, gender was not much discussed, nor was sexuality; the fact of blackness was seen to be the key focus. I would argue that a key differentiating factor, not expressed by Mercer at the time of this debate on the new Black vernacular in filmmaking, is the focus on gender. This was also a time in which different interest groups were pitted against each other amid a perception of there not being enough pie for all. If there was a need in the 1980s for the voice of blackness to emerge away from white hegemony, a non-patriarchal language also needed to emerge – and is still a project in emergence. This is not to essentialize any grouping but to acknowledge experience as a defining force of self-interpellation. Kodwo Eshun, speaking to John Akomfrah from Black Audio Film Collective, described it as about 'a question of the form of politics and the politics of form and this articulation came to the fore very much throughout the 1980s and into the early 1990s' (Eshun and Sagar 2007: 131).

For the filmmakers I discuss in this chapter and in this book it is through the cinematic representation of experience that a woman's voice emerges. At the time of the late 1980s and 1990s to talk of work in terms of experience or expression was often to belittle the work and render it narcissistic and indulgent in a post-conceptual moment. However I would argue that through this voice the transformation of film itself occurs – there is, as posited by Eshun, a dialectical relationship between the cinema and experience.

The Passion of Remembrance (1986), while made by both men and women, has a clear agenda to question the male domination of the legacies and self-representations of the Black activist experiences of the 1960s and 1970s and to challenge homophobia. Its unique groundbreaking contribution in the United Kingdom – and the United States according to Coco Fusco (1985) – I would suggest can be seen through the contrast with *Pressure*, which is an unequivocally male film about male concerns. *Passion* conversely questions this through an intersectional understanding of the processes of racism and of the varied construction of the Black community. It was directed jointly by Isaac Julien and Maureen Blackwood with an equally mixed team; the process of equality in the production of the film is a testament, I would argue, to the counter-hegemonic position of Black homosexual subjectivity.[33] Here, famously, the viewpoint of women, of homosexuality and of the young is proudly represented. Sankofa came together as a collective of gay and lesbian filmmakers, and it was their sexuality that formed an integral component in their intersectional approach: of not giving a hierarchy to the different racism, sexism and homophobia.[34] The conversation in *The Passion of Remembrance* was not just about racial stereotypes but about the elision and suppression of women in the Black anti-racist activism lauded in the previous generation, about the homophobic prejudice within the Black communities. In contrast to *Pressure*, *The Passion of Remembrance* constituted its visual language within a fragmented schema that speaks to the multivalent experiences of communities as perceived through their subject position as women and as gays. While this film has a voice of gravitas and didacticism that would set it apart from many of the works in my argument, the defining cinematic language of this work is the episodic, the lo-fi and the heterogeneous genre-mixing *mise-en-scène* that can be seen in Bette Gordon's *Empty Suitcases* (1980) or Vivienne Dick's post-New York work such as *London Suite (Getting Sucked In)* (1989), albeit with different musical or political references.

The Passion of Remembrance opens with found footage of the Grunwick dispute in 1976–8, a strike in which Asian women were prominent activists. It then cuts to the main strand, that of realist vignettes of a Caribbean family and their associates in a London inner city estate. This ongoing strand presents, in episodic narrative form, the conflicts between the immigrant and British-born generations within a context of police and civilian racism and harassment. As if a soap opera or an educational film, each episode focuses on an example of tension, with mediated footage breaking through from time to time. Interspersed between these concrete examples of life lived, there is a set of scenes in what might possibly be a sand quarry but reads as a desert. In these interludes, what could be seen to be a classic Brechtian chorus, a man and woman, symbolic ciphers, conduct a debate, calm but pregnant with suppressed anger, on gender relations and Black activism; they perform in words the tussle they speak of. These scenes are in a landscape that is out of time and place, setting the discussion in historical time rather than the 'real time' of the documentary footage or narrative scenes.[35] The camerawork is different in the desert scenes, composed around the portrait, focusing on the faces and the single figure. These scenes not only lend a motif from science fiction that allows for a meta-conversation of gender relations and activism within the Black community but also draws from the Romantic traditions of the figure in a landscape that speaks to the utopian. In contrast to the slice-of-life vignettes, these landscape scenes are a moment of estrangement, yet also of taking control of the narrative without the daily struggles and concerns. The utopian in this context, I would suggest, represents the desire to live life without the struggles and concerns of racism and patriarchy that is the norm. Patriarchy is acknowledged here as an equal scourge to racism – an unusual intersectionality.

Another layer that moves through the film is of mediated footage of Black involvement in union action and street protest. This kind of footage was ubiquitous at the time in the Black video workshops and each film works it differently. An extended passage of this footage opens *The Passion of Remembrance* and punctuates moments in the film like a spine, so reminding us of the central position of media representation in how the sense of self constituted – and more, to recalibrate the mediation to one of action rather than one of victim. In this device can be seen the influence of Stuart Hall. Deep in the middle of the film, a key female character, after an unsatisfactory evening out, returns to the youth centre alone and puts on a VHS tape to watch some protest footage. This shift moves the footage from an ever-unfolding reportage and lived experience to history and representation; the woman is looking, implicating gender and generation into the footage as an active and critical device. Later, others join her and look with her as a tool for existential self-reflection by the young adults in the community centre. The youth leader in the community centre is a proponent of Black power, continually urging the youth to stand up and be conscious. Thus the multi-layered fragmentation through these many types of chorus within the film does not merely represent – while doing this also – but urges the viewer to interrogate the mores of the 'community' through the subjectivity of woman and homosexuality. At the time the film was criticized for being awkward and self-consciously proffering stereotypical positions: cardboard cut-outs, symbols rather than characters or narratives with verisimilitude. From the vantage point of today, the awkwardness looks more like a stylistic choice, and is more in line with some of the other films in this volume that positioned themselves within a discourse of lack rather than the Hollywood-induced finessing of style that dominates today.

Despite Isaac Julien claiming that punk led him to go to art school, Sankofa are not an obvious part of the punk trajectory I am forming. Julien was one of the founders of Sankofa and he, like many of his peers, eschewed the emphasis on form from many of their structuralist teachers in favour of narrative as expressions of feeling and experience.[36] As a result they were marginalized in the experimental film world: the dominant paradigm being structuralist materialist film. Isaac Julien escaped this elision at first by aiming for the mainstream with *Young Soul Rebels* (1991) and then through the gallery system.

Sankofa, Vivienne Dick and Ruth Novaczek are interested in operations of power in their work. However, they all demonstrate an acute sense of their own otherness, wanting to widen the chain of equivalences through drawing the heterogeneity of the multicultural into their purview. An analogue of sorts can be delineated here between the positing of experience by John Akomfrah as a Black male who describes watching the programme *Police Five* on TV as a child and feeling implicated as well as being actually bullied the next day when the criminal was identified as Black. What matters here is changing the dialogue that informs the world about who you are who you or might be. Women, who are misrepresented and invalidated in a ubiquitous way, also may need to represent themselves and reframe their experiences to lend agency to their subjectivity that is so often out of their control.

So while the works of Sankofa and Black Audio Film Collective were not part of the punk trajectory, they were nevertheless an important landmark for the thinking of, for example, Ruth Novaczek, who knew Isaac Julien at art school. He was a year above her at St Martin's school of art and they had a dialogue while in college about race and identity.[37] As such Novaczek was aware of Sankofa's aims and work. Novaczek's work may not have taken the form it did without multiculturalism and the underground, which, as I explore in an earlier chapter, had deep connections as well as divergences with punk. Indeed, Novaczek's work would not have been made without punk and the part it played in finding a visual language for the work through Rock Against Racism. While Sankofa should not be confused with that particular force of change, of punk, they were, however, part of a concomitant transformative trend.

Novaczek's degree show film *Tea Leaf* (1986[38]) bears some confluence visually with Julien's own degree show film *Territories* (1984), made under the auspices of Sankofa, and like Julien, she explores the intersection between race and sexuality. Both *Territories* and *Tea Leaf* use distortion and heightening colours of handheld documentary footage. *Handsworth Songs* (1986) by Black Audio Film Collective also uses this device, but Novaczek and Julien use it to intensify experience that particularly fuses sexuality with politics. Julien slows the footage down to accentuate the visceral effect of the black and white bodies held together in the master-slave dialectic of desire and power. Novaczek uses road movie footage from a car with fast edits of fragmented close-up movements montaged on top. She continues to develop this methodology through many of her future films. Fragmentation and montage are devices that denounce transparency or authenticity through the real: these modes of production assume representation as a fiction but one that can be repurposed to elicit a freedom from containment of stereotype and assumption. Unlike Julien's film, it is not an experience into bodily desire that Novaczek is conveying but an escape from the toxic bodily experience of abuse: a freedom that she chose through poetic decisions – and possibly the interest in the New American Cinema. The specific approach that I describe below is glimpsed at in *Territories*, in a short passage, but focused on as the central language of Novaczek's film. Sankofa might have felt that they could not afford such

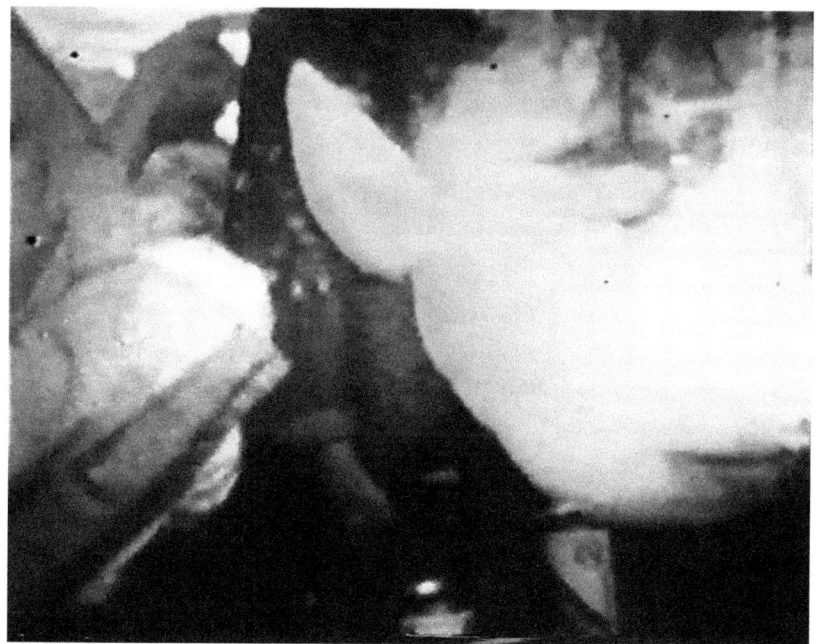

Figure 9. *Tea Leaf* (1985, Ruth Novaczek). Courtesy of the artist.

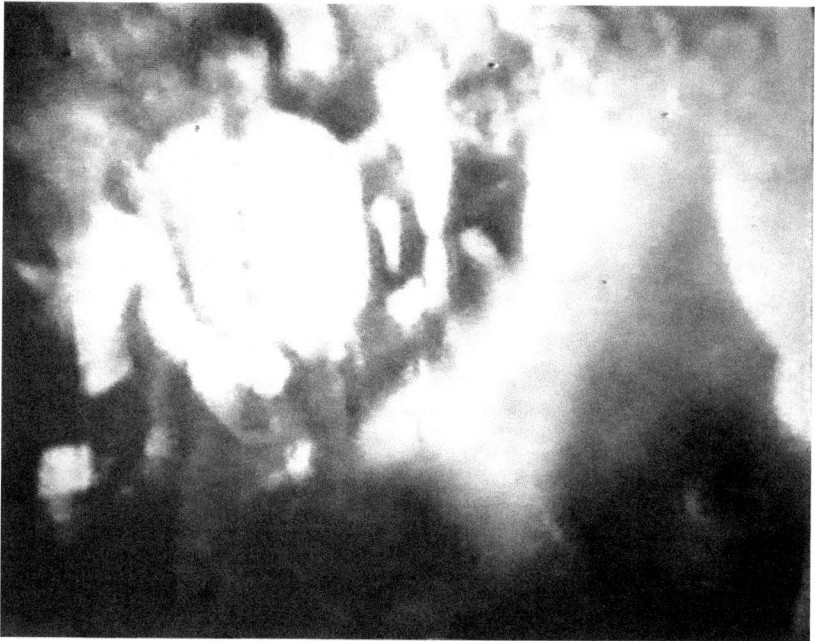

Figure 10. *Tea Leaf* (1985, Ruth Novaczek). Courtesy of the artist.

release from the foregrounding of political statement because of the overt racial discrimination in British society.

In *Tea Leaf* (1986) the authenticity of the narrative for the filmmaker presented as a first-person voiceover narrative is not in question. The music and pace lend a sense of farce as a distancing device to what is the recounting of an abusive relationship with her babysitter. As a film about the abuse of an older woman on a younger, the form the film takes is central to its watchability. Watching the film is like experiencing the discombobulation and chaos that such abuse engenders. Its impact, as explored in the film, is that of interweaving Jewish identity and sexuality and how abuse, self-esteem and relationships are bound up with racism. The film brings this all together through the absurd disjunction between the narrative of child abuse and the speedy upbeat klezmer, reggae and calypso music.[39] Two women are the subject of the film, brightly tinted and continually flitting across the screen in different configurations: in the supermarket, on the street, dancing. They are both subject and object as the voiceover is assumed to be of the artist talking about relations with a woman when she was underage and the shadow this cast upon subsequent relationships. It is both brutal and beautiful.

This possibility of softening these distinctions can be seen pulsing through the work of other filmmakers who were active at the time but in different locations. Lizzie Borden and Vivienne Dick both situated outside the British trajectory of Sankofa to Ruth Novaczek can be seen through the same prism and the many interlacing influences. There are obvious links between Borden and Dick that can be seen in *Liberty's Booty* (1980) and *Born in Flames* (1983), most forcefully. To be noted for the purposes of my argument, while neither of these films are about Black subjectivity as their prime focus, in both films normative value is given to the Black players and Black subjectivity. This is a profoundly different sensibility to the films and intentions of Clarke and Sankofa – even in their obverse contexts – who feel the need to represent blackness through the contexts and urgencies each has to their time and location. The works also speak to a brief moment before race became about rights of ownership and the ensuing vetoes to do with who could speak for whom. Borden and Dick's work operates through an intersectional approach to race and class drawing out from gender relations. Dick's *Liberty's Booty* is a film that shows more complex structural consideration than the earlier *Guerillere Talks*. It also uses a hybrid non-fiction form that fictionalizes lightly. Ostensibly it is close in attitude and subject matter to the Bette Gordon film *Anybody's Woman* (1981) except that while Gordon's film focuses entirely on the representation of sex and women within the sex industry through a naturalized whiteness that is ubiquitous, the Dick film explicitly intersects class and race and explicitly makes the point that the struggle for decent working conditions crosses lines of race, gender and class; that while each condition, say that of the prostitute or 'working girl', is specific and particular, it is also subject to the same struggles as employees of McDonald's for example. In *Liberty's Booty* (1980) blackness is incidental but present and it is the incidental nature of the Black inclusion that is important; there is no re-inscription of the exoticism or underwriting of value in relation to blackness here. The trajectory formed by looking at *Liberty's Booty* (1980) and the later *London Suite* (1989) is perhaps the most paradigmatic of the links that I am building in my argument.

Liberty's Booty (1980) is set in the lower east side, in the apartments inhabited by the filmmaker and her friends. The economic deprivation in the neighbourhood is clear. There are several moments in this episodic film that speak immediately to the cosmopolitan. The sweep of city street scenes, namely the lower east side, in the opening shots includes Black and white people playing and interacting together – incidentally. There are precedents, such as Helen Levitt's film, *In the Street* (1948), that depicts Spanish Harlem as a short documentary film, shot with a concealed camera. This can be seen as a precedent of sorts. Both films posit the city as a site of equivalence where race is subordinate to class as an organizing factor. The key difference – apart from the concealed camera, a device that can be analysed in several ways – is the visual language of the work. Levitt's film aimed to show the dignity of working-class people in the city; the point of view in the film is of the silent observer looking into a world. The orchestral classical music, soundscaped for the film, creates a distance and a melancholic dignity to the people observed. The observing camera has been argued retrospectively to have set up a hierarchy between the viewer and the viewed where the eye of the camera has dominion. There was for the time a tacit politics in making visible the ordinary lives of Black working-class people that Levitt shares with Clarke. However, in *Liberty's Booty* (1980), by contrast, several factors are key in offering a nuanced reading that moves away from a hierarchy of subjectivity through the speaking subject.

One of the opening passages in this fragmented episodic piece is a woman describing why she does 'tricks'. She is paying her way through college and it pays well. Inequality, labour and gender thus immediately set the agenda. It also establishes a nonstereotypical vision of the working girl as aspirational rather than a more common assumption of a 'loser on drugs'.[40]

A later scene is of the 'girls' sitting in a McDonald's café where an Irish voice cuts in, recounting a pivotal strike in Ireland against McDonald's. Another key scene is of an Hispanic woman speaking in Spanish. The scene opens with Angel, one of the characters saying, 'Now we'll pause for a few messages' so it is set up like a TV ad interrupting a programme. In the shot we see some graffiti by Samo – aka Jean Michel Basquiat – and his friend Al Diaz which asks, Which of the following institutions has the most political influence: (a) television, (b) the church, (c) the state and (d) McDonald's? Angel then continues to recount how she bought a McDonald's burger which made her ill and gave her diarrhoea.[41] There are no subtitles or framing for this passage of the film, just a woman standing in front of an urban playground with political graffiti in Spanish, speaking. In the use of her vernacular the

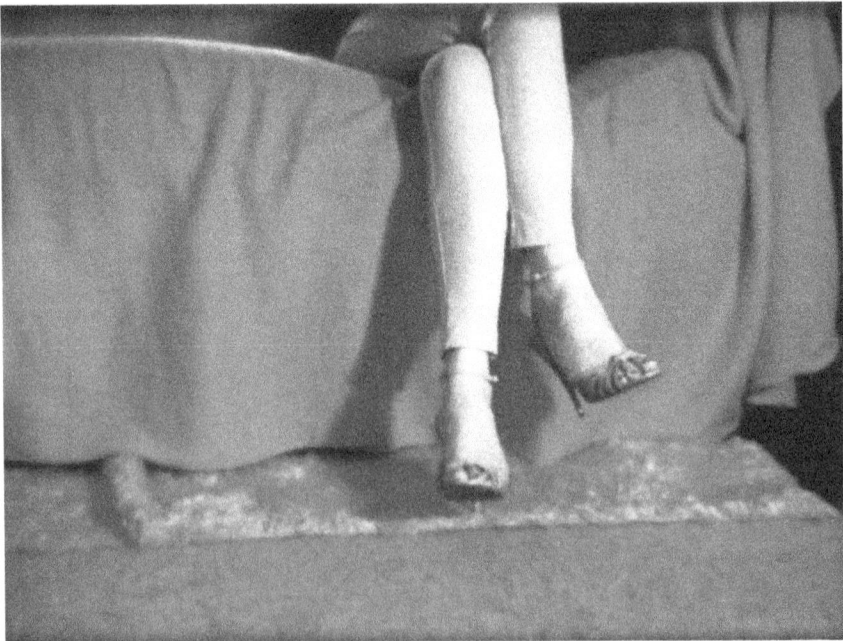

Figure 11. *Liberty's Booty* (1990, Vivienne Dick). Courtesy of the artist.

assumption is either of a Spanish viewer or of indifference to the viewer. Either way this section forces a vision of multiculturalism on any viewer. Importantly it questions the hierarchy of whiteness in the assumptions of the hegemonic Anglo-Saxon viewer or the US audience, forcing this notional viewer to confront themselves. In this film hierarchies of victimhood as well as attendant notions of authenticity and artifice are thrown into disarray as everyone, no matter their skin colour, is patently and obviously dealing with the same issues: that of working conditions.

The flattening of hierarchy is mirrored or perhaps constituted through the methodology of the filming where some of the actors are Dick's friends and some of the actors are actual prostitutes and political activists – again, building here on precedents such as Clarke's *The Cool World*. Different from *The Cool World*, *Liberty's Booty* is not concerned so much with authenticity but with horizontality. The horizontality is also emphasized in its episodic nature of the form. Furthermore, each of the episodes is inserted without build-up, explanation or establishment shots. The lack of explanation and denouement naturalizes and equalizes each aspect of identity as they are presented side by side, so normalizing the cosmopolitan nature of city living and of humanity making itself fully visible, without fuss but with total acceptance. In the heterogeneous structure is the absolute assumption of different people living agreeably alongside each other. There is no question here of the 'dignity' espoused by earlier generations – conveying dignity assumes the power of the gift in the hands of the giver – which to contemporary viewing smacks of the snobbery of the deserving poor. In the structure and form of the film there is inherently no judgement. Each instance is presented as self-contained, each dealing with oppression in its own way, hence the lack of translation. There is no asymmetry, just an equal fight for equal rights.

Lizzie Borden identifies Vivienne Dick as an influence and this can be clearly seen in *Born in Flames* (1983), which is a low-fi science fiction mock documentary film. It is set ten years following its making in a notional socialist United States and focuses on two pirate radio stations that become the locus of a feminist revolt when an activist is arrested then found dead in police custody. The film is utopian in envisioning socialism and dystopian in the continuation of sexism and misogyny. The socialist state conjured in the film effects equality in class and colour. The equality of the Black and Hispanic communities is

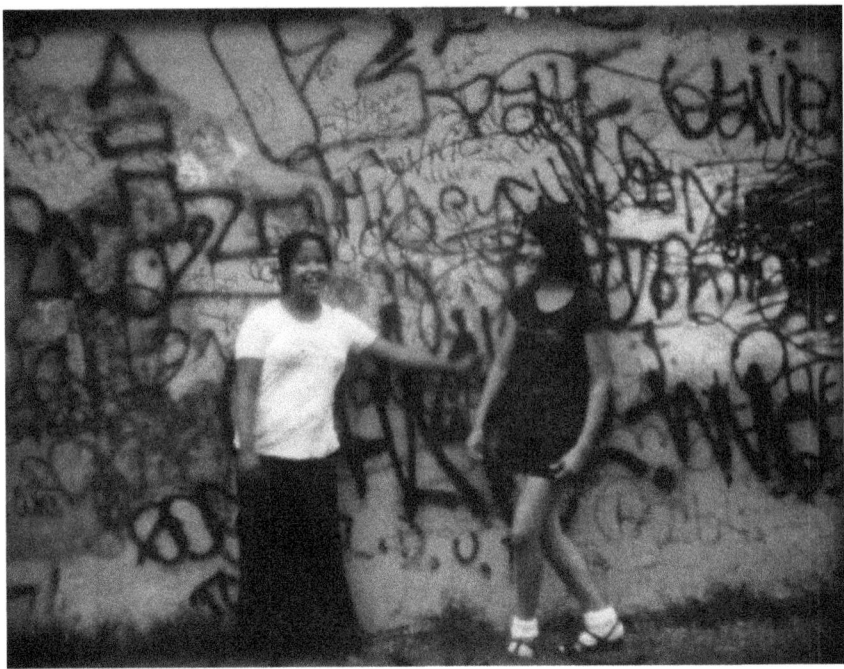

Figure 12. *Liberty's Booty* (1990, Vivienne Dick). Courtesy of the artist.

notable and a foil to the inequality of the women. The point of the satire is that the socialism figured in the film does not give women the equality that they should expect, thus commenting, like Sankofa, on the failure of actual and current – male – socialist activists to take on gender politics. Underground groups like 'the women's army' have formed around radio stations to combat the sexism that is everywhere. The art punk band Red Crayola's scratchy atonal music is worked into the film. The cityscape is semi-derelict and bereft of the wealth and cleanliness, for which New York is currently recognized: it is the bankrupt New York of the 1970s and 1980s in look, and of course the lo-fi film stock adds to its sense of being out of time. There is voiceover of police commentary of the women under surveillance and interviews of key players in the women's army, speaking to camera as well as vignettes of examples of women's direct action on the streets. The radicality of the film is to envisage the way in which different equalities are pitted against each other and therefore arguing for an intersectional socialism. This film is commenting on the same problematic as *The Passion of Remembrance*, albeit using a very different device, but arguing that even within radical movements, like the

Black Panthers, which fought against inequality many socialist radicals were still blind to gender inequality.

The film explores various ways in which the women are discriminated against or come into physical danger and the ways in which women form activist groups to protect other women through direct action, activism and consciousness-raising, through the radio and the formation of political cells. Like *The Passion of Remembrance* (1986) and the films of Vivienne Dick, *Born in Flames* (1983) is episodic. The inner-city urban setting as the backdrop is common to all these films. *Born in Flames* (1983) is particularly like *Liberty's Booty* (1980) in the seemingly casual relationship the actors have towards the narrative drive of the piece. The jump cuts and fragmented narrative as well as the interweaving of professional actors and amateurs deliver the same kind of mood, despite a very different kind of soundscape and narrative. Like Dick, Borden also figures an assimilative community between the Black and white women: the gender inequality here foregrounds the equality between the Black, white and Hispanic people in the film. This is significant particularly in the United States, where race is so overdetermined by the history of slavery, the laws of miscegenation and the vast economic inequality that still exists as a legacy of this historical reality. The overburdened history of Black America can be seen in the contrast between US-made *Born in Flames* and the UK-made *The Passion of Remembrance*: while the out-of-time sequences in *The Passion of Remembrance* offer hope for change, *Born in Flames* is darker, with the police state crushing the female activism by burning down the radio stations.

As the 1980s became the 1990s, an approach that aims to depict a normalized intersectionality appears in Ruth Novaczek's *Rootless Cosmopolitans* (1990) and Vivienne Dick's *London Suite (Getting Sucked In)* (1989). Novaczek's main preoccupation between 1986 and 2000 considers Jewish and Black identity in dialogue. In *Rootless Cosmopolitans*, Novaczek continues to draw links between different minority groups as an aspiration towards a coalition of the diasporic. 'What is a Jew?' begins the film of *Rootless Cosmopolitans*. Filmed in black and white, both colour and origin are questioned in the film, wrought from the confines of racism, and ethnic insiderism – each seen to be a condition of possibility rather than a limitation. As a response to this question, the film offers an episodic set of vignettes of women in the city, who suggest some kind of female equivalent of Woody Allen and their interior world. The narrator,

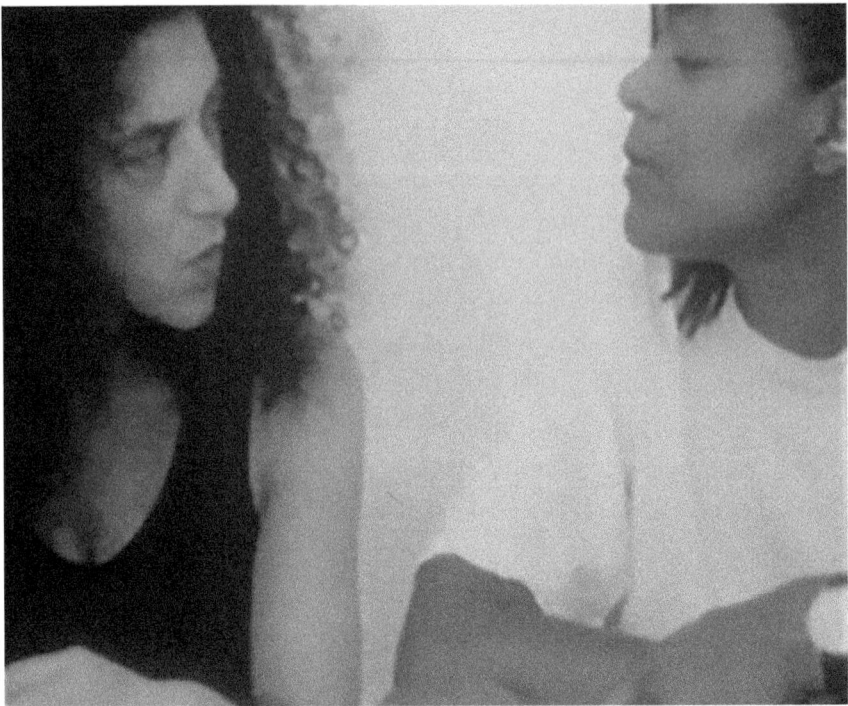

Figure 13. *Rootless Cosmopolitans* (1990, Ruth Novaczek), screen grab. Courtesy of the artist.

as in *Tea Leaf*, introduces two women as friends. The film very quickly moves to a conversation between them that draws an equivalence between Black people and Jews and questions of who looks Jewish and who looks Black. The film centres on the identifications and mis-identifications across the two groups – the identification of some Jews with whiteness and the anti-Semitism of Louis Farrakhan. The ease of the discussion in the film between Black and Jewish women in itself sets up a counter-narrative to the cited identification. The narrator is a minor player in the sound as multiple voices begin to tell their stories. 'She comes from a travelling family. Jews they live here then the borders change'; all the while the subject is silently smoking and a voice talking over the image. 'I came here in '39. I just earned a living … '; the subject speaks but the voice is disconnected from the image of her smoking and talking and walking with her daughter in the street. Lily, the subject, then moves back to the existential questions, talking about accepting her Jewishness and what it

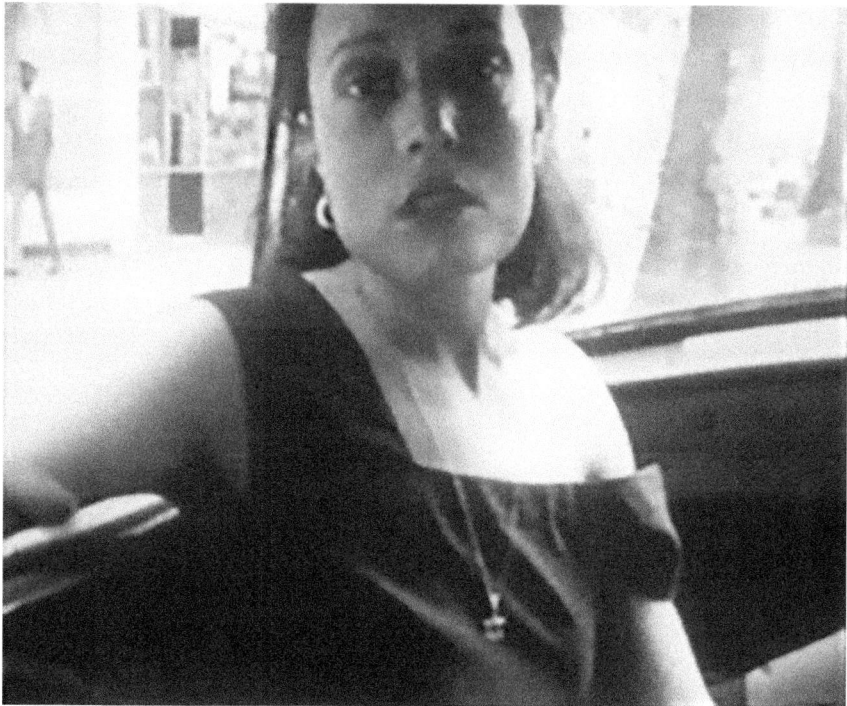

Figure 14. *Rootless Cosmopolitans* (1990, Ruth Novaczek), screen grab. Courtesy of the artist.

means, thus moving from the existential to the personal and back again – in this way the everyday and history are intertwined.

In this film, there are multiple voices, disconnected from the image to make equivalences between people and peoples – in a later passage the subject tells the story of her grandmother getting elocution lessons and the image shifts between what seems to be two elderly women: a European-dressed woman and the same woman in what appears to be a white hijab[42] – the narrative could apply to either of them and thus confounds assumptions of community, belonging and identity at the very moment that it identifies it. Unlike *The Passion of Remembrance*, the main focus here is to use representation to confound expectations of community through play and indeterminacy. Through the play of disjunction it explores the importance of personal perceptions of the world to reconstitute the political through widening the chain of equivalences. The significance of placing Novaczek's work to this trajectory of women artist filmmakers who have been working with identity is to do with the almost total elision of her 'identity work', possibly because Jewishness did not equate with the post-war diasporic idea of an immigrant community that was built around the idea of the postcolonial nor the third-generation ideal of proclaiming difference instead of assimilating – or, as Novaczek – through Judy Waldman's Brooklyn voice – states in *Rootless Cosmopolitans*, 'Let's face it, it's not trendy to be Jewish'.[43] Central to the idea of multiculturalism is speaking from one's subject position, and some of its failings are to do with the hierarchies it sets up between groups defined by their victim status – in relation to some notional centre – and the rigidity of the borders between 'differences'.[44] While Sankofa were marginalized by the 'white' art world but maintained an influential position within the narratives of the 'Black' art world in the UK.[45] Novaczek was marginalized by both the 'Black' art world as not belonging to their narrative and the 'white' art world, as focusing on racism and anti-Semitism rather than assimilating into ethnic invisibility. Punk offered a moment of possibility for these distinctions to be flattened out: that artists even tackled these subjects is axiomatic of this possibility.[46]

London Suite (Getting Sucked In) (1989) was made after Dick had moved to London. This was fifteen years after Rock Against Racism had first emerged and multiculturalism is at the core of the film. As with her other films, a class perspective is paramount and the interlacing of the economic realities: the message is that working people are bound by their lack of affluence irrespective of race. The main protagonist, who is the artist herself, lives in an inner city London, council-owned tower block and her normative context as presented in the film is of Asians – as those of either Pakistani or of Indian East African heritage – Afro-Caribbeans – as the communities with Caribbean heritage were then described generally – and whites – the rest – living together. The viewer sees, early in the film, incidental footage in the lobby of the flats with British-Asian families waiting for the lift interacting with Dick, her friend and her son. This is cut to a scene where two women are sitting and then wandering around an urban wasteland, sharing boyfriend troubles; one of them is talking about a man who is meant to be the boyfriend but he has not been calling her. Her friend is listening and making sympathetic interjections. The teller of the story eventually reveals that her boyfriend is Caribbean. Dick could be criticized for bringing this Black-male-not-taking-a-white-girlfriend-seriously

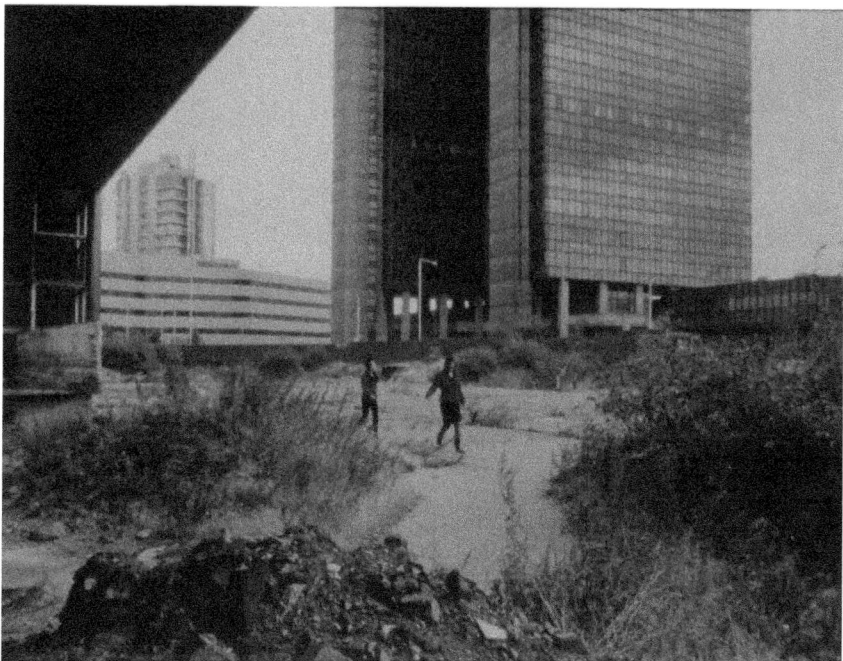

Figure 15. *London Suite*, Fiona Dennis and Beate Wilson (1990, Vivienne Dick). Courtesy of the artist.

stereotype into the film, and while that observation stands, that it is conceived as a minor detail inflects the nuance of black-white relations as normative into the narrative. What is striking within the context of so many heavy-handed films that still focus on issues of race as a feature is that this fact is presented as incidental within a scene that is presented as incidental in a film of heterogeneous voices.

So *London Suite* is a film that typifies a multicultural sense of arrival: the notional boyfriend is merely one of several Black voices in the film at this time which moves away from the burden of representation, worried over in the 1980s, towards a complexity of representation that posits a Black man as just a man, amongst many types of men of any denomination. To exemplify this, the following scene is of a rooftop interview with an older Black man in a suit. He is African American, telling us through the direct address that 50 per cent of Londoners come from elsewhere and for many different reasons stay there. This man, through the device of the interview, his age and the formal manner of his dress, is given the gravitas to comment on life with authority. He is speaking

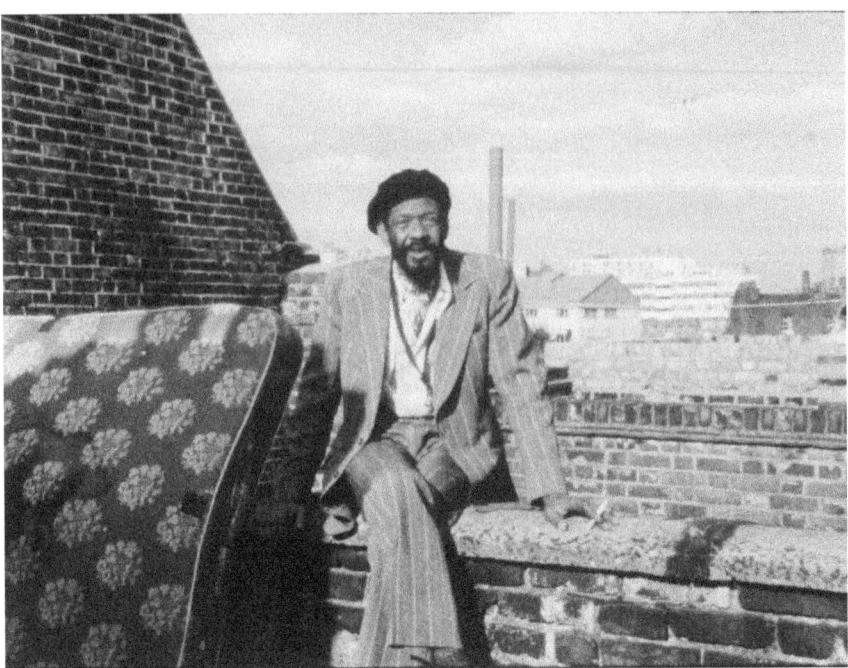

Figure 16. *London Suite*, Sheik L Thomson (1990, Vivienne Dick). Courtesy of the artist.

from the rooftop yet the deflationary aspect of an old mattress resting against the wall at his side and his obvious poverty, signalled by the worn quality of his suit, highlights the contrast between the lack of authority conferred on him by society at large and the authority given to him by Dick in this film.

These key scenes address the issue of multiculturalism directly; however, there are other scenes, seemingly random, that attest to an intersectional approach where race, class and gender are all part of a wider discourse of debate about lived experience in twentieth-century urban life. That each state of inequality is not foregrounded particularly, and not the main theme but just an integral part of a structurally horizontal reading of experience, is significant and unusual. This work naturalizes the issue of race as a mere integrated and incidental aspect of lived experience rather than the core subject of the film.

Filmmakers such as Novaczek and Sankofa in this generation had emerged through the 'new' disciplines of media studies, sociology and, of course, fine art in new universities and art schools in the UK and Ireland.[47] They had benefited from both the avant-garde debates within the film world and the debates framed through Stuart Hall, Frantz Fanon or Homi Bhabha. These latter debates gave academic legitimacy to the experiences of diaspora and immigrant communities in the UK for the generation of artists who were emerging at that time. However, these new debates gave rise to further questions such as: In whose community are you situating yourself? Whom are you addressing, and what is your language? The argument over provenance and reference that dominated the argument for a Black vernacular in the 1980s, with the proliferation of work by Black artists, seems moribund now in the twenty-first century. What is clear is that the power of this mix produced a significant move in terms of how film could offer a transformative and self-reflexive aesthetic that built a language for future generations of artists.

Notes

1   It is beyond the scope of this book to discuss in full the problematics of identity politics in this context; however, it is a discourse to which I have contributed elsewhere such as 2019: 99–113; 2015: 19–25; 2008, Luxonline unpaginated; 2001: 63–70.

2   Poly Styrene https://www.youtube.com/watch?v=NznmF9cyFpw. Poly Styrene had made a reggae record earlier in 1976 entitled *Silly Billy* https://en.wikipedia.org/wiki/Poly_Styrene (Accessed: 2 August 2020).

3   I am looking here at a particularly British context.

4   The notion of what is Black music is a highly problematic term and it is important not to essentialize this in any way. What I am more concerned with here is the perception of what might be considered 'inside' and 'outside'.

5   While I am positing a linear trajectory of sorts, I would want to distance myself from any notion of belatedness here within what is a very small grouping that derived from the socioeconomic conditions of the post-war social contract that gave rise to an unprecedented modern class mobility that is now stagnant.

6   http://www.screenonline.org.uk/people/id/521843/ (Accessed: 3 May 2016).

7   Sankofa and Poly Styrene might demonstrate the tensions of the time between burden of representation and the desire to be free of constraints that would now be an anathema to contemporary artists such as Martine Syms.

8   Stuart Home describes the context in some detail (2005).

9   The sense of embeddedness that is characterized by the series on the BBC *Black and British* (2016), which was a showcase for the new Black middle classes in the UK. This programme in fact demonstrates, despite the differences between assimilation and multiculturalism as discourses, that class is still the defining factor in acceptance in the UK.

10 The SUS (stop and search) law allows the police to search anyone who they even suspected of breaking the law. It was originally introduced in the nineteenth century to control vagrancy but was used extensively and controversially against Black men until it was repealed in August 1981.

11 The lineup was The Clash, The Buzzcocks, Steel Pulse, X-Ray Spex, The Ruts, Sham 69, Generation X and the Tom Robinson Band. According to Syd Shelton, Poly Styrene was one of the first artists to sign up to perform at the concert in Victoria Park in April 1978. https://www.youtube.com/watch?v=kQs8gfiUnCE.

12 Rachel Garfield, unpublished interview with Syd Shelton, 10 September 2015.

13 Michael Jackson and Stevie Wonder tried to organize a boycott allegedly because not enough Black performers were invited (Eclipse 26 August 2016).

14 The inclusion of reggae on sound systems at venues might have been because Don Letts was the DJ at the 100 club on the night of the Sex Pistols gig there, so the link may have been more of an accident than by intention.

15 'I only hope they spell my name right in Who's Who, and get the dates of my prison record straight, and don't forget to say "Race, Negro"' (Damon 1997: 172).

16 Even here there is discussion to be had, given Black's elision of her Jewishness.

17 Anne Robinson was a member of Wildtrax Collective along with Jenya Iljon, Caroline Sheldon and Claire Glassman.

18 I do not have the scope to look at all of these examples here.

19 Although there are other women such as Germaine Dulac (1882–1942) and Alice Guy (1873–1968).

20 This is as much to do with Clarke's communist sympathies.

21 As discussed in Butt (2007: 36–55).

22 Clarke has been largely written out of this history in part due to the ways in which the formation of the Anthology Film Archives consolidated a particular history (Rabinovitz 1991: 140).

23 Also pointed by Nogués (2015: 138).

24 There has been some scholarship regarding collage and discordance as a Black trope (such as Kobena Mercer's work on Romare Bearden) (Mercere 2002: 29–46) or Paul Arthur in *Lines of Sight* on African-American experimental filmmakers (2005: 111–31).

25   Phone interview with Naseem Khan, 18 April 2016.

26   Paul Gilroy points this out in relation to several songs by The Clash that express a kindred experience with young blacks (1991).

27   Although hip hop later took this ground and rock and roll was an earlier aspirant, punk had a particular relationship to race and class that – as I describe – brought a change of policy as well as youth cultural rebellion.

28   Even today, important writers such as Eddie Chambers, who framed the period do not include filmwork from that time. Chambers will focus on Steve McQueen in a later chapter while not mentioning Isaac Julien nor Sankofa.

29   This new subjectivity has a very long history, written about by many theorists on the continuity of Blacks, Jews, Chinese and other non-hegemonic communities in Great Britain. It is the explicit exploration of it through art that was new and was described as such by Zoe Whitley in her introduction of the Sankofa screening of *The Passion of Remembrance* (1986).

30   Neither of these artists would be described as Black but fall under the vaguer but connected nomenclature of a postcolonial subjectivity in art.

31   This is corroborated by Karen Alexander, who states in *Visibly Female* (ed. Hilary Robinson 1988: 35–6) that she joined white women's collectives such as Albany video, to make films as there was not anywhere else for her to go at that time. There were Black men making film and video on white women: she noted that things were getting better with the establishment of Sankofa and Ceddo then recently formed.

32   https://www.theguardian.com/artanddesign/2017/mar/21/whitney-biennial-emmett-till-painting-dana-schutz and http://www.artnews.com/2017/03/21/the-painting-must-go-hannah-black-pens-open-letter-to-the-whitney-about-controversial-biennial-work/, (Accessed: 19 December 2018).

33   Although the film does not differentiate between Caribbean and African or Asian: in that sense there is still an assumed homogeneity.

34   Isaac Julien stated that Sankofa would discuss everything very intensely all the way through until the film was made and in this way they were a true collective. 7 September 2015, Rewind: Sankofa, Tate Britain talk.

35   I would note that this is a problematic assumption but one that was prevalent in the 1980s within both the debates on community needs and the burden of representation.

36   Claire Holdsworth describes the influence of Derek Jarman, who visited St Martin's during Julien's time there (2017: 74).

37   Unpublished interview with Ruth Novaczek (2014).

38 There are various dates for *Tea Leaf* but I am quoting here from the artists own website.

39 Novaczek recently re-edited the film with new sound that no longer has this combination of music. However, it is pertinent to my argument to cite the original soundscape.

40 This might be referencing *The Prostitution Papers* (1975) by Kate Millet.

41 Email to the author (Novaczek 18 August 2020).

42 The two images are in fact 'the same woman, Manya Jurmann, her scarf is a head covering not a hijab but the allusion is there'. From an email to the author (Novaczek 10 August 2020).

43 The Irish are subject to a similar historical positioning. For the Jewish experiences, see Brodkin (1999) and Bauman (1988), Steyn (2000) and Stratton (2000).

44 Even though the notion of centre and margin has been critiqued theoretically in terms of geography and postcolonialism, hierarchies of victimhood still operate.

45 The importance of a discourse around the work is to be noted here. The re-emergence of interest in Black Audio Film Collective and Sankofa could arguably be attributed to the legacy of the writings of Kobena Mercer, Stuart Hall and Coco Fusco: there is no such equivalent in British Jewish discourse.

46 Novaczek was also a DJ and in bands in the 1980s. She also was influenced by punk and world music. Email to the author (Novaczek 10 August 2020).

47 Although Vivienne Dick studied French and Archaeology at undergraduate level, only studying for an MA much later at the LCC in London in 1996–8. From email to the author (Dick 19 August 2020).

3

In praise of the fragment part one: Feminism, visualizing the kitchen table and do-it-yourself

It is a collage experience to be a woman artist or a sociopolitical artist in a capitalist culture.

(Raaberg 1998: 157)

Orgasm Addict was released in 1977. It was a single by the Manchester band The Buzzcocks. The cover had a photomontage by the artist Linder that was to define a generation. Although now well known for her montages in the United Kingdom, at that time she was a student of graphic design at Manchester Polytechnic and connected to a young milieu that included Howard Devoto and Pete Shelley of the punk band The Buzzcocks and the music journalist, Jon Savage. The record cover of *Orgasm Addict* was a monochrome in blue with an image of a grey naked female torso, her hands held above her head as if swaying to a dance move.[1] A domestic iron had replaced her head. There was a smiling open mouth, red lipstick and white teeth prominent on each breast where each nipple would be. The body is glowing as if sweaty. This is her most famous image, an important icon that arguably forged a visual aesthetic for British punk. American Punk was probably more the rock-and-roll-derived Ramones record cover of guys in torn jeans, tee shirts and leather biker jackets. Within punk, there were other models. From a very early point in punk history, the use of anarchic forms of cut up and paste to make posters and fanzines was widely adopted in the UK. However, the reach of the image for the single *Orgasm Addict* went far beyond the fanzine aficionados to make that montage an iconic and key image through the immense circulation of the seven-inch single.

The core argument for this chapter is the examination of the ways in which the image *Orgasm Addict* used contemporary currents in feminist art and brought them into dialogue with earlier Dada and surrealist movements as analogous to the filmwork in this chapter. Key to understanding the work is some interrogation of collage in its different forms. Crosscurrents of punk, feminism and art from the Weimar Republic served to create a new vision that differs from some prominent second wave feminist examples in art but that can be seen in more recent work such as Abigail Child and Leslie Thornton in the United States and Susan Stein and Ann Robinson in the United Kingdom, artist filmmakers whom I will focus on in this chapter. Although the connection between Linder and, say, Child may look tendentious at first, I will trace here several strands of interest and convergence that can tease out the reasons for my approach. In formal terms the methods of fragmentation, montage, use of found footage and shocking juxtapositions draw these artists together through an attitude that has underlying philosophical foundations common to them all. I will differentiate this work from the stylistic methodology of serialization that marks conceptualist and post-conceptualist modes of production, both of which aimed to critique the authenticity and originality of the single art object which is not so much a concern of the artists I discuss here. I will also articulate the differences between the trope identified in this book and the methodology of breaking or interrupting the flow of narrative that aims, after Brecht, to make the viewer aware of their rational presence to aid a political awareness and agency – not that these artists did not benefit from the knowledge gained from other artists who explored this as a primary concern. Central to the approach of fragmentation and one that I will discuss in the next chapter when analysing the artworks by the younger generation of artists is the intellectual scaffolding of Siegfried Kracauer (1889–1966), the critic who wrote about popular culture, modernity and film. I will be particularly thinking through an early work of Kracauer, the *Mass Ornament*, to reflect on Abigail Child's *Is This What You Were Born For?* (1981–9) and Leslie Thornton's *Peggy And Fred in Hell* (1984–2016).

Kracauer saw fragmentation and disintegration as axiomatic of the historical moment in which he wrote. I will draw parallels between the late 1920s and the late 1970s in terms of the psycho-social moment and if not the political moment precisely, the sense of the urgency of change and the disintegration of the current order that were at the forefront in both decades in these different urban locations in Europe. Recalling Badiou's teleology of the twentieth century in *The Century*, that of the Russian Revolution (1917) marking the beginning of the twentieth century and the fall of the Berlin Wall in 1989, marking the end of the century, both *Mass Ornament* written by Kracauer in 1927, and punk fall about a decade either side of these evental moments. Both *Mass Ornament* and punk could be seen to be bookending the processes of these historical events of the beginning and end of the USSR that mark the cultural feel of that century and might help us reflect on what is useful for taking forward from that historical moment in contemporary art practice as we move into the twenty-first century.

In this first part of the chapter I will be developing another lineage through feminist art practices that takes us through the relationship between Linder and Child to collage that existed within that important emergent context for Linder as she was developing her visual language. Given the debates of the 1970s and 1980s in art, of conceptualism and the force of feminism within art schools and in the public sphere at the time, it is noteworthy that both Child and Linder do not draw from the methodology or debates in collage that were set out by the American second wave feminists, such as Miriam Schapiro or Lucy Lippard. Lippard and Schapiro both insisted on collage as a feminist strategy, but Child and Linder went instead to a previous generation of work for inspiration.[2] Perhaps also this is axiomatic of the marginality of Schapiro's position – and indeed Betye Saar – as a painter in the 1970s at a time when painting was in retreat by the avant garde: the dominance of the lens in arguments put forward for the avant garde sidelined painting practices in discourse. The logic of this rendered painting old-fashioned and above all tied to the commodity value system that the avant garde critiqued.[3] Moreover, collage has a history of association with critique and iconoclasm within its very process of making that I would argue is core to its use by punks.

Linder and Abigail Child are both admirers of the pioneering Weimar artist Hannah Höch (1889–1978), famous for her photomontages and credited with being one of the first artists to adopt this way of working as central to her oeuvre, indeed credited with inventing photomontage. Child has been likened to Höch through the shared interest of 'the social circulation of signs' of *détournement* of images of women (Turim 2005: 83). The interest in *détournement* can easily be assigned to Linder in her work and I would extend this case study to bring Höch and Child into dialogue with Linder through these shared interests and processes. Child also makes actual collages as single-image objects.

The leap in generation, from Linder back to Hannah Höch, could also be argued in a similar way to the earlier differentiations in Chapter 1 regarding the previous generation of boho deflationary films – Frank et al. versus Dick et al. – that is tied to a different temporal moment of economic expansion.

While it is easy to think now that 'feminist art' was of a single broad trajectory – and the term itself implies singularity – there were, in fact, several hotly argued positions that represented different areas of thinking and working methods that made claims within the multivalent discussions that artists exploring feminism were engaged in the late 1960s and early 1970s. I will rehearse some of it here by way of a context for Linder's montages that demonstrates her unique approach for that moment and why I am picking up on her work for my argument. Later in the chapter I will draw feminism, collage and film together through an examination of the importance of montage in filmic terms using some classic film theories of Siegfried Kracauer, and Mary Ann Doane's explanation of parallel editing, positing it as a form that has been particularly exploited by women filmmakers as a way of envisioning a personal cinema of their own.[4] However, first I will set out some positions within feminist practices by way of a broad-brush picture of the field.

Within second wave feminist practices there was a widespread focus on fragmentation, seriality and interruption; each brought different contexts and positions with them that require some differentiation. Apart from these formal differentiations, there were several broad strands with contrasting provenances. Crudely put, on the one hand is the practice of negation, that is, the practice that is exemplified by semiotics and the critique of representation. This approach is one that can be characterized by, say, Martha Rosler's famous work *The Bowery in Two Inadequate Descriptive Systems* (1974–5), which articulates the inadequacy of language, visual or verbal, to describe reality by presenting a series of photographs of the Bowery, a place notorious at the time for homeless alcoholics, with accompanying descriptive terms. Many of these artists relied generally on photography as a critique of assumptions of truth and of notions of 'the natural' in representation or performance as a critique of male representations of the female body. On the other hand is the practice of excavation of self-identity through history or mythology, such as the works of Betye Saar, Ana Mendieta or the later work of Alexis Hunter.[5] A third area, one that I am exploring here, can be seen through the generation following these pioneers, a generation of artists such as Linder, Robinson, Child and Thornton, who worked through fragmentation.

A key factor that gave rise to the divergent form between the previous generation and that of Linder's generation is to do with living amidst the disintegration of post-industrial West – as it was called at the time – in the post-1974 climate. The 1980s was a decade of both enormous social expansion and emancipation interlaced with a decade of contraction in the public sector and cuts in jobs, resulting in a culture of scarcity and uncertainty. In the UK at the time there was the concomitant and added threat of fascist-fuelled racist activism, as I outlined in the previous chapter. The generations coming of age in the 1970s and 1980s built on the initial battles for emancipation of the 1960s, but in generational terms, they could not build towards success in the same way economically at that time as the previous generations born in the 1940s and 1950s. The economic panic in 1974 after the oil crisis had an inevitable impact, and this continued well into the early 1990s as the industrial base of the United Kingdom and the United States was decimated and continued to be so in the shift from industry to financial services – in the UK at least through the vision of Margaret Thatcher, leader of the Conservative Party from 1975 to 1990. The north of England and Scotland were hit particularly hard by the economic policies of those governments (Beckett 2009: 157–82). 'Our own times have, in Britain, their own particular difficulties: a crisis of profitability, de-industrialisation, mass unemployment and a sustained attempt to dismantle both the ideology and structure of the Welfare State' (Harvey 1982: 46).

Similarities can be drawn from a comparison between the period from the early 1970s in the UK until the fall of the Berlin Wall in the late 1980s, which heralded the end of the Cold War and that of the anxieties of the Weimar period. The combination of profound economic instability, the beginning of the withdrawal of the welfare state and open, fierce battles between the left – the striking miners, CND activism and anti-fascist activity – and the rise of fascist groups such the National Front, British Movement and British National Party may explain why Linder, and others such as Peter Kennard, in the UK drew from Höch and the more overtly politically active John Heartfield rather than from others. Both Höch and Heartfield were involved with the Dada movement in the aftermath of the First World War period. This particular mix of politics in 1970s UK might also explain the way in which the work of artists like Chicago, Kelly or Schapiro did not speak to the next generation in the way they worked with subjectivity through gender and history in a personalized way. In contrast to the sense of possibility that characterized the work of Chicago or Schapiro and also in contrast to the academically engrossed Lacanian approach of Kelly in the UK, Dada attracted artists like Linder precisely because of the shared outlook and approach that the aesthetic devices of the pre–Second World War generation of artists spoke to.[6] Both the Dada and punk generation explored the possibility of a critical form of an expressionist tendency within art.

Born in 1954, although older than some of the punk generation, Linder was a generation younger than many of the second wave feminist artists who were born in the 1930s and 1940s, including Jo Spence, who came to art later in her life.[7] The younger generations lacked the economic security or belief in a better future that marked the 1968 generation, for whom economic expansion and belief in a better future were naturalized. As Linder stated

> Cut ups were in the air in 1977, a way to cut through the detritus of 20 years' plenty – all the living things you never get to touch applied to old copies of National Geographic and Picture Post, women's magazines – Family Circle, Women's Own, G Plan catalogues and pornozines, the knife offered a certain visceral brutal control: it was a process at once violent and peaceful, which allowed the subconscious to come through.
>
> (Linder 2006: 12)

The irony and humour of the following generations are axiomatic of the inability to be optimistic and would be the decisive winner in the dominant language for art in the UK particularly until the 2010s.[8]

The change that the punk generation brought was profound even though it is not accounted for in art historical terms as much as the 'feminist generation', because the feminist kitchen table aesthetic – as opposed to the male version, the potting shed of the amateur hobbyist – combined with the do-it-yourself of punk, took the idea of de-skilling together with the idea of fractured imagery to a different level that spoke to the politics of the moment. The feminist approach, born out of the domestic constraints of time and space that women often experienced, was brought to the purposefulness of the homemade and lo-fi through the economic unviability of the punk generation – of which the two are, of course, connected – which again fed back into feminist punk in the 1980s. This feminist punk was of a different order to the previous generation not just in terms of the processes of montage and DIY but also in terms of their questioning or rethinking some of the previous orthodoxies of feminist practices as they had emerged. Key examples are to do with the use of pornography (Bette Gordon, Cosey Fanni Tutti), the use of the street as backdrop (Betzy Bromberg, Vivienne Dick or Abigail Child) and the backdrop of the nuclear holocaust or wasteland as a space of agency (Leslie Thornton, Anne Robinson).

In sum I would suggest that the optimistic conviction in the power of a semiotic reframing of representation championed by the feminist artists such as Alexis Hunter or Mary Kelly might be linked to the forms in which the idea of transformation took hold in different conditions. Whereas the work of the conceptualists, for example, was cool and pared down to revealing immanent critique through form, process, rationale or semiotic readings of representation, the next generation of punk posed their critique through an expressionist exposé of the lived contradictions of subjectivity.

Although the 1970s and 1980s were, of course, distinctive, there is in some ways a conflation of the 1970s and 1980s when looking back. The violence and bitterness of the social and political struggles of the 1980s can be seen, in the build-up of the strikes and fascist activism in the 1970s, as a context to the form of Linder's work – the cut of the image, the brutal juxtaposition of domesticity and pornography. The shock and violence of the art and discussions in Germany in the early twentieth century spoke to Linder, as she states, 'the dismembering done by Max Ernst and Hannah Höch, the political savagery of John Heartfield – whose summer exhibition 1977 at the ICA was a major stimulus' (Linder 2006: 12).

Linder's attraction to the brutal and candid imagery of Heartfield can be understood through the shared experience of artists living in a period of economic turbulence in Europe and the rise of fascism. Heartfield's work spans from 1916, through the Dada years, and some of his best-known work was in response to crisis: that of Hitler and the rise of fascism in the build-up to the Second World War. It was work that spoke to crises. In addition to two devastating world wars, the early twentieth century saw the rapid increase in Fordist mechanisms of factory work, and a sense of the disintegration of the previous forms of community and working relations. The late twentieth century saw a continued assault on collective working relations through a sustained attack on the unions and on the post-war contract of social democracy in the UK even while the Cold War offered the ever-present threat of nuclear warfare. The nuclear threat was a constant background noise exemplified by the profile of CND that increased dramatically in the late 1970s and early 1980s. Many of the artists here such as Anne Robinson, Sandra Lahire, Bette Gordon and Leslie Thornton directly reference the threat of the bomb in their work, as I discuss in the following chapter.

By contrast the late 1960s, when many of the second wave feminist artists were at art school or in their early career, was a very different political moment for the United States and the United Kingdom. There was a belief in the possibility of social and political transformation. This was coupled with an economic stability which gave confidence to the activists in their sense of agency. The oil collapse – and a collapsed art world – inflation, mass unemployment and fear of an economic slump of the kind that characterized the 1970s were not unlike the memory of the 1930s. The 1970s saw a transformation that led to the emptying out of the inner cities leaving them economically unviable, particularly in the United States.

It is not surprising, then, that the interest of the young artists of the 1970s would jump a generation back to a previous time of intense economic volatility. What was at stake here was the urgency of the period to forge a new language for art that was distinct and that spoke to women's lives, constituted by their lived relationship to this disintegrating world:

> From Manet onwards the anti-aesthetic (the awkward, the ungainly, the ugly, the unassimilable) has been appropriated as a means of testing the ideological boundaries of the real and the establishment of non-avant garde taste. This taste of necessity has defined itself as anti-bourgeois. Sometimes however, it is able to define itself not just in the negative but in the positive as pro-working class.
>
> (Roberts 1998: 47–48)

I discuss the lo-fi in relation to anti-aesthetic elsewhere in Chapter 1. However, what is useful to retrieve from this line of thinking is to do with the way women situated themselves in relation to the avant garde. I would argue that the idea of the fragment was and is tied to the condition of women making art and to the desire for accessibility. The demand for accessibility required a flattening of hierarchies of taste and aesthetics through de-skilling, through the acceptance that there are different forms of knowledge, that there is no comprehensive body of knowledge nor totalizing vision to be in command of.[9] Lens-based work is now an acceptable if not ubiquitous form of practice, amongst many others, and has many collectors and art prizes. This is a relatively recent phenomenon. By contrast at the time of the feminist pioneers, broadly speaking in the 1970s, photography was used partly because it did not look like art and was not subsumed into the art market or the museum. Photography was seen to be everyday, deflationary and ephemeral. Despite being a form that was championed by the avant garde, especially the surrealists, it was not generally accepted into the art market until the 1990s. Before then photography was often used by artists as a critical tool that stood against the authentic genius, mark-making notion of the artist in favour of an everyday, technological sign of modernity. In an analogous way in the 1970s and 1980s, film was seen to be more purist and less democratizing than the cheaper and more immediate video.

In this way the what can be called a 'kitchen table aesthetic' is the opposite of the Romantic notion of the artist. It is not just a symbol of not having access to a studio in order to finesse your capabilities in a prolonged apprenticeship and then consolidate in sustained full-time levels of practice. The kitchen table aesthetic is also to do with not requiring access to a 'room of one's own', as Virginia Woolf famously identified it, in order to make art. Anyone may have access to the kitchen – hence the 'kitchen table aesthetic',[10] while excess money is required for an artist's studio: 'the studio and the gallery are not separate. They form interdependent moments in the circuits of production and consumption of culture under capitalism' (Pollock 2003: 220). Making work on the kitchen table, without money, is a de facto form of resistance to art in the service of capital as well as a resistance to patriarchal forms and canonizations. In itself it produces its own kind of work more akin to the cottage industry than an industrial scale production of post-war European and American art. The bombast of the industrial attitude may be exemplified equally by the fabricating artist of the 1990s, such as Damien Hirst, or the warehouse productions of post-war sculpture, like Donald Judd, but is out of the scope of the domestic scale. The scale in size should not, however, be confused with bombast and scale in ambition, which can be epic in anger such as the work of the Hackney Flashers or Linder.

Collage is the ultimate kitchen table work. It can be made with no technology, few materials and with little time. Collage has built into its condition a lack of seamlessness and lack of totalizing vision. David Batchelor in a similar approach to his analysis of art aligns minimalism and monochrome with the entitlements of the bourgeoisie and by so doing reveals colour as a marker of the *arriviste* according to normative notions of taste as he describes it (Batchelor 2000: 9–10). In this way, working with collage can be seen as a way of aligning with the idea of the working class as outliers to the art world, not only in terms of its conditions of making but also in the effects of its making. The artist-filmmaker Abigail Child, after a short career as a documentary filmmaker, decided to work experimentally and has been working in experimental montage ever since the 1970s. She describes how she encountered melodrama through montage when making *Mayhem* and through this identifies the 'hot' aesthetic of melodrama as an antidote to what she calls the 'Western cool posture of neutrality (objectivity)' (Child 2005: 22). The fragment and the lo-fi are thus linked to the sweep of debate that turned away from the coherent, seamless, beautiful art object as a sign of the political potency of art, fuelled by the translations and publication of the discourses as discussed earlier of Bertolt Brecht and Louis Althusser in *Screen* magazine in the early 1970s. For Brecht a re-evaluation of method was imperative for art to illuminate the processes of capitalism, but his programmatic Greek chorus-inspired stance did not account for the anarchic multi-directional fissure of collage rather than the linear interruption that was the main paradigm of the serial image of conceptualism.

Linder's image, constructed for the Buzzcocks' single, is a case in point. It was not made for the gallery but for a punk record single – a vinyl record with a single song on each side. *Orgasm Addict* was an iconic collage for the punk generation precisely because it lacked the earnest reclamation and instrumentalization of some of the most celebrated – and of course important – works of second wave feminism such as *Nightcleaners* (1975) by the Berwick Street Collective, Mary Kelly's *Post-Partum Document* (1973–9) or *Who's Holding the Baby?* (1978) by the Hackney Flashers. Instead, it aimed to shock in a visceral and non-instrumentalist way.

Nightcleaners is a particularly interesting comparison, as it too uses fragments and layers of footage which juxtaposes meaning. In this way it could be seen as part of the same cinematic trajectory of, say, Abigail Child.

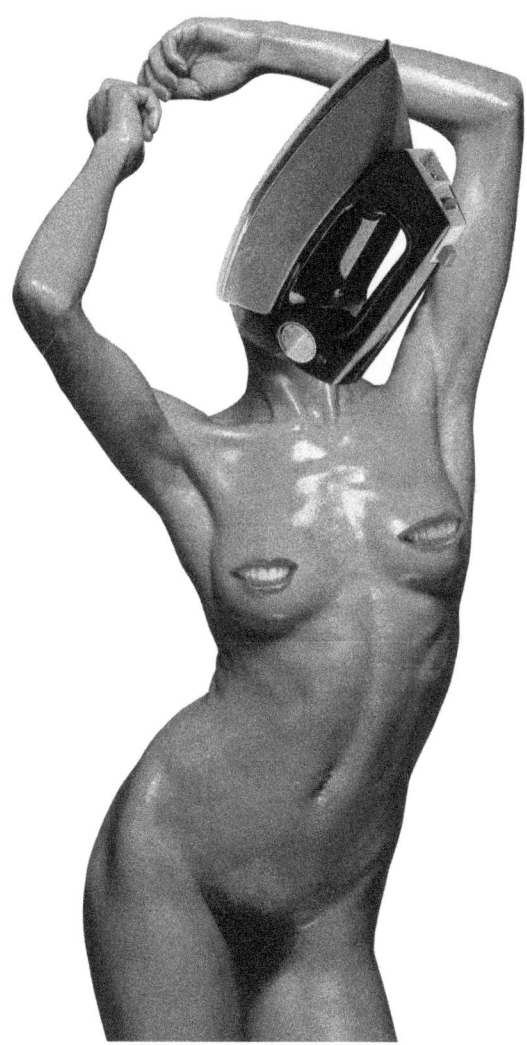

Figure 17. *Untitled* (1976, Linder Sterling) © Linder. All rights reserved, DACS/ Artimage 2021.

However, the cinematic structure and form have a completely different effect despite some formal similarities. The difference I am describing here could be analogous to the way in which a blues guitar speeded up produces heavy metal, for example: that is, a similar musical route that produces another genre entirely.

Nightcleaners was produced by the tensions between political activism and theoretical discourse.[11] It was a film that was made by the Berwick Street Collective over a two-year period and became an experiment in Brechtian distanciation, using an office cleaners' strike as a starting point. This film is held up as a prime example of political film by some because of the ways in which it uses the documentary form but also interrupts and fragments it through slow motion and jump cuts, thus allowing the viewer to understand the ideological drives of the film. This film is not, however, about the subjects but more to do with conveying the tensions between form and content. Within this context, I would argue that the subjects of the film, working-class women, have diminished agency in the way that they are presented by the artists.[12] From the commentary it is clear that the artists were involved in the strike. They were shown to be leafletting and attending – at least filming – union meetings. The art historian Sheila Rowbotham, who shared a house with Mark Karlin, one of the filmmakers, also describes how the 'Cleaners' Action Group', a campaigning group formed to unionize the cleaners, was started in her bedroom. One of the clear differences that I am discussing, however, can be characterized by the comment of Karlin that the film is about 'distance' (Rowbotham in Kidner 2018: 23–36). Despite involvement in the process of filming through collective discussion, the distance that the artists explore theoretically and formally means that the working women themselves are mediated to the extent that they become a cipher rather than agents. The effect of this operates in a similar way to the ways in which Warhol's *Chelsea Girls* was compared to Dick's *Guerillere Talks* in the discussion in Chapter 1 regarding distance and proximity: the difference between being inside the work and observing the work demonstrating the long shadow of Kant. In the same way it is clear in the making of the film, in its structural set-up, that the striking nightcleaners become subjects observed and as such different to the filmmakers in their aim to think through political filmmaking. Thus, the aims of the filmmakers to forge a political language of film to underline the politics that it portrays through a Brechtian distanciation are done ultimately at the expense of the actual subjects, which in fact takes it away from the communist aims of Brecht towards claiming a new aesthetic device. At the time of making this film Peter Gidal was a key proponent of distance as seen in his polemic first published in 1974 entitled *Theory and Definition on Structuralist/Materials Film* – so much so that he gives the paragraph a subtitle of its own. This paragraph entitled 'Distance' goes some way to explain the role of the device of distance in the making of *Nightcleaners*. He states,

> Through the attempted non-hierarchical, cool, separate unfolding a distance(ing) is sought. This distance reinforces (rather than denies) the dialectic interaction of viewer with each film moment, which is necessary if it is not to pass into passiveness and needlessness. This interaction on the physical level and on the level of critical praxis is obvious. The real time element demands such a consciousness and will. I can here only hint at the deeper problematic within the 'real time' 1:1 relation between viewer and views is located [*sic*].
>
> (Gidal 1996: 154)

This can be seen in the effects that are used: through interrupting the women speaking mid-sentence; through the slowing down of footage to the extent that the women become iconic – their image becomes estranged, morphing into grotesques. These are merely a few devices that render the relationship between the viewer and subject asymmetrical: while the aim of *Nightcleaners* was to set the viewer apart so they could think politically through the film, it does so at the expense of the humanity of the women strikers.[13] This differentiates it from the empathy seen in the immersive films of Vivienne Dick, particularly given the subject matter of a strike by women: the interplay between the politics of materiality and the politics of material existence is here at odds, not in convergence. Not that Dick's work lacks the devices that set a framework for cognitive work by the viewer: the moments in, say, *Liberty's Booty*, where there is a collision of space and time, is also constituted through the example of the merging of the images of the sex workers sitting in a New York McDonald's, while the sound is of an Irish male voice describing a famous McDonald's strike in Dublin, Ireland, where the strikers prevailed. However, this powerful momentary example of distanciation is inserted into a film which is primarily experiential in focus. What I am emphasizing here is the difference between abstraction and the concretization of the idea compared to the ways in which the film *Nightcleaners* appears to be the result of the experimentation with an idea in which the concrete context of the striking women was just the initial spur. Dick's work instead appears to be producing the results of experimentation with the negotiation of lived experiences of the subjects she engages with rather than the cipher for another idea of the artist.

Linder's collages, also in contrast to the structural strategies of *Nightcleaners*, are speculatively playful with their use of images, which are often ambiguous. This work is freed from the burden of representation that documentary requires, and therefore is not vulnerable to claims of the submerging of the subject to the requirements of visual experimentation of *Nightcleaners* nor does it rely on the originary claims of form bound up with the authenticity of the indexical link to the real. The playfulness of Linder can also be seen in Child's work. As she explains, 'Through montage and rhythm I was able to forge new connections and dissemble existing ones, but as I approached the body more intimately, giving myself at one point the direction to "embarrass" myself, as I approached narrative language and the Forbidden, *unloosening* subjects that had previously been untouched, excess and gesture accompanied the fragmentation. I encounter melodrama' (Child 2005: 21–2).

Child's undoing is of a different kind. Like Linder, it is an excessive melodramatic undoing rather than the cool dramatic undoing of *Nightcleaners*. Interestingly, melodrama was an 'important representational mode', according to Patrice Petro in her book *Joyless Streets* (1989: 24). Melodrama was a way of 'allowing the repressed to achieve material presence' (Petro 1989: 30). The process here becomes the progenitor in visual play where the meanings are not contained. The readings of melodrama for Weimar film are in contrast to the retrospective readings of Kracauer that focuses on broken and oedipal masculinity, in his book *From Caligary to Hitler*, which served to explain the role of popular culture in the development of fascism. The alternate reading of Weimar film by Petro through Peter Brooks (1976) offers a new approach through the process of play that produces critical and productive ambiguity that can be seen in the works in this chapter. Purposeful ambiguity through the use of parallel editing will be developed in the following chapter, according to the readings of Mary Anne Doane. The idea and processes of play give rise to the ways in which artists using film and video can develop visual indeterminacy that is nonetheless of political impact. This single factor points to a different provenance than that which preoccupied many second wave feminist practices that dominated at the time that Linder was emerging. For while Linder would certainly have been aware of these new feminist works, it was not conceptualism that excited her so much as the possibilities of the excess and *informe* of surrealism that spoke most clearly to Linder through John Heartfield and Hannah Höch, who both used shock, irony and play to hone the politics in their artworks. Part of this differentiation is to do with the ways in which the reductive seriality of much conceptualism produces a contrary effect to the additive and repetitive overloading of much punk. In the reductive seriality, questions are posed that form a new seamless resolution; in the repetitive excesses of punk, an undecidability of heterogeneity is proposed – with no resolution. 'In the fragments which refuse to be reunited or even imagined as parts of an original whole, difference and heterogeneity are postulated in more radical terms' (Pollock 2003: 241–2).

An example of second wave additive seriality might be Alexis Hunter's work from that decade but possibly specifically *Approach to Fear: Masculinity – Exorcise* (1977), which is a series of photographs of the artist's hand spoiling another photograph of a naked man's genital area by scrubbing it with black ink. A further example might be the African American artist Adrian Piper, who moved from working through abstracted seriality to embodied and lived seriality in *Catalysis* (1971). Important though these works are, in fact, some of my favourites, these were still distinct from the fragmented visuality of the kind I am approaching in this chapter that is to do with the spatial leap of parallel editing as well as the lo-fi. All these second wave feminist artists were working with domestic, lo-fi, lens-based imagery. Their work did not have the slickness and production values often expected of the 1990s onwards. However, the punk work of Linder is compounded by further fragmentation, situating a language that developed a hybrid form out of conceptualist practices that would become part of the toolbox to which she had access as an art student.[14] This would offer a different vision to that of, say, the art historian Rosalind Krauss's influential position on the order of the grid. Krauss states, 'In the spatial sense, the grid states the autonomy of the realm of art. Flattened, geometricized, ordered, it is antinatural, antimimetic, antireal. It is what art looks like when it turns its back on nature' (Krauss 1979: 51).

Krauss discusses the ubiquity of the grid in modernism to its sources in optics of the nineteenth century. Germane to my argument, she describes how the grid is a structure that is spatial and static, a rectilinear structure that does not allow for development but is merely etiologic; that is, the focus on the grid is the focus on one instance of change. It is about origin not development: in this she cites Piet Mondrian and Josef Albers, whose work did not move forward in their last decades. The fragmentation of Linder's work and the others in this chapter is often based on the diagonal, not the grid, which has a dynamic motion of continual change with no beginning and no end – much like collage. It brings back nature in all its nonconforming messiness.

Away from the rectilinear rigours of conceptualist-derived approaches was another framework that impacted on artwork made by feminist artists: that of the concern with herstory and identity.[15] In some ways this can be seen as a rival form of practice as both the provenance and intention are set in quite different terms. This work aimed to change the conditions of women not through the art of negation such as activism, documenting or intervening in the lives of working women, but by an art of celebration, redefining what and who women could be by reclaiming lost histories and practices of women in order to find a new visual language of elevating the power of women exemplified by Judy Chicago, Ana Mendieta, Carolee Schneeman and, of course, Schapiro herself.

Gwen Raaberg's excavation into the genealogy of collage as a feminist trope is useful here. To some extent what was at stake in the choices of approach between collage and seriality in second wave feminist art was to do with the politics of critique and negation as opposed to the politics of repurposing art and its languages for an enabling sense of self-worth and celebration. The taxonomies of collage can also be seen to be drawn from sociological thinking. Raaberg cites Lucy Lippard's argument for collage as a positive use of fragmentation and a dominant form in feminist practices of 'putting things together without divesting them of their own identities' (Lippard cited in Raaberg 1998: 205). One of the case studies is Miriam Schapiro and Melissa Meyer who wrote several essays on collage and were the inventors of the neologism 'femmage'. Schapiro and Meyer gave clear guidelines of the parameters of women's collage gleaned from the observation of marginal women's work, developing a formal justification for contemporary feminist collage on a lineage of practice drawn from folk history of women's practices. In their article in the vanguard feminist magazine, *Heresies*, they delineate the manifesto for 'femmage'. This taxonomy of what constitutes femmage could be used for the films I focus on – even while the visual language Schapiro and Meyer were describing would not normally be discussed within the same category as the work I write about in this book.

> 1. It is a work by a woman. 2. The activities of saving and collecting are important ingredients. 3. Scraps are essential to the process and are recycled in the work. 4. The theme has a woman-life context. 5. The work has elements of covert imagery. 6. The theme of the work addresses itself to an audience of intimates. 7. It celebrates a private or public event. 8. A diarist's point of view is reflected in the work. 9. There is drawing and/or handwriting sewn in the work. 10. It contains silhouetted images which are fixed on other material. 11. Recognizable images appear in narrative sequence. 12. Abstract forms create a pattern. 13. The work contains photographs or other printed matter. 14. The work has a functional as well as an aesthetic life.
>
> (Schapiro and Meyer 78: 69)

In contrast to the grid and its static nature of singular transformation that Krauss argues, Schapiro and Meyer posit that collage is both forward-looking and backward-looking: it allows women to make sense of the fragments of recovered history as the only history that they will ever be able to recover and as a way of using those strategies in the contemporary in order to forge a new language for the future (Schapiro and Meyer 77). Abigail Child echoes this sentiment in her book *This Is Called Moving*, particularly her chapter 'Poetry in Motion', which describes the provenance of her methodology (2005). In Schapiro and Meyer's writing the strategic aim is not the absolute call for an alternative radicality of the avant garde.[16] The claims of such absolutism are hard to adhere to in any case in a post-Rancière understanding of the ways in which art operates. Instead the power of the collage is an expression of an experience of the world that still has power to confound and question. An anecdotal example might be my own encounter with the collective work of Jo Spence, Rosy Martin, Maggie Murray & Terry Dennett at *Documenta* in 2007. What was unique about the encounter with this particular iteration of display was that amid the high production values and large epic offerings that is the usual presentation of work in these global survey shows, this lo-fi, small, humble work, modestly pinned up, was highly noticeable as completely out of step with the main trends and tenets of art of the time. In its stuck-on, awkward way it stood out and made me stop and look in a different way to the rest. It made me reflect differently on that work than merely what it purported. In the contrast with the mainstay of the display, this work looked at first odd and amateurish, but then as I recalibrated my vision towards the dominion of the Spence work et al., it worked on me to regain its stature, rendering the work around it ersatz and mannered in its overproduction. This is not to denigrate recent work, made within its own context, however; it merely highlighted an approach that has been sidelined but which requires some recalibrating of its own as a legitimate approach to current art production. It also highlights the need to look beyond the lo-fi appearance of the work I am discussing in this book.

Furthermore, Schapiro and Meyer articulate their views on women's art activities and the 'femmage' tradition as a process that developed out of the experiences of women's lives, fragmented by domestic and nurturing duties and limited by patriarchal cultural privileges. Analogies can be made in a variety of direct ways through some of the films of Su Friedrich that invites the viewer to experience emotion through the gaps she sets up. Friedrich is an American filmmaker who, working through experimental documentary, has done much to develop a language that brings together different forms in a palimpsest of imagery. One example of fragmentation is an early film of hers, *Scar Tissue* (1979), which is a film made from found footage of street scenes from the 1940s. Each fragment of these black-and-white shots is divided by black lead-in. This is an abstract film, although linear in its construction. Each image is fragmented as the viewer only sees a partial shot: never the person's head, only feet, hands, waists. In a different way *Gently Down the Stream* (1981), a slightly later film of Friedrich's, reads very much like a collage in the image. Each shot shows a rectangle within the frame – the frame being a rectangle in itself, of course – of a film of a woman rowing a boat, and later a child stepping into a paddling pool. Beside and around this found footage is written in chalk. The writing is the narration of a short set of stories. Together it is composed and reads like a series of still images, not a film. The mixture of found footage and drawn footage is what gives a sense of collage and visual richness to the work. It is visually layered and operates through a disjunction of immanent critique that is familiar in still images. Susan Stein's imagery is both shot and found. Her films *She Said* (1982) and *Tracks* (1989) are also good examples of collage, using a mixture of personal experience and images to explore women's lives.[17] *She Said* starts with a forty-second handheld shot of a close-up of the fragment of a door. A third of the frame is the wood frame and two-thirds of the frame is the bobbled and frosted glass window in the door. The door opens and in the darkness the viewer can just about see the stairwell and silhouettes of two people as the cameraperson goes into the house. Then the viewer will see Black leader for several seconds until a female narrator recounts a woman's reminisces of her work in a metal factory. There is Black leader between sections – just the kind of mannered use that Peter Gidal railed against in its pretence of making the material the process (Gidal in O'Pray 96: 150). It is a fragmented narrative divided into several sections. The first is of women talking about their work as a sheet metal worker, a domestic servant and a typist. They are recounting details of objects and tasks, and the images are of black-and-white photographs sliding across the frame top to bottom, left to right, back to the front. Stein was and still is interested in women and work; however, this is a very different approach to the subject than *Nightcleaners*, using the rostrum camera to reflect on histories of women's labour from the seventeenth century to the time of making the film. Each section is divided by Black leader as voices become more poetic and oblique, speaking to the emotional experiences of women's lives and the effects of labour rather than the particular details of their working day. The film becomes more and more elliptical as letraset slogans start appearing interspersed between the other black-and-white photographs of 'learning femaleness', 'secret. Secretary', 'free to buy'. These slogans refer to the wider context that women inhabit in culture and that denotes their sense of being in the world. The viewer now cannot help but realize that the piece randomizes the information provided so the images and voices do not cohere. While the experiences of the narrated snippets are clear to start with, their relationship to the images is not explained. At times the images are moving too fast to hold on to the information of what they depict, and other times it slows down completely so the viewer can absorb every detail. As the narrative becomes poetic and oblique, the relationship between image, text and narration changes again. The film ends as 'work in progress/Stein 1982', thus inscribing provisionality into the work.

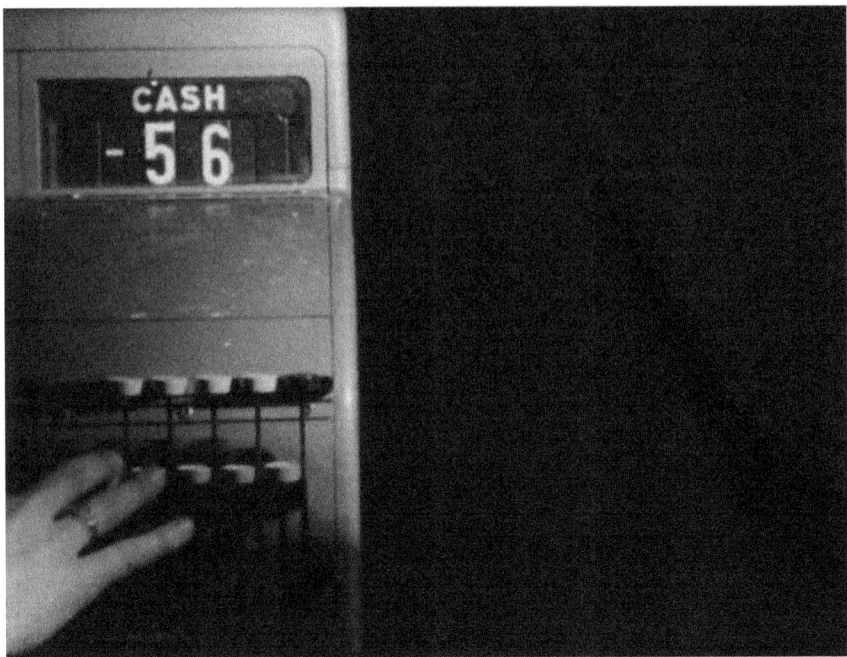

Figure 18. *She Said* (1982, Susan Stein). Courtesy of the artist.

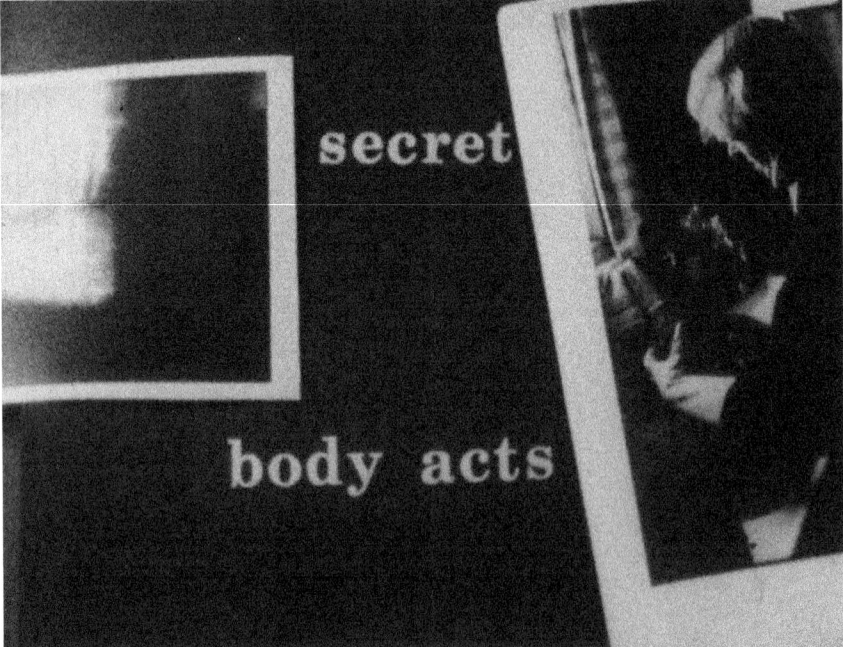

Figure 19. *She Said* (1982, Susan Stein). Courtesy of the artist.

These two films by Friedrich and Stein are not obvious ones to bring into the framework of punk as they do not possess the grunge aesthetic of many other filmmakers here, such a Vivienne Dick or early Novaczek, and their objective is to convey a singular idea, consciously working with form as an alienating factor. Yet the way in which the subject matter and material concerns coalesce coupled with the use of images and sound that aggregate towards a composite bring these films into the purview of this account and demonstrate the range of approaches to the idea of collage in moving image during this period by women.

The spatial and temporal leaps that Friedrich and Stein are making here and that Child, Dick and others in this book habitually use can also be characterized through the use of parallel editing. Janet Harbord, building on Mary Anne Doane's suggestion that parallel editing introduces a spatial leap, develops this thinking as an approach to making films that opens up an imaginative space for the spectator to think between the frames. Unlike the classic shot/reverse shot, parallel editing produces no linear accumulation of meaning, but instead a disjunctive range of shots that fold in a leap of time or space, creating meaning in a different way. While the chase edit 'aggregates regularity' and creates normality, parallel editing creates suspense through desire and fear, which, according to Harbord, 'displaces the temporal logic of film, creating a simultaneity that requires the spectator to insert herself into the relationship between images, to forge connections' (2007b: 72) where often these connections are not self-evident in the film itself. It is an edit that has a gap in meaning through its contingent incoherence. Into that gap our own imagination may roam to make connections. This is a cinematic way of approaching the idea of collage that is to do with a textured layering of imagery. Parallel editing is essentially a kind of montage that can offer an effect of collage through contingency like no other cinematic form, which is itself an effect – contingency, that is – of the simultaneity.

Harbord posits that we might think of editing as assemblage rather than a cut, thus interweaving space and time. 'Editing as assemblage, a bringing together of parts into unforeseen relations, requires us to think about films' spatial relations, as a fabric that spreads itself across space linking atomised images and producing new lines of connection' (2007b: 80). In this way it privileges heterogeneity rather than singularity. Heterogeneity flattens out the hierarchies of the temporal, as an equalizing force. It increases the violence of the cut because it eschews both the linear seamlessness of Hollywood and the current prevalence of the Bazinian long look, forcing us to look deeper between shots rather than into the shot itself.

A different kind of example that might be brought into the frame from Schapiro's idea of collage is through references to folk. Folk is probably the other end of the spectrum to the obvious regard of the disinterested in critique. However, a dialogue between folk genres and use of collage, as Abigail Child's works show, can produce critique of the form through an experiential subliminal recognition of traditional narrative reframed without recourse to the traditional functions of shot sequencing that would usually explain the narrative flow. The classic film genres of slapstick and noir are the folk of cinema: they are excavated as a foundational form of expression with wide appeal that speaks to people's ordinary experiences in a way that can be taken forward in new ways. Abigail Child's series *Is This What You Were Born For?* (1981–9) could be seen to be just the kind of manoeuvre that Doane, Harbord and Schapiro in their different ways are suggesting: a response to feminist discourses that uses assemblage as a way to find a language. Through using the folk of cinema in its many forms, not only noir and slapstick but also found footage of porn and documentary, Child is *détourning* these forms as a woman. However, while the methods are similar in some ways, the effect is not analogous. This composite work, made up of seven short films of different lengths and foci, reshapes previous mediations of film – Hollywood narrative films, documentary film, home movies, found footage equally – through extensive reframing. 'Editing film let me think about music, sound, image, language – the *multiplicity* of the thing is what drew me' (MacDonald 2005: 203).

Contrary to any assumptions about Child's work is to know that in the 1970s Child worked for NBC and made several documentary films for WNET-TV until developing her reputation as an experimental filmmaker in the 1980s, so the sense of the random is not to do with lack of understanding of filmic language or skill but to do with a desire for reinvention, to find a language of her own, and in fact Child's work, as with much of the work in this book, is deeply engaged with film history and reference (MacDonald 2005: 201). William Wees makes this point: the very defiance of category in itself creates new definitions of what makes good art and is to do with the way these artists 'participate in rather than rise above media-saturated modern life. Not passively nor in a shallow postmodern spirit of pastiche ... but analytically, critically and sometimes appreciatively too' (Wees 2005: 26). Interestingly it was through seeing a Hollis Frampton film that Child realized that she could do *anything* she wanted (MacDonald 2005: 207) and her work builds on the cinematic insights of films such as Peter Kubelka's *Unsere Afrikareise* (1966) but develops it profoundly to a degree that reinvents the language thoroughly.

Much of the commentary of Child's work explains the careful crafting of rhythm or the Eisensteinian dialectical editing, but, as a thought exercise, if I were to posit the opposite, the inversion would bring a reading to the work that aligns with the punk aesthetic that is attributed to her work as an anarchistic editorial gesture. To reframe Child's sophisticated and extensive work through a purposeful lack of discernment may bring it into the frame of the punk deskilled scattergun approach to learning; in fact, many of the previous generation, according to William Wees, saw Child as those amongst her generation, demonstrating a 'falling off in quality, artistry and originality' (Wees in Petrolle and Wexman 2005: 23). Like Wees, I do not agree with that analysis. Wees identifies three ways in which the women represent what he calls a paradigm shift: firstly, that as women, they present issues like patriarchy and sexuality in their films; secondly, that their films engage 'dialectically' with the media and popular culture; and thirdly, that the works, as I posited earlier, 'defy categorisation'. In all these ways, particularly the latter, these filmmakers produced work that confounded what constituted previous markers of important avant garde or experimental film.

So if, as Wees suggests in the same article that the women like Child – and Thornton, whom I discuss next – purposefully rejected the notion of the 'great man' canon of work, then this kind of intervention, that of 'defying category', offers a purposefully oppositional proposition. The seemingly random set of choices á la the de-skilling of Dada in itself suggests a virtuosity *via negative* through differing means and a differentiating subject orientation than the 'men' their predecessors. So rather than reclaim virtuosity which could arguably fall into the same cul-de-sac of depth as the purists, we could posit a kitchen table aesthetic of a purposeful randomization of the collage. The point for me, of the epic seven piece *Is This What You Were Born For?*, is that it keeps moving, keeps defying development through working through different genres and a range of speeds and approaches. While each film uses different approaches and genres, each filmworks with assemblage and parallel editing. In this epic work breadth rather than depth is the point. Breadth has usual connotations of the dilettante, the superficial – she who has no time – or inclination – to spend time painstakingly researching, in the way that is usually recognized as fostering excellence, until she becomes an expert, but instead flits across the surface never really understanding what is going on – following any fashion going. I would argue against this understanding of breadth and argue to see it as a form of expertise. Comparison across time, genre, position, field of knowledge can create its own form of expertise that is able to critique by comparison and testing across the fields.

Each film in Child's epic series *Is This What You Were Born For?* deals differently with the world and obviously engages classic film history as well as experimental film. This is an ambitious piece, both epic and deflationary: epic in number and in the overall vision while also being deflationary in its fragmentation and approach. Each film is made up of outtakes, or seemingly so, and the denouncement of narrative drive of the films in favour of a spatial imagist collage also confounds any intention that a viewer might have of finding coherence in any usual sense. If there is any forward drive, it is a rhythmic one as movements or shapes are repeated, not abstract painterly shapes as in Len Lye for example – another early influence – but filmed events and found motifs. In much of her work there is some footage obviously taken from TV documentaries and possibly shot by Child, outtakes from her own documentaries. Each film has a different feel and could be described as considering different genres for more examples; *Covert Action* (1984) reframes home movies, silent movie slapstick in the case of *Perils* (1985) and *Mayhem* (1987) reframes film noir. Child's use of cinematic genres is a way in which she thinks through estrangement and the alienation of capitalism and heteronormativity. For example *Perils*, which I describe later in this chapter, is a take on the silent era but renders it incoherent, not only through the lack of narrative structure but also through the lack of coherence to the actions, movement or sound in the work. However, there is a 'look' of the silent era slapstick short that Child captures. Reframing the operational disjunctions that the technologies – or lack of sound – of the silent era required, Child amplifies it towards an hysterical reaction, which will be explored more significantly in

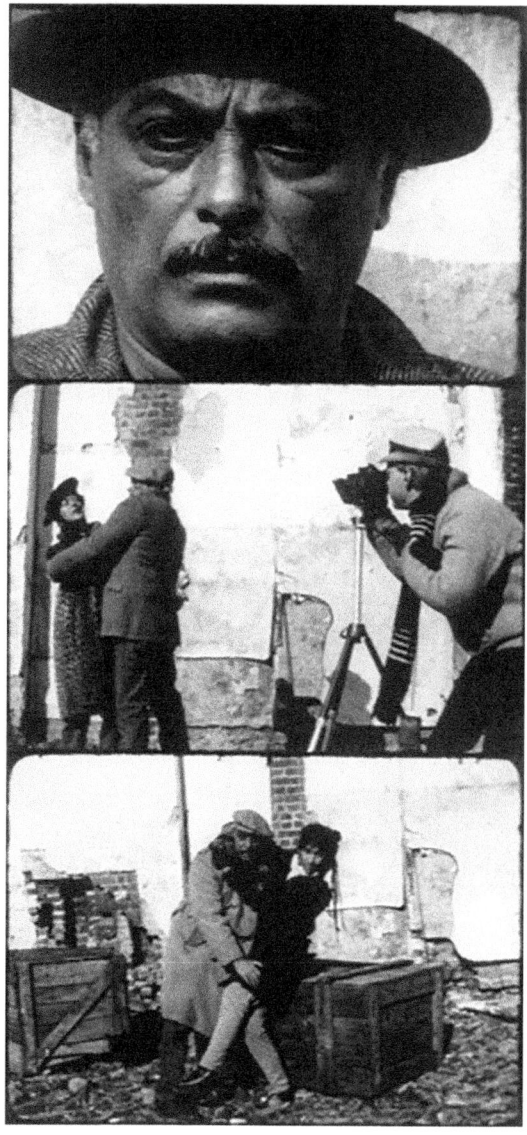

Figure 20. Diane Torr, Elion Sacker, Jim Biederman and Sally Silvers. From *Perils* (1984, Abigail Child) © Abigail Child.

the next chapter. More pertinent to this chapter is the relationship between film, collage and contingency that Child exploits in her work to the full.

Unlike many filmmakers who reframe in order to explain or to clarify for the viewer what is really going on, many of Child's films seem to celebrate incoherence – and in their totality as a series, it is incoherent – through the editing of sound and image. This obfuscation is not to do with presenting smoke and mirrors but, like Su Friedrich and Susan Stein – only more so – in exploring the affective possibilities of experiencing the world through its rhythms and impressions as an alternative form of critique to that ruled by reason, although can, in its own way, access reason. As Maureen Turim states, '*Mayhem* stresses the shards of a broken order into a new configuration. Certainly Child's cutting strives to maximise our appreciation of disorderly conduct, giving us playful gestures in odd retakes of film history intercut with found footage.' And as Child states herself in Turim's text, 'I'm trying to break the adjacencies' (2007: 265). Thus, these films from *Is This What You Were Born For?* are structured so that the viewer must struggle to make sense of the maximalist scale of the thousands of moving images montaged together in each film and then also in relation to the other films brought under the umbrella of the same series of films. Interestingly, the maximalist effect is brought together through a kind of 'making do' of collage: a making a lot out of little. As a feminist practice, collage can be seen in Abigail Child's and also Leslie Thornton's – discussed below – mix of found footage that is wrapped in footage shot by the artists themselves. Child, particularly through her use of genre, her use of a range of genres within the one composite piece that makes up the film series *Is This What You Were Born For?*, can in some ways be likened to the folk histories that Schapiro draws from. Child works through the genres that are the folk histories of film such as the aforementioned slapstick, noir and home shot porn. Furthermore, through her own interventions Child also works over the gaps in an analogous way to the quilting that Schapiro traces.

The way that Leslie Thornton (b. 1951) makes use of the quilting together of styles and footage is more protracted and creates greater leaps that get held together through the rhythms and repetitions of sound and image, but that stretches the form and increases the viewer's requirement to insert herself between the different modes and types of footage. Thornton is a filmmaker of the same generation as Abigail Child (b. 1948). She studied in Buffalo, New York, under Paul Sharits, who was an important influence.[18] She was also taught by Peter Kubelka and Hollis Frampton, both of whom deconstructed the image and representation in film, but in a way that was to become the *doxa,* that is, in a minimalist way of paring down the information to reveal its construction. Conversely, Thornton does this through a maximalist epochal sweep in her *Peggy and Fred* work, an approach that she shares with Child. A part of the epochal sweep is to endlessly remake the work into many versions of different edits that defies the new – and singular – vision proposed through a reconfiguring of image that, say, Frampton or Kubelka tend to do. The multifaceted forms of image-making and versions create a heterogeneity and multi-faceted vision that goes beyond the predecessors. Thornton has been remaking this film since 1984 and was still changing versions for her installation at London's Raven Row gallery in 2015–16. The version of the film shown at Raven Row then became the final edit, although there are occasions where Thornton will exhibit several versions at once.[19] So while in *Peggy and Fred* the anchoring motif is the children acting in a constructed room, each film reconfigures footage bringing in different passages and references. Thornton plays with the narrative by inserting shifts in focus and mood, working with a range of footage and sound; in a few places she uses appropriated footage from well-known historical documentary events and some random finds, but most,

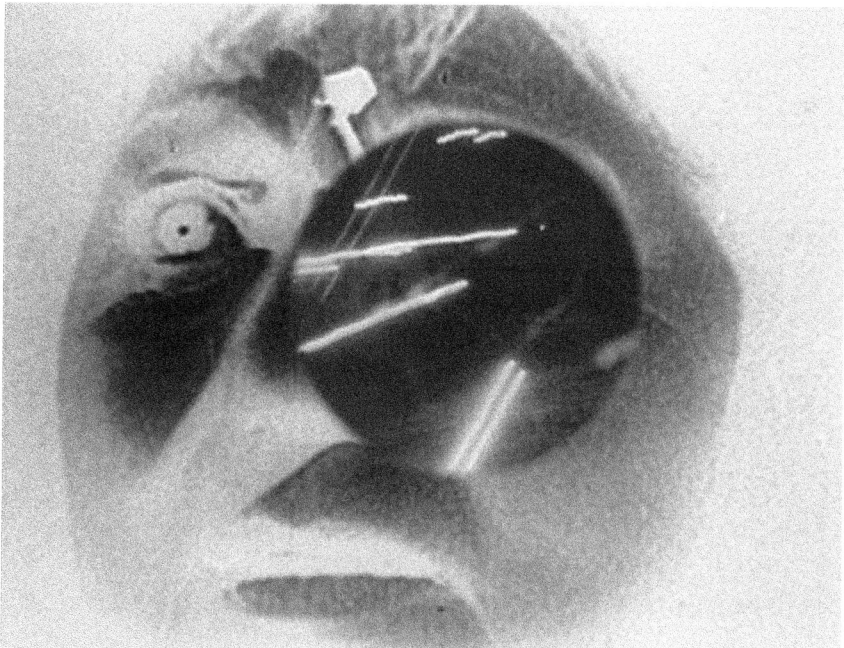

Figure 21. *Peggy and Fred in Hell* (1983–2015, Leslie Thornton). Courtesy of the artist.

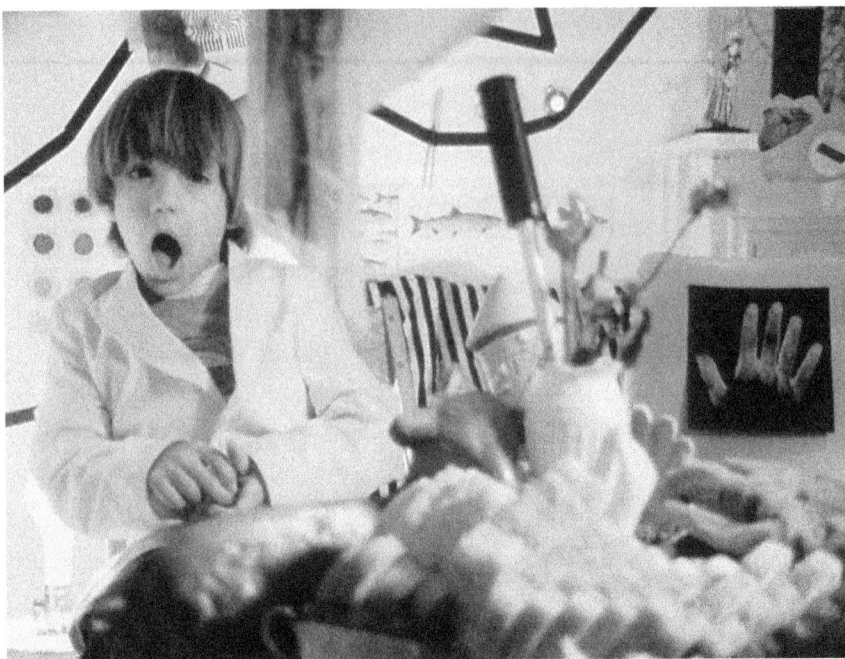

Figure 22. *Peggy and Fred in Hell* (1983–2015, Leslie Thornton). Courtesy of the artist.

including much that looks archival, is shot by her. Thus, collage in this film is used as part of a world-making strategy. As Thornton herself states,

> I *appropriate* material, and embed it in such a way as to bring it into a kind of present tense. Thus, rather than looking to found material to construct an argument or narrative, as is often the case in documentaries, I use it as an ambiguous and indeterminate reference, to expand the visual vocabulary perhaps, but also to draw attention to its presence as an image to re-experience. It is [a] component of the found world of Peg and Fred. Two notable instances are the use of footage from the Library of Congress Paper Print Collection, and the appropriation of audio from Polanski's 'The Tenant'.[20]

The core, or maybe I should say, spine of the film takes place in a bespoke room dressed up to be post-apocalyptic in which Peggy and Fred – her upstairs neighbours, Janice and Donald Reading – perform their various interests. Sound is an important driver of the film, its rhythms denoting editing choices and constituting moods. Central to this is Peggy and Fred, often singing songs to camera, such as Janice singing 'Billy Jean' by Michael Jackson, or Donald singing a half-remembered biblical song from school; this footage offers an interesting prototype of sorts to the early work of Ryan Trecartin and the questions his work poses around the real and the performed and the post-human subject constituted through the screen. In *Peggy and Fred* the concern is not with naturalism, nor with the authentic subject, but with a subject that interacts with a fluid space that it experiences with no a priori proof: the significance of parallel editing here is completely bound up with the flattening of experience through a lack of linear dénouement, or integrated building. The film has large temporal and geographical shifts between the room the children inhabit, shots of penguins or vocal chords in use and unpeopled landscapes; the children who are the main protagonists do not learn from any experience and there is not the satisfaction of any suggestion of conclusion or closure in the film. The lack of closure and tendencies to prioritize process is amplified by Thornton's continual reworking of the various versions over the decades, reinforcing a sense of provisionality that is part of the condition that I am aiming to outline here.

In collage, provisionality is integral, as the process is to do with endless possibilities that collage presents through its use of mass-produced images that are represented often again and again. The visibility of the cut and paste in the image reinforces this as it emphasizes through its lack of seamlessness or what I would rather call a seamfullness, a choice amongst many that has been made. The inability for the collage to present seamlessness is a testament to the in-built provisionality of the image. This work, made and remade in various versions over three decades, constitutes a studied contingency in its reformation through different incarnations. Thornton's voice is less frenetic than Child's and works with a different maximalism, one of duration that works through a slow, long form and incoherent juxtapositions rather than the fast-firing maximalism of Child. However, like Child, Thornton plays with a narrative structure that de-centres from the children as the primary subjects, with no dénouement and no obvious ending.[21]

As stated earlier, apart from the *Peggy and Fred* detail and the obvious TV footage, the film is constructed so that it is difficult to tell how much is actually shot by Thornton and how much is appropriated or indeed how much shot as if to look like found footage.[22] Thornton consciously plays with the footage and, like Child, shoots as if to create a semblance for the real in different state. For example, she shot the Reading children on stock that would look old even when new (Halter 2012: 514–21). The sequences are shot on a range of formats. The different formats from 16 mm to video and then digital add to the texture of the overall work and also to the sense of a collage. Ed Halter, in his text on Thornton in *Close Up* (2012: 514–21), suggests her work as 'punk inflected, apocalyptic, content-maximalist' (Halter 2012: 517) and so divergent from the work of her structuralist tutors who were, it may be worth repeating, the *doxa*. It is also interesting to note, as with say Susan Stein, that looking at Thornton's aesthetic one may not associate it with a punk aesthetic as one would say a No Wave film. However, this film, like some of the others in the book, becomes punk in its irreverence to the normative approaches to experimental film in ways that I delineate throughout.

The repetition of footage is a usual trope in experimental film, and often it is used to re-vision the image, look closer to structure an abstraction or to question the form or material. Child and Thornton use repetition not to

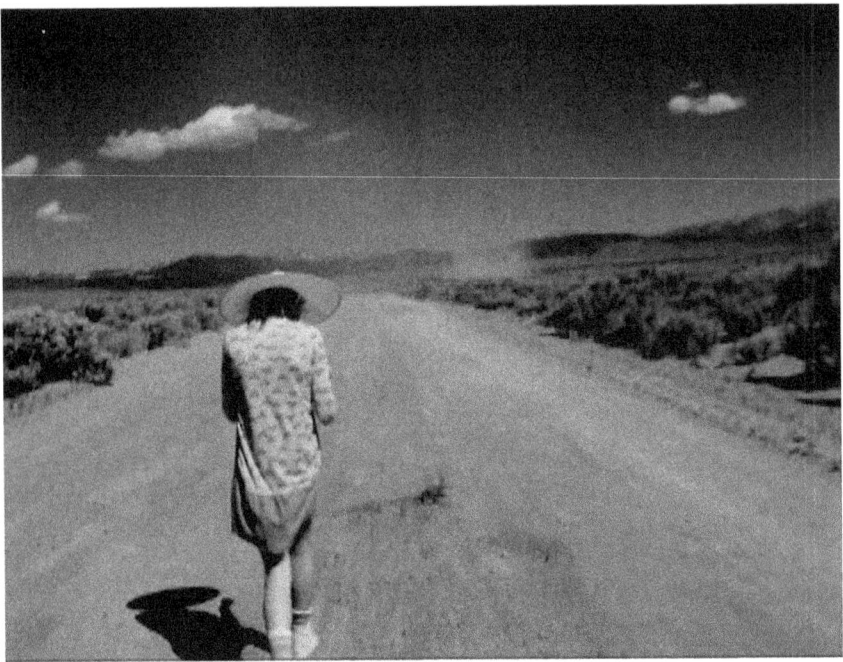

Figure 23. *Peggy and Fred in Hell* (1983–2015, Leslie Thornton). Courtesy of the artist.

unpack the narrative magic of film as an analogy to Plato's cave in the way of their previous generation of tutors. On the contrary, they both in their own ways use repetition as a device to interrogate the formation of subjectivity in the interstices between normality and estrangement.

Appropriation can be used to serve many different requirements, the need for nostalgic desire, the interrogation of historical truth to name just two, but in both these artists the appropriative gesture is used to pose questions of the contemporary life as lived. Their command of the material that looks 'found' but is their own shot material lends the kind of ambiguity that confounds the critique of appropriation as nostalgic yet while employing its tropes. Therefore the past is reconstituted as the present. The present can be enriched by reframing the past. Through this methodology of self-shot imagery that looks appropriated, the past is constructed and reconstructed and the present is reinvented through this process. The aim is to foster a mutability in the present moment as a force for change. This is the case for women, especially whose cinematic past is one of patriarchal sexism, where women were only allowed to 'look good'. Films in Child's epic series remake the lives of the women by including them in the genres in a contemporary way. Another way of conceptualizing the form is by working the fragment to speak to the contingencies of women's lives in two ways. Firstly the documentary form is a comment on the political and the social, to reflect back on the world for the edification of the viewer. To appropriate the documentary form critiques the original form, however, it can also mutate it to rethink the present circumstances. Child's work in this way allows the viewer to see, through repetition, the condition of women's lives in complexity. Secondly, and this is a point inextricably connected to the first, the frames and images through repetition are reset and nuanced through the multiple repetitions alongside different frames and images. This reframing through repetition comments on the precarious contingencies of the formation of women's lives.

What both artists share is a sense of the possibilities of the contingencies of montage. Child and Thornton not only re-use footage but re-use film genres, re-appropriating them for another epoch to comment on film history at the same time as commenting on how you can only live the present through what you understand from the past. They both reveal the wonder of the scope of possibility through the estrangement of juxtaposition, and in both artists, montage represents a normalizing of estrangement, if those antimonies can be set together: 'Beauty will be convulsive. Or not at all', quotes Child in an interview, revealing her appreciation of the creative juxtaposition that parallel editing can bring as well as her interest in and debt to the contingencies that the surrealist artists enjoyed (MacDonald 2005: 219). Both contemporary artists suture these antimonies of the strange and everyday in their work and unlike the surrealists, they use no symbolic or psychoanalytic underwriting. Despite this, both artists borrow in some ways the feel of surrealism in their creation of a believable but still altogether strange world. The estrangement however is brought down to earth through the humanity of people, their physicality and their exultant enjoyment of a peopled world. Through this joyful playfulness they – in a very different way to, say, Sandra Lahire or Ruth Novaczek who actively work with colour and tinting habitually to celebrate the world – both reach out to the viewer. Ultimately their concern is with what Stephen Dwoskin in his book *Film is…* (1976) called a 'personal cinema',[23] and in this way all these artists share a lineage with the New American Cinema.

This chapter began with Linder and her relationship with second wave feminism and collage. Abigail Child not only works in film but also writes poems and makes photomontages. The choice to work in film, photography and words rather than paint points to different conditions of making that ties into the feminist discussions of the modus operandi of artists: painting requires a daily ritual, needing money, space and time. Lens-based media is cheap and can be made either on shared equipment or today on a small laptop, which takes us back to the kitchen table. Work that is ambitious in scale does not need actual scale in production, unlike painting and sculpture. This is where Linda Nochlin's classic text *Why There Are No Great Women Artists* (1971) still has much traction.

Nochlin posited in her landmark text that the conditions that produce genius are structural and social, implying that total immersion, support and focus – in addition to financial support – are critical to the term of 'great artist'. This is a well-known and much discussed text, however, still pertinent to the way in which art is seen and legitimated in various ways even today. Assumptions of value in art production still impact on people with the least access to income.[24] As I will argue later, the long-look form, one of minimalist seamlessness, reflective of, and constituted by, different set of working practices than those many women have access to through their lives. Working, as many women do in conditions of structural fragmentation, particularly those women who become mothers, favours a fragmented form: the time to hone work to its optimum in virtuosity takes time, space and focus, all at a cost inaccessible to the majority of women, regardless of their mothering status, who are still paid less than men for the same jobs. The condition of coming back to the same work again and again over time, picking away and taking it up again later, in between other necessary tasks, produces a different kind of work to that which can be made over many continuous hours of focus. In this case, discontinuity has the political import of recuperating an aesthetic that is constituted through the condition of women's lives. With little bits of time to make work, little bits of work are often the way of hanging on to a practice under duress and, for the period of the 1970s and 1980s often under erasure. I posit this advisedly, even with the backdrop of a range of elite women artists who have access to large funds and the support to make high-profile, extended and expensive works.

To not be part of the elite, to be battling with structural fragmentation, should not be seen as a failing for the artist – nor should the work be assumed to be work that should not be taken seriously; on the contrary, after Nochlin these forms of practice should be looked at carefully to draw out the way in which they work *qua art* as well as an expression of the conditions of the maker and as such say something about the world: they should be acclaimed, which is the aim of this book. To be clear, conditions of making determine a work and work made through a prolonged fragmented existence is hard won and no less professional nor seriously conceived. The conditions of making merely change the form of the artworks themselves. Nochlin's point in the final analysis was that it should be recognized and acknowledged by the art world at large that ambition takes many different forms.

In what could be seen as a direct response to Nochlin, and a slightly different but related response than the one I am suggesting directly, Lucy Lippard wrote the text *Making Something from Nothing (Towards a Definition of Women's 'Hobby Art')* (1978: 128–38), first published in *Heresies* magazine in 1978. By offering 'hobby' as a model for women artists she is proffering, in a contrary gesture, an oppositional model to that which will allow the artist to be taken seriously. This is because the hobby is rather like the decorative, most often in modernism – particularly the latter – seen to be superficial and lacking in serious intent – or any intent at all. This, like Schapiro's recourse to collage, was a recuperative act that was part of a historical trend particular to second wave feminist discourses on art and practices by artists searching for a language. Her argument here rests in part on her criticism of what she calls the 'paternalistic noblesse oblige' (Lippard 1995: 130) form of political art practice that tells people how they should think. She is arguing for art from below and an acceptance of different forms of opposition than that of an intellectualized critique that is not from below at all but derives from the elite, 'yet such borrowings from "below" must still be validated from "above" … ' (1995: 135)[25] and therefore is inherently asymmetrical in nature, which undermines its supposed ethics. Situating and elevating the artwork of women, historically relegated to the hobby is a brave act – even while, say, the Marxist conceptualist art collective *Art and Language* had championed the 'amateur'[26] – given the increased requirements of professionalism and ambition that infuses the expectations for art in a biennale and commercially driven art arena. However, it is central to Lippard's intention of redefining what art could be: like Nochlin, she is attacking the hegemonic male definitions and the structures supported by them. In this article Lippard identified collage as a transformative act, as an act of people who are marginal to the powerful centres of art creation and the gatekeepers of display. She sees collage as a powerful metaphor through the systemic 'gluing and ungluing. It is an aesthetic that wilfully takes apart what is or is supposed to be and rearranges it in ways that suggest what it could be' and links collage to the bold claim that modernism's collapse began with the birth of feminist art, 'around 1970', by stating this claim in the following sentence. It was thus seen to be a form redolent with possibility, that of changing the language of art, akin to the liberation that Linder describes (Lippard 1978: 25).[27]

Insofar as the spectrum of artists discussed in this chapter are in confluence, it is through a concern with the social and how that interacts through fragment and dissonant form. Even when some of the form may be familiar, the foregrounding of relationships is what marks these works out. However, in part because of the contingencies of time that brings different conditions to the fore, the concern with the social took a very different form within punk to these frameworks delineated here above. The focus is neither on activism nor on celebration, neither provenance nor theoretical frameworks for destabilizing the system. Instead the punk collage of Linder and what links her to the other artists in this chapter is the relationship in their work to the detail of the everyday, distraction and shock. These artists are just a little too young to be incorporated into the second wave feminist movement, in age as well as stylistically. Yet the work makes important feminist interventions not just through the obvious subject matter of questioning the extant role of women in the domestic sphere but, for Linder in particular, through the brutal portrayal of the violence of the status quo for women in the 1970s.

In an indirect response to Nochlin's position and with a tacit historical understanding, these artists, as pointed out by William Wees about Leslie Thornton, Abigail Child and Su Friedrich, 'contested the whole notion of "giants". They rejected its Romantic, Emersonian, Great-Man Theory of individual creation as well as its perpetuation of a canon of great films and filmmakers and they were all well aware that, with the exception of Maya Deren, all the "giants" were men' (Wees in Petrolle and Wexman 2005: 22).

What separates Linder and the other artists in this chapter from what is loosely referred to as second wave feminist artists is that her reference points stood against the main thrust of feminist art discourses and practices of the time. Much existing enquiry in art was particularly of the sort that was sneered at by punk: rather too earnest, seen to be patronizing, lacking the humour and particularly the concrete material and chaos that punk often injected to these forms and subject matter. Despite these factors, feminism afforded Linder the possibility to make the images she did. At a point where women were redefining their social role, Linder was redefining a visual language that borrowed from Hannah Höch and John Heartfield, both artists of the Weimar republic. It is no accident – apart from the serendipity of the ICA exhibition – that Höch also made her images through the liberatory moment of the Weimar republic when women were redefining their social role (Lavin 1993: 1). The context of punk, however, gave rise to the conceiving and production of images far more shocking and brutal than viewers had been used to, even than the brutal juxtapositions of Martha Rosler's *House Beautiful: Bringing the War Home* (1967–72). Rosler's work is powerful and performs the outrage of the atrocities of the Vietnam war, particularly in its aim to collapse the geographical distance and so effect an end to the war. This is work that performs political agency, and because the point is clear and obvious, the shock is absorbed – at best – into action: this is the aim of the work. The collage work of second wave feminist artists such as Betye Saar and Miriam Schapiro is of a gentler and more optimistic sort where we can see the chasm between these generational shifts in approach. Schapiro presents it as a strategy by which contemporary women can gather together an artistic tradition, a heritage and a technical procedure in literary, musical and plastic arts that feminists may draw upon for 'aesthetic direction' out of the fragments of their cultural past (cited in Raaberg 1998: 158). By contrast the work of Linder is unforgiving for the viewer except through a kind of gallows humour, if you will. Linder's work performs the aftermath of failed agency. It is a different radicality altogether.

Montage and collage, then, at the very least have different provenance and references, but operate in some similar ways – and it is no accident that Abigail Child works in both filmic montage forms and collage. With the use of film and video by artists, a recuperative reading is possible through weaving together the aims of feminist collage and ideas in independent film. A recuperative reading reframes these terms together as a lo-fi amateur strategy or device through the cut and appropriation. One thing about appropriation is that it is cheap. As is collage. You do not need to shoot new footage; you can find some old stuff and re-use it. This framework of making art out of almost nothing, out of detritus of the ordinary, is central to the attitude of punk that celebrated anarchy, destruction and the extremities of lives gone to waste. It is through the use of collage that the artists can deliver their sense of fragmentation without a redemptive tendency and it is the possibilities of the negative – as opposed negation – that the next chapter will be investigating.

Notes

1   In the original collage the torso is taken from a colour magazine image – so the body is not grey but 'white' skin toned.

2   There were, however, a range of discourses in different art schools. In Manchester Polytechnic, painting was dominated in the early 1980s by male abstract painters.

3   In fact there was a brief return to painting in the early 1980s. Alexis Hunter is an example of an artist who in the 1970s made important photographic work exploring feminist possibilities for reframing sexist representations of women in photography. In the 1980s she turned back to painting towards pre-modern myths of *wimmin* as figures of power and positive identification rather than

critiquing stereotype and negative messages. This is within a context of a return to male-dominated expressionist machismo such as the exhibition 'The New Spirit in Painting' at the Royal Academy London in 1981. See Pollock (2003) and Cottingham (2000).

4   In this chapter I do not aim to discuss the distinctions between collage, montage, appropriation and photomontage. They each have different qualities that rest on the method and process but I do not believe that each offers inherently different meanings because of these varied processes of making.

5   Alexis Hunter's work had a radical break from a serial-based photographic practice that critiqued assumptions of femininity to a painting practice in the 1980s that explored the mythology of her Maori background.

6   Martha Rosler in the United States or some of the eastern block feminists like Sonia Ivekovic in former Yugoslavia may be exceptions to this.

7   Jo Spence could well be brought into the purview of the punk aesthetic as outlined here.

8   There were a few exceptions, notably *Live in Your Head: Concept and Experiment 1965–75,* curated by Clive Philpot and Andrea Tarsia in February 2000, and *Protest and Survive*, curated by Matthew Higgs and Paul Noble, September 2000, both at the Whitechapel Gallery. This could be seen to be a turning point in the re-emergence of interest in conceptualism and art from the 1970s.

9   This is to be differentiated from kitsch. The aims of this generation were elevated through political motivation even while the language was of deskilling. Kitsch had a different provenance, possibly closer to some AV punk aspirations than documentary as used by conceptualist feminists.

10   Thanks to Rosie Martin for alerting me to this term.

11   For a more nuanced and developed thesis on the emergence of the Berwick Street Collective and *Nightcleaners*, see Kidner et al. (2018).

12   Proponents of structuralist/materialist film would also agree, stating that only by critiquing the form itself would political transformation prevail; however, my criticism is somewhat different (see Gidal in O'Pray 1996: 145–70 but specifically 146).

13   This may also have been to do with the anti-humanist Althussarian politics prevalent within film discourse.

14   Later, in subsequent decades, photography would be taken in another direction and reach towards fine art, making a case for its inclusion in the art market. Photography then pushed that medium to unprecedented levels of finish, also encompassing model-making and fiction-making.

15 Interestingly Alexis Hunter moved from concerns with the semiotics of women's stereotyping to reflecting with history and identity following a reverse evolution from photography to painting.

16 Peter Bürger (1984) claimed that collage failed in its attempt to undermine the notion of the autonomous art object and so continued to act in the service of capital.

17 *Tracks* is a theoretically loaded film that also incorporates disjunctive abstract and collage insertions.

18 Unpublished email from the artist, 18 August 2020: 'And early Yvonne Rainer and Bruce Conner were the strongest influences while I was a student. Also early Warhol.'

19 From Q&A of screening at Close-Up cinema, 19 February 2020: 'I've only done this once, for my BAM retrospective, that is, shown two different full length versions. On the other hand, I have shown many incarnations of Peg and Fred, and felt I had finished it many times, tho I kept returning to the itch of it. The final and definitive cut was made in 2016' (Thornton 18 August 2020).

20 Thornton, unpublished email to the author, 14 August 2020.

21 In a cinema screening on 19 February 2020, Thornton had to actually announce 'This is the end' for people to start clapping.

22 Almost all the footage is, in fact, shot by Thornton, except for a few iconic documentary images, such as the Egerton photographs of the milk drop, or the nuclear testing for example. Interview 2017.

23 In *A Critical Cinema* (2006), Child decries the personal cinema but expands that her work is about personal relationships rather than about herself.

24 Merely one anecdotal example is the common place assumption amongst artists and curators that if you teach full-time, you cannot be a serious artist. I also know of at least one gallery that will not let its artists take on teaching and insists they do casual work such as occasional decorating if needs be.

25 She cites how William C Seitz's 'Assemblage' exhibition elided women's crafts as he did not see that work 'as the classic *bricolage*'.

26 Art and Language gave a paper at the ICA in 1995 titled, 'We Aimed to Be Amateurs' http://createinnovation.org.uk/resources/conference-papers/pragmatics-and-problematics/. See also Hostage series XIX (Art & Language 1999: 102).

27 Despite Peter Bürger's assertion that the shock of collage was over by 1923 and that it failed to change the relations of art with the bourgeois subject, the ability of collage to put together realities has purchase in opening people up to new possibilities, arguably.

4

In praise of the fragment part two: Kracauer, disintegration and punk

The previous chapter served to contextualize some of the concerns and motivations for second wave feminist use of the collage and explain why it is important for the moving image work of Abigail Child, Leslie Thornton and others. A point of differentiation in the drive to use collage between second wave feminists and the work of Linder for example is to do with the strategies used by the artists as described by those artists. The kitchen table was the symbolic association rather than the studio, characterized by a turn away from virtuosity towards the lo-fi. This chapter builds on the previous chapter by bringing together seemingly disparate elements from early twentieth-century Vienna, and late twentieth-century bomb culture. What links these elements is a moment where the fear of catastrophe and emancipation were both in operation. The tendencies and strategies I discuss in this chapter are to do with Linder's Dada-esque and punk dialogues read through Siegfried Kracauer's work on cinema. Kracauer is brought to the discussion as a way of contextualizing and reflecting on the properties that the artwork engenders and why the link with Höch and her generation is important. Collage, despite the case made by feminists as outlined in the previous chapter, is not the preserve of women by any means. Collage has an ongoing currency as a critique for the status quo and has, of course, been used by men as much as women. Nevertheless, the women in this chapter have used film to put forward a particular vision of the world that has only been able to function through collage, bringing heterogeneity together, in a deflationary way through a temporal medium.

If there is any purchase on collage and its effects, the interpretive texts by Janet Harbord and Miriam Hansen on Siegfried Kracauer offer some interesting insights pertinent to the purchase of these works, and what is at stake for me in collage as an assemblage of fragments. Collage has long been associated with the kind of dissociative, shocking protest that punk represented for the ways in which punk had been engaged with the idea of upending the rules of beauty, of bad taste, of shock tactics. Famously Walter Benjamin used the fragment as a methodology in his text *One Way Street*. His friend Siegfried Kracauer, writing specifically about film, understood the fragment as a necessary and fundamental building block of the making of the film through the way in which film had to be broken down into pieces then put back together into a specific sequence. The fragment, deriving from Nietzsche's eternal return, could be seen – in a positive light – to be a way of recuperating meaning from a meaningless existence of the rationalism of modernity (Frisby 1985: 34). Unsurprisingly, a focus on the fragmented would emerge to be a dominant trend for artists at times when modernity would disclose its cost – as opposed to its opportunities – to the next generation. What I mean to say is that the fragmented often emerges as a trope at a time of scarcity rather than plenty. The do-it-yourself, kitchen table approach that I discussed in the previous chapter was in itself the constituting force of the form, not only musically but also visually; however, there were other contexts and motivations at play that are important to interrogate. The ghosts of surrealism and Dada in punk have been well covered by Greil Marcus in *Lipstick Traces*, which, published back in 1989, first argued the trajectory that linked punk with Dada, situationism and collage. Very quickly within punk circles an aesthetic was established that developed an ongoing engagement with collage that can be seen in early punk fanzines and agitprop. These methodologies of the cut-up, the lo-fi and appropriated imagery were followed in order to make the images speak to the second hand, make-do culture of photocopiers and images derived from magazines and newspapers. It was a purposefully degraded aesthetic that was in a visual opposition to the excessively indulgent aesthetic of the previous hippie or prog rock forms of stylized and psychedelically infused imagery – and I am thinking here now specifically of image-based artists rather than the conceptualist precursors. There is an obvious visual link with Dada in the layout of the fanzines and record covers in punk. The anti-aesthetic in Dada was by the 1970s an aesthetic in itself and one that lent itself to be taken a step further in punk through cheap printing and photocopying methods that had not existed in the Dada era, and from pop iconoclasm. As Linder stated, 'punk was cutting out the question, "can I do this?"' (Edmund 2016). So whereas feminist collage, particularly from the United States, was a statement about gender, the condition of women's working and creative lives posing a positive critique of possibility, punk collage as represented by Linder was absolutely about class – or the unschooled – at the intersection of gendered interests and working practices. The collage of punk drew out the anarcho-communism of Dada that punk unwittingly aimed to change much more than just the focus on gender relations.[1] It evoked Dada to bring down bourgeois notions of the professional artist – even while many of those such as Linder who made the collages, fanzines and posters for punk went to art school. Dada was a constituting cipher because of the impact of the double effects of economic downturn and the endgame of the Cold War, with its underlying nuclear threat. Like the Weimar period, this was also a period of women finding their voice, of being more visible in the workings of society. While there are different claims for Dada, punk also had advocates for a range of positions both political and apolitical. However, punk was not a campaigning forum in the way that, say, the feminist collective The Hackney Flashers were incorporating politics into their art.[2] Like Dada it was not programmatic but was, instead, a burst of anger at a world where the problems seemed overwhelming and the solutions elusive.

Hannah Höch is the artist par excellence who links the artists Linder and Abigail Child, two artists who emerged from different locations and artistic contexts. They are both discussed at length in this and the previous chapter. Also discussed in this chapter is Leslie Thornton's ongoing major work *Peggy and Fred in Hell*, and *Marasmus* (1981) by Betzy Bromberg. These works show significant strands of analogous methodology through Siegfried Kracauer. Kracauer who was seen as a turncoat by his erstwhile friends, Theodor Adorno and Walter Benjamin, is an important figure for this book for several reasons. Kracauer was against the instrumentalization of film. He was interested in form and argued for film having special and exclusive properties. However, he saw the subject as being at the heart of what the cinema is trying to do in ways that are about interrogating the world through the camera, not interrogating film through its unique material properties. Importantly for artists in this book and the framework through which they are analysed, Kracauer argued that central to film was 'the problematic of the subject, as both a practical critique of bourgeois fictions of self-identity and a discourse for articulating the historical' (Hansen 1993: 444). In this he sets himself against structuralism, conceptualism and neo-conceptualism in film practice and offers a middle ground between the instrumentalization of film and its opposite – an antipathy to the bringing together of art and politics.

Many of the women in this book use documentary in its various and expanded forms to explore the effects and interactions between their subjectivity and the politics in the world. Kracauer is usually associated with arguing for documentary as the main legitimate focus for film as proof of the material world in a literal way. However, the antinomy that he set out was that of documentary as opposed to what he considered to be the conservative and regressive lofty aims of aesthetic forms of narrative film that relied too much on the conventions of theatre or art. He argued passionately against the aestheticization of the lens-based image in the way it was conceived by Edward Stieglitz, preferring the magic of the everyday as seen by Cartier-Bresson on the street. As with photography he states that film *is* art rather than being made *as* art (Kracauer 1960: 22). However, his thinking is both more complex and more problematized than is often characterized. I would argue his account of film is infused with undecidability, much like the artworks that offer heterogeneous propositions through diverse and sometimes contradictory or confusing strategies, often within one film. Kracauer's arguments for film do not offer manifestos or answers and rely on the accidents of contingency and the inability to completely control the flow of life. His documentary method is one that would align itself in some ways with what later became the lineage of the Free Cinema, or in the United States the New American Cinema, both forms that rely on the passage of the world and what is captured when the camera is turned on.

Much of the criticism of Kracauer derives from his late book *Theory of Film*. This book aims to schematize film but is, like the films themselves, full of caveats and contradiction. His desire to schematize is in itself a contradiction and rather an odd pursuit as he sees film not merely as an intellectual pursuit but as an all-encompassing medium that grasps the whole of reality as a physical thing. He identifies an embodied experiential reception as a positive feature of film – rather than one to be excised – and as a point of resistance, described very well in the earlier *Mass Ornament* but also present in *Theory of*

Film through an embodied response that is not fully encompassed by reason but mired in contingency and context at all times (Kracauer 1960: 27). The artworks described in this book and especially this chapter also have claims to undecidability – or the indeterminate in Kracauer's parlance – which adds richness to the art through what he calls 'Psychophysical correspondences … for shots not yet stripped of their multiple meanings'. This is one of Kracauer's inherent properties of film as he describes in *Theory of Film* (1960: 69). In this list he identifies a range of properties such as endlessness, fortuitous, indeterminate – each describes properties that I consider to be analogous to the work in this book. He describes the street for example as where the flow of life asserts itself, but that in filming the flow of life the camera goes beyond life. A key form of resistance for Kracauer, seen in the films, is through depiction of the forgotten debris of life. The forgotten, the left out and the debris are key themes and to varying degrees form the methodology for the artist filmmakers such as Vivienne Dick, Abigail Child, Anne Robinson, Sadie Benning and Ruth Novaczek. Miriam Hansen, who wrote on the Frankfurt School including Kracauer, and a key touchstone in my interpretation, cites from his Marseille notebooks that form the basis for his *Theory of Film*:

> Film brings the whole material world into play; reaching beyond theater and painting, it for the first time sets that which exists into motion. It does not aim upward, toward intention, but pushes toward the bottom, to gather and carry along even the dregs. It is interested in the refuse, in what is just there-both in and outside the human being.
>
> (cited in Hansen 1993: 447)

Kracauer moves beyond the dialectical filmmaking of Eisenstein,[3] that is judged by him to be too didactic in later life at least. Instead, he discusses chance and a more randomized contingency as the driver of the politics of film.[4] He sees film not as being about controlling the world but instead as the seed of creative life – as being lack of control. Furthermore he argued that film did not have a political destiny to fulfil; instead, '[t]he dimension which defines the phenomenon of film at its core lies below the dimension in which political and social events take place' (Hansen 1993: 446).

We can see these earlier delineations and oppositions between Eisenstein and Kracauer mirrored in some of the divisions in the debates of the 1970s between signifier and the signified as being the primary carrier of meaningful change. That is, on the one hand those who proscribed narrative-led works – through an extension of Brechtian concerns with false consciousness mixed with Greenbergian notions of the autonomy of form. This view reached its apogee in the 1980s, a decade in which those arguments coalesced around the Film Makers' Co-Op through the debates with materialist film. Other prohibitions that emerged were to do with the perceived male gaze that put an embargo on the representation of women in art and film. The most famous advocate of the proscription of the image of women was Mary Kelly, in a Lacanian manoeuvre to circumvent the problems of women being the object of the male gaze. In direct opposition to those attitudes were the artist and filmmakers who were specifically interested in narrative form, desire, subjectivity and the body as a legitimate way of exploring the world in a way that would elicit awareness and change. Some of the artists who exemplify this other strand were VALIE EXPORT, Stephen Dwoskin, Derek Jarman in Europe or Chick Strand and Jonas Mekas in the United States, at times marginalized in the discourses of experimental film in these countries.

In Britain, Derek Jarman was a central figure who, with the younger artists around him such as John Maybury, Cerith Wyn Evans and Richard Heslop, turned away from the politicized theoretical framework of filmmaking towards a different form of estrangement, closer to that of surrealism, through excess and a Dada-esque grunge. Tellingly Jarman embraced punk with his film *Jubilee* (1978) that harnessed the punk vision of nihilism as analogous to the husk of humanism that Thatcherism represented. He continued this vision in *The Last of England* (1987), which interestingly has obvious links with the work of Georg Grosz, another Weimar artist. So, thinking about Jarman particularly and his period of punk grunge, I would argue rather than a rejection of politics *tout court*, this kind of work was merely a turning away from the overdetermination of theory-led filmworks. To be specific, this represented a turn away from a particular methodology of critique of the material as the only marker of the political drive for change and linking back to the even older debates on realism and politics as set out earlier in the book.

Instead, and this is where it links with the main examples in this chapter, the focus was on a visually led trajectory of excess and complexity building in different viewpoints through parallel editing and a mix of genres and methodologies in the same work. The tendencies to narrow the focus by excising the extraneous, which had marked much work since conceptualism, had led to an artistic as well as ideological cul-de-sac with the films lacking in Kracauer's 'psychophysical correspondences'. These younger artists, Child, Dick, and others, were in favour of a move towards different kinds of political thinking and its relationship to the visual world. They were less interested in proposing solutions than posing questions and often did this through turning the camera to the world, to the flow of life on the street, subverting the documentary form. This was art that was not bound to a manifesto – such as a quasi-Brechtian methodology – but was searching for what the new questions might even be – although one could argue that these artists were following a libertarian manifesto drawn from the lineage of the underground film. The moving around between different foci in one artist's trajectory or even within one film itself poses new existential questions which in the case of these artists was how to live in this world of theirs at that particular time and place.

So the punk generation embraced a different approach than their art school mentors; they looked to precursors in the underground, such as the Kuchar brothers or Jack Smith, rather than the avant garde, towards those who embraced visual pleasure, sometimes even in narrative form, albeit also in a way that was oppositional to Hollywood. This was an approach that encompassed reflections on the body and subjectivity in alienation and embraced the shock of cinematic violence or the deflation of humour.

This chapter is about the relationship between the fragment and dissolution for women. Building on their work, Kracauer seems a useful jumping-off point as someone who was thinking about modernity, dissolution and the body. Kracauer saw political possibilities for film. He argued for film as transformative through its reception and the physical investment that it invokes. Possibly the theoretical scaffolding that Child invokes is from Benjamin and the radical possibilities of the spark of contingency; however, even here there is a link through Kracauer, who was part of a wider dialogue that Miriam Hansen interrogates.

Kracauer's primary interest is documentary. Like Benjamin, he is interested in the relationship between shock and technology, that technology transforms being through shock. He was very much against art film, which he saw as bourgeois. Instead he was interested in the transformative properties of the everyday. He abhorred the long shot which he argued came from theatre and gave a stable totalizing view of the world and 'a distance from reality that only the bourgeois can afford'; instead, he argues for cinema that combines intention with being (Hansen 1993: 450). Partly, this was why he loved vaudeville and comedy as being closer to the materiality of life as well as the ability of comedy to interrupt the closure of narrative form (461). It is interesting then that one of the key films in Child's seven-part series, *Perils* (1986), is a play on slapstick.

Perils opens with a series of cinematic sounds: a screech, an exclamation, a musical introduction and then a shot of a woman standing against a wall. The whole *mise-en-scène* is in a derelict, grassed space in front of a crumbling wall on a street in Lower Manhattan. What contributes to the startling effect of the film is the lack of concern with the crumbling and derelict nature of the 'set' which is in a public space; the characters are dancing and smiling, creating a fun and funny mood on a street corner of rubble. It is shot in black and white. The first shot is a woman's face. Then some more faces: it has the air of a police line-up, all seem vacant, staring into space for the few moments on the screen. The third or fourth face is of an older man wearing a cowboy hat, who seems weatherworn, staring into the camera. A series of shots ensues, fragmented and repeated of several people in front of this derelict wall that acts as a stage backdrop. It is funny, however, as the sound and form of the acting recall classic slapstick film.

Perils was filmed just the other side of the wall of D.W. Griffith's studio, where he filmed *The Musketeers of Pig Alley* (1912), allegedly the first gangster film, referencing an earlier moment of struggle in the city (Turim 2007: 273).[5] This film also references the struggle between the anarchy of crime and the imposition of order. The anarchy here is a playful anarchy that acknowledges the violence that got them there yet in a tableau-esque way that both cites and critiques theatre. The earlier film is a classic silent movie. In contrast the Child film is an evocation of mood; it goes against the grain of the previous tragedy, offering a deflationary and absurd comedy in its stead. The comedic and the outtake together set up a very different relationship to the viewer than the mawkish farce it refers to. Child wanted a sense of 'the resonant voluptuous sense of history and the face' (Sitney 2008: 286).

In part two there are some implications of jealousy, with shots of two women and then much play fighting. It is shot on 16 mm black and white. It is dark, with high contrast like an Italian neorealist film. It also has a slapstick quality to it, which is to do with the mock fight and the cheap clothes as well as the obvious black and white. The imagery has a simplicity in its portrayal, that of a repeated tableaux configuration against the wall, in the rubble. In its continual repetition that seems without a structurally informed rhythm, the pace is quick and the imagery is jagged in its jump cuts and repetition. There is no segue to any kind of final denouement, except an intertitle 'to be continued... '. It is thus – like Susan Stein's film described in the previous chapter – structurally incomplete, and like Thornton, binding provisionality into its ontology. *Perils* is radically deflationary, defying every expectation set up by cinema, yet playing with it, offering a witty alternative.

In her book *This Is Called Moving: A Critical Poetry of Film* (2005), Abigail Child discusses the importance of editing and montage to the process-based visuality in her work. 'I borrow the dynamic of collage', she states, and '[h]ere there is to an outcome that I planned, merely a sifting and sorting to enable a subjectivity to emerge' (64). Child also maintains that 'we don't see in long looks but in impressionistic collage'.[6]

The film, like many others in this book, is a kind of disjunctive episodic 'I'm trying to break the adjacencies' (Turim 2007: 265) – as opposed to an ordering intention towards the episodic – and here divided up into numbered sections. In the first numbered section there is an establishing shot of two people walking towards a wall – the famous wall of Griffith's – then four against the wall, then a close-up of the man and woman looking at each other. There are posed shots with a tripod and stills camera being moved around while the man and woman pose in a dancing position: an acknowledgement of the staging. It is all slightly absurd due in part to the incandescent sounds and also due to the lack of narrative, the sense of things happening but without any clue why they might be so. Furthermore, the viewer does not know why these people are in this place, nor really what kind of place it is.

Although different in many other ways, in terms of time and place, this use of wasteland can be linked to the use of unreadable spaces in some of the other films discussed in this book. It is a collectivizing factor in the works, that all use some sort of device of an-out-of time or out-of-place *mise-en-scène*: in *Passions of Remembrance* (1986), or the use of the wasteland in Vivienne Dick's *London Suite (Getting Sucked In)* (1990), or the room that Peggy and Fred inhabit in the *Peggy and Fred* series of films. In each of these films, through the device of siting, a new reality has the possibility of being forged unfettered by the clutter of life's operations. Each of these spaces is transformative in their suggestion of a sense of reinvention out of the ashes of the wasteland, from ground zero up.

Unlike today in the urban centres that have been subject to intensive gentrification over the last four decades, the wasteland was a common-enough motif. Whereas the focus on modernity had previously been also a focus on the future as a positive, building new homes, new public sites for the future, artists now turned to the wasted spaces between, which had been under erasure – much like the lives of women and minorities were. The spaces of Thornton, Child and Dick have not the utopian hope of modern pristine spaces of the future as it was meant to be. Nor do they have the dystopian drama of beautifully composed wastelands such as Patrick Keiller's laments to a modernity destroyed, such as in *Robinson in Ruins* (2010) – a relatively recent film. On the contrary, the spaces in Child's film and the aesthetic milieu I am describing are a wasteland at the end of a process, which are unused and uncared for – although loved and used in these films. What differentiates *Robinson in Ruins* from *Perils* is that the latter uses the space as a place for play, rather than a place from which to propose solutions. Without the romantic dressing of music or beautiful long shots, they become not a passive lament but an active repurpose. The former is about doom in the ruins and the latter, hope, albeit an absurdist kind. In *Perils* there is no instrumentalization of the image unlike *Robinson in Ruins*, where Keiller chooses sites of significance for rhetoricizing the dystopian future of mankind. This non-space is the site of the whole film in *Perils*, not a chorus or interlude as it is in *Passions of Remembrance*. The interlude is the film: a film of outtakes. In *A Motive for Mayhem* Child writes, 'I had long conceived of a film composed only of reaction shots in which all causality was erased' (Child 1989: 11). This is a film made from outtakes of other films; outtakes are the non-spaces where nothing happens – maybe the conceptual non-spaces of Augé rather than his own propositions of actual spaces. Nothing rides on these clips that Child uses, these clips, which by another filmmaker, would generally be excised. As such they represent the negation of the drama of Hollywood cinema and the negation of narrative drive.

Another way of conceiving this negation is as a metaphor for the undercutting of the ideology of the cinematic instrumentalist drive. This linear drive is equated with a linear idea of life as continuous progress towards the suburban dream that is represented in such a film: that is the way in which the capitalist imperative – of getting a life equals getting a job, having kids, having grandkids, dying – is perpetuated within the Hollywood model par excellence. If here in *Perils*, life is constituted from the outtakes, then agency is evacuated along with the assumption that we can know the world. Furthermore, if action equals time in Hollywood, then this film does, in fact, represent Augé's non-spaces of modernity after all, thus the negation of time and, of course, time equals money so in effect it is the negation of capital.

Much of the work that takes this approach, of outtakes, shock and extreme disjunction, was profoundly affected by the backdrop of the Cold War and the constant threat of the dissolution of society through nuclear warfare. Kracauer states that film comes about through the organization of disintegration. Although this analysis of his would be for any film, disintegration, as Kracauer saw it for the possibility for film, could have been a key term for 1970s urban life, much as it was for the 1920s of his early writing. These 1970s and 1980s artists faced the disintegration of a nuclear threat head-on and asked what life was about under this constant threat. They highlighted the inconsistency of life through the formal devices of extreme montage and discontinuity while foregrounding through these formal devices the importance of personal investment of social relations in the politics of society. This might have been to do with the ways in which feminism, poverty and the nuclear threat rendered abstraction too passive a response for these extreme times. Both periods – of the Weimar and the decade from the mid-1970s to the late 1980s – saw an expansion of women's rights and the questioning of gender norms. Punk, which questioned femininity, gave way to the New Romantics, which questioned masculinity.[7] And while punk was concerned with an exteriority, with the street and the flow of life, New Romantic film was, like the music, concerned more with interiority and the gothic.

The film *Eerie* (1992) for example, by Sandra Lahire, is set in the mountains and features two women, one dressed in a tuxedo, both dancing to the sounds of piano music. The film is heavily montaged and elliptical, the sound floating as they are over a ski lift supposedly in the Alps. It is a mere one-minute long. A

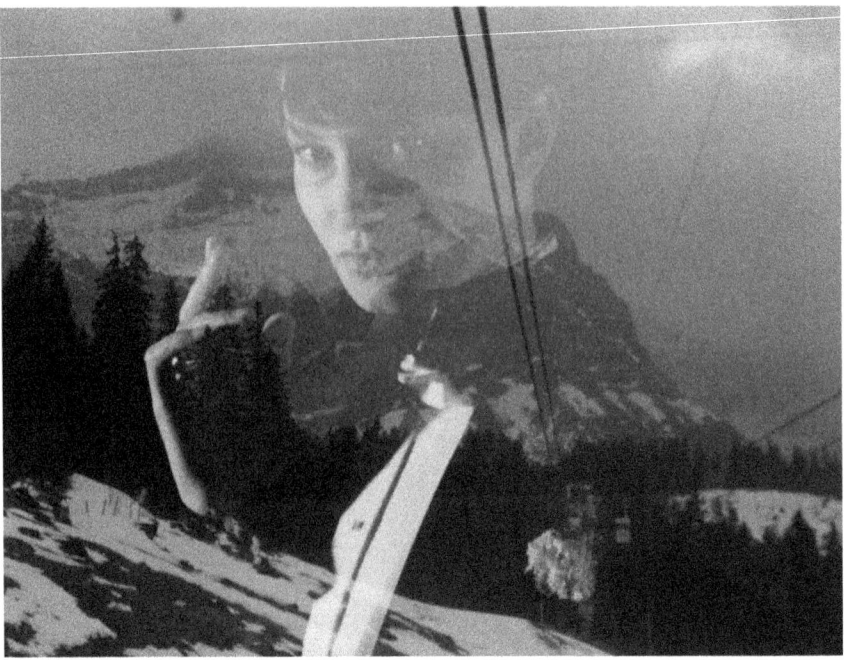

Figure 24. *Eerie* (1992, Sandra Lahire). Courtesy of Sandra Lahire and LUX, London.

woman is in the ski lift, possibly one of those dancing. They dance, one woman in a tuxedo, the other in a dress. That is the film. A fragment of expressionist melodrama, demonstrating a nostalgia for the lost gender emancipations of the Weimar Republic made at time in the early 1990s when feminism was in retreat. As Peter Brooks states, 'Melodrama starts from and expresses the anxiety brought by a frightening new world in which traditional patterns of moral order no longer provide the necessary social glue' (Brook 1976:29). It was also a time when the tomboy alongside the hyper-feminine looks of punk – that could be seen to be a critique of normative femininity – had given way to a more normative femininity of the New Romantic (Halberstam 1999: 153) as opposed to the queering of masculinity central to the New Romantic sensibility. Punk and the New Romantic are often conflated these days, and I would want to differentiate these distinctive but connected moments in British culture. This is an attenuated link that is really a long way from punk and much closer to New Romantic.[8] And yet, the desire to evoke a former moment of freedom from constraints on gender normativity that is at the heart of the choices of Lahire and other women filmmakers exemplifies a link between the punk and New Romantic movements as between these two moments through Dada, photomontage and political outlook.[9] The New Romantics came after punk; however, there was a connection between these very different movements – and moments – through the idea of an end time.

Kracauer started to write his *Theory of Film* at a time when he thought his world was going to end, holed up in Marseille with the Nazis on his heels, himself 'archiving the disintegrated particles and of reconfiguring them toward a different, a yet unknowable order' (Hansen 2012: 256). He finished the book in the United States, after the war, with its shadow ever-present in the book (Schlüpmann and Gaines 1991: 112). This 'unknowable order' in the *Theory of Film* is not one of redemption but merely of the tenets of Dada, that of 'the concrete and chaotic instead of the transcendent' (Lavin 1993: 14), a phrase which could easily describe the works in this volume with their interest in the everyday coupled with the deliberate confounding of normative cinematic narrative structure and a response of sorts to the violence of disintegration around in both periods.[10]

Kracauer saw film and photography as the only media capable of dealing with disintegration 'in a material, sensorially graspable form, of archiving the disintegrating particles, and of reconfiguring them toward a different, as yet unknowable order' (Hansen 2012: 256). The relative bleakness of the 1970s and 1980s seemed here to require the embracing of the concrete reality for these artists rather than a withdrawal into abstraction for the older generation.

While the interface between the concrete and chaotic is ever around, it might link to the way in which Kracauer foregrounds contingency as a key component in film. The comparison can only go so far of course, and the 1970s and 1980s saw the chaotic in particular ways that is different from the Weimar period. The possible disintegration of the status quo during the Cold War into a nuclear holocaust was 'a material, sensorially graspable form' (Hansen 2012: 256) of horror and could be seen to offer a distinctive and new feature of much of this work from this later era.

To return to the film *Eerie*, the film can be read not only through the signs of gender representation but also through its ability to conjure the potential of doom through the feel of the music, the precariousness of the moving cable car and the montaged dancers waltzing in slow rotation over the Alps. The viewer might be left with an overarching sense of vertigo, of being on the edge of the danger that would severely punish and eradicate any non-normative gender relations, particularly through the hindsight of the late twentieth century when the film *Eerie* (1992) was made. In this case the sense of danger cannot be fully disentangled with the impending doom of Nazism conjured in the film's focus on the *mittel* European moment. The sense of dread that the film ultimately effects is the violence of the imagined future that is not depicted in the film – *via negativa* what is depicted is love – and the knowledge of the actual violence that ensued in that future.

The foundational cinematic moment for the relationship between violence and montage is established by Maureen Turim as the cut of the eye in the surrealist film *Un Chien Andalou* (1929) by Luis Buñuel and Salvador Dalí (Turim 2005: 71). The centrality of the relationship between violence and desire is established here and offers a lineage not just in the action but in the affective force of it. The eye is cut with a razor, a fast movement that then leaps to a cloud moving through the moon, leaving the impact of the actual implied cut in the imagination of the viewer: the imagination being much more extreme than any depiction could be. The edit thus amplifies the physical effect of the meaning *via negativa*. The cut works both on a physical and metaphorical level. Turim invokes the Buñuel/Dalí film to discuss Abigail Child's work here and the direct link that her work and avant garde art of this generation of women has with the violence and disintegration of surrealism. Child's series *Is This What You Were Born For?*, which is the title for her seven-part film odyssey, is a title drawn from Goya's *Disaster of War* (1810–20) series of etchings from the peninsula wars in the aftermath of the Napoleonic wars that devastated Europe in the eighteenth century.[11] While Child's work does not depict war itself, the metaphor is clear, referencing a time when it seemed the world was torn apart by warfare. The form of the film(s) is an analogous methodology and works as a metaphor of disintegration and discombobulation which, in the violence of the editing, sweeps in the zeitgeist of the Cold War and the sense of an endgame everywhere at the time of the making of this work, that is in the 1980s.

In the UK, Linder's work, from a slightly earlier period of the mid-1970s, relishes the darkness of what was wrong through the cut in her montages. Like Linder, Child's work did not directly engage with the concerns of possible feminist mentors such as Judy Chicago or Mary Kelly and looked elsewhere towards a liberatory aesthetic that used the body and the world in a direct way – hot work that spoke passion not reason, but an unreason that made political sense in disturbed times. In a similar way, slightly later, Child was also developing a methodology and creating meaning out of unreason as political reflection on the world – also much like punk music.

Subject matter notwithstanding, the form in this work is at least as important as the content. As Linder says,

> I remember the pure pleasure of photomontage. I had spent three years working with pencil, paint and pen trying to translate my lived experience into made marks. It was a moment of glorious liberation to work simply with a blade, glass and glue. Almost a scientific methodology. Sitting in a dark room in Salford, performing cultural postmortem and then reassembling the corpse badly, like a Mary Shelley trying to breathe life into the monster.
>
> (Linder 2015: 12)

Linder described the process in the recent monograph that draws analogies with the darker side of surrealism. She was interested in the violence of Hans Bellmer, who used mannequins to put the female body together in shocking ways, or the radicality of gothic romanticism, both of which are drawn on at times within punk – which developed into goth through a particular strand. It was thus no accident that Linder chose collage. The dissonance of the cut and paste was an obvious choice for a movement that was intent on destroying in order to rebuild, a musical form that made a glory out of social and political disintegration. It is also of note that many filmmakers embraced a mode of working that is analogous to Linder's cut-and-paste inscriptions. In this approach – of Kracauer's reorganization of disintegration – there is a closer link between the montage of Linder and her progenitors from Dada, and of the filmmakers that I exemplify here. The close linkage acts as a precursor to the films of the 1980s that worked through some similar conceits of melodrama, superficiality, detritus and apocalypse as the collage of the second wave feminists.

Hansen writes that for Kracauer,

> The valorisation of self-shattering shock and sensation in the film experience was fuelled by the hope, even in darkest times, that the cinema could stage, in an institutionally bounded form of play, encounters with a

historical experience marked by rupture and displacement, fragmentation and reification, but also by the possibilities of self-alienation and alternative modes of engaging with the material world.

(Hansen 2012: 263)

Both Linder and Child cite Hannah Höch (1889–1978) as an important precursor. Höch, one of the originators of photomontage, made *Cut with the Kitchen Knife* in 1919. Despite the jump of sixty years, Child's *Perils* and Linder's untitled collages from 1977 could be discussed together with this earlier work through the methodology of collage and the intentional violence through which they cut and shape the work. Works such as the *Cut with the Kitchen Knife* or *Deutches Mädchen* use the cut to render the present strange and to shock the viewer as an allegory for the bifurcation of the position of women in Weimar Germany. Linder's work could also be seen to be a cipher for the tensions in the expectations of young women who are trying to rethink their status in relation to the domestic sphere, marriage and the body beautiful. The all-pervasive pressure to conform is the corollary of the extremity of the response to it: as a way to break out of conformity. This was a profound impulse in this period, where there was a dearth of contemporary women role models in a world that also seemed brutally on the edge of annihilation.

The process that Linder worked on consisted of having two piles of magazines, one of women's mags and the other pornographic magazines – the former the women's pile, and the latter the men's pile. 'I wanted to mate the G-Plan kitchens with pornography, see what strange breed came out' (Morrissey and Hoare 2007: 12). Further analogies can be drawn here to the work of Child where the use of porn in the montages by Linder stands in for the role of women in the domestic sphere as wives and mothers.

The binary polarization draws directly from the debates at the time and the extreme polarization of the pro-sex and anti-sex debates. The pro-sex position is what would be more accurately described as those who explored the representation of sexual gratification and pleasure as empowering. Feminists such as the writer and artist Kathy Acker, famed for her punk sensibility, explored sexual and violent imagery in order to critique class mores. However, they were countered by the anti-sex feminists such as writers and activists Susan Brownmiller and Andrea Dworkin. Dworkin's own thesis on heterosexual sex was that there was no occasion when penetration was not rape, and that there were no circumstances in which pornography was okay.

> The psychic violence in pornography is unbearable in and of itself. It acts on one like a bludgeon until one's sensibility is pummelled flat and one's heart goes dead. One becomes numb. Everything stops, and one looks at the pages or pictures and knows: this is what men want, and this is what men have had, and this is what men do not want to give up.
>
> (Dworkin 1988: 23)

In addition to the pro and anti – or sex positive and sex negative – positions, there were outliers such as Shulamith Firestone, who was arguing not only for a rethinking of the family structures and gender roles but for a release from any bodily functions, particularly childbirth, through technology as the only way to establish gender equality (Firestone 1979). Thus, the rhetorics of feminism at that time included many versions of what might have seemed in the last few decades as quite extreme language that discussed patriarchy in terms of relentless violence against women.

Punk, as a libertarian tendency, did not in general take the anti-sex approach as I describe in chapter one through the films off Bette Gordon and Tessa Hughes Freeland. However, in some ways the approach to gender non-conformity in the period can be exemplified as much through the Crass single *Shaved Women* (1979) – that equated women who shave their legs and arms as collaborators and traitors in a genocidal war that evokes the concentration camps of World War Two – as through Siouxsie Sioux's quasi sado-masochistic leatherette costumes.

Not all works were so sober – and sobering – and extreme. *Screaming Babies* needs to be seen against 'sex positive' feminist artworks that were more aligned with the punk approach such as Cosey Fanni Tutti in the UK or Annie Sprinkle and Kathie Acker in the United States, both of whom used pornography in the 1980s in their artworks. One of the features of punk was its lack of seriousness and its intentional superficiality. Annie Sprinkle in the United States and Kathie Acker as well as Linder in the UK are further examples of the uses of humour to deflate the shock of the imagery and counter the angry earnestness of writers such as Dworkin. Whereas Annie Sprinkle uses feminist strategies of self-presenting performance in a deflationary way, Acker and Linder draw from Dada and surrealism. It is not that Linder et al. support the violence meted on women by patriarchy and misogyny;

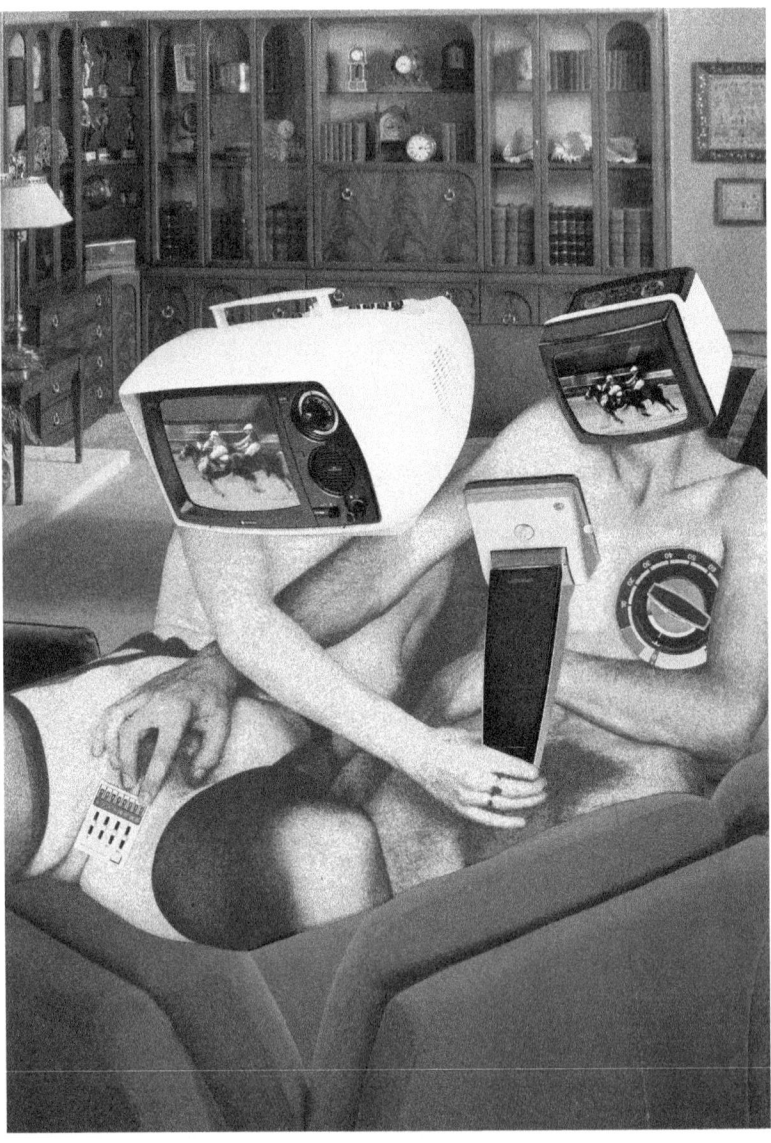

Figure 25. *Untitled* (1976–77, Linder Sterling) © Linder. All rights reserved, DACS/Artimage 2021. Image: © Modern Art.

instead, it is a strategy of gaining power by making the contradictions of the sex industry visible. For example, in *The Secret Public* (1978) Linder and Savage used magazine images of naked women and men with TVs for heads or a hoover for a penis in a domestic setting. In the scenario both men and women are victims of the idiocies and exploitation that give rise to the alienated engagement with porn. One image for example depicts a kitchen with a woman who is propped from the knees up in a saucepan that is on the kitchen counter. The woman is naked, with her hands behind her back and her face staring out from the inside of a food liquidizer. This is a shocking image but is rendered more humorous when juxtaposed with several other images in the series. Another image, for example, is the image of a man and woman masturbating each other, both of them sitting on a sofa with TVs for heads. The woman has a transistor sheet partly covering her vagina and he has a hoover where his penis would be. Another is of a woman, again naked, reclining on a sofa, with cakes pasted on her head and below her chest. All that can be seen of her is her torso and so her breasts. The absurdist humour of these other images – hoover penis, cake head – challenges or at least complicates the savagery of the woman through ambivalence – who has a head in a liquidizer and feet in a saucepan. Maybe it is all funny or maybe it merely highlights the tragedy of the situation of women. Like Höch the works turn on the funny/violent axis much like the slapstick of Child's *détournement* in her film *Perils* (1986), where Child takes out the narrative thread completely, keeping merely the gestures, repetition, absurd sounds and looks of the form of slapstick. *Perils* is the photomontage of Höch in temporal form, using cinematic histories and languages to develop new forms of viewing. Slapstick, as Kracauer sees it, offers redemption that can be seen in the relief from the violence of the image in the humorous moments that make happy endings ubiquitous but also puts them 'under erasure' (Hansen 1993: 467); in this way slapstick offers an antidote to the system through its bifurcation through humour. The humour also sets out a difference between the main thrust of second wave feminist art, the No Wave movement in New York and punk.

The humour in these works, either absurdist or slapstick, often goes together with violence. Many of the artists in this book use montage in a violent way that both gives and withholds the desire in the image shown. This is a gallows humour, brutally interrupting the flow that goes further than the Brechtian imperative to make strange. Connected to the brutal imposition of cuts is the use of appropriation which is a central theme of collage and of some of these films. Abigail Child and Leslie Thornton appropriate imagery, although mainly from their own archive of previously shot footage, as well as methodologies of montage: the violence of the imagery echoes the violence of invisibility. As does the use of appropriation: Ruth Novaczek often appropriates and juxtaposes Hollywood norms of femininity as a foil to the Jewish woman or the narratives of romance. Maureen Turim uses Abigail Child to think through the importance of appropriation as a tool to *détourne* the history of erasure under which women and, arguably even more so, lesbians have had to operate. Turim's analysis could, in fact, be brought to bear on many of the artists who appear here in addition to Child: appropriation is fundamental to almost all the artists I cite. Through Child's work in *Mayhem* (1987), part six in the series, Turim positions the power of *détournement* in appropriation. In fact the way in which Child's work is analysed in relation to Höch could have been written equally about Linder's work from this period, and beyond. The violence and shock of Linder's early punk work in a similar manoeuvre can also be recuperated via the work of Hannah Höch herself.

Thus the work of Höch and also Heartfield had a renewed sense of urgency in the violence of the cut and the disjunctive juxtapositions of an earlier moment for many artists held within the ripples of punk that still has currency amid twenty-first-century turbulences. Akin to the thinking from Kracauer of the possibility that film offered is the reorganization of the photograph to try to make new sense of the world, the endless replay and the focus on an articulation of process that is not overdetermined by instrumentalizing formulas but alive to its ongoing contingencies.

In addition to the examples of the drama and violence of the cut that Linder and Child's work draws from, other strategies to destabilize fixed meaning are habitually used, such as the redeployment of salvaged images to reframe in a new moment. It is the extent to which Child particularly uses this strategy that renders it unique. It is the specific way and the purpose in which many of the artists in this book use this strategy that makes it particular. Child, probably more than any other in this book, works to put the viewer's understanding of what is happening always on the edge of disintegration. In *Mutiny* (1983), the

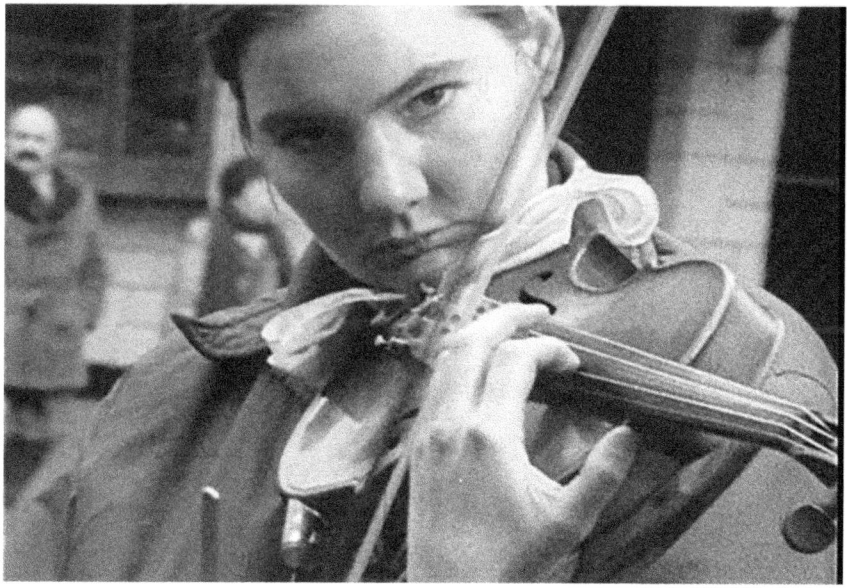

Figure 26. Polly Bradfield from *Mutiny* (1992–3, Abigail Child) © Abigail Child.

second film in the series, Child uses appropriation at its minimum. Here the violence is in the lack of continuity and its corollary, the constant interruption. There is little that the viewer can hold on to in order to make sense of the film, and like many of her films, it is the sound that holds any sense of continuity to be found. The film is destabilizing because it is almost completely abstracted by the speed of the fast montaging of self-appropriated footage. In *Mutiny* people everywhere are moving and reacting to the world in this film and the viewer keeps trying to make sense of the people flashing past in their fragmented movements. This is unlike an abstract piece per se, where the primary aim of the viewing is to do with form, for the viewer to make their own sense of the images, free of the world – in a broad-brush encapsulation of abstraction. It is also distinct from the Brechtian distanciation in its speed and relentlessness of delivery that holds the viewer's attention and allows for no outside. In this film the world is everywhere in an agitated but carefully orchestrated mash-up of signs. There is so much of the world flying past, yet not for long enough to see why. The cause and effect of narrative structure is completely broken down. It goes further than Thornton's narrative as 'freefall'. It is a work 'of detachable parts' (Wees 2005: 38). And yet the viewer cannot overcome the desire to follow a narrative because she sees people moving, dancing, working, walking. Child maintains enough of the documentary from where most of the footage must derive, for the viewer to be involved and for the humanity of the cinematic subjects to keep their hold on the viewer.[12] While moving too fast to fully hold a narrative, the images are too potent to be completely abstracted. The fragments of gestural movement are a stopping point for the viewer, slowing down the stream of life. However, even so, this tension stretched to extreme points produces anxiety, even while the images also constitute a rhythmic and colourful flow that is a beautiful and constant movement. It is ultimately life-enhancing through the dynamic and rhythmic movement of people through the film: dancing, talking, playing instruments, and even after all these years, the visual shock is still not exhausted.

From the context of Kracauer's cinematic observations of the Weimar period, Child's *Mutiny* can be seen to have some echoes of the Tiller Girls.[13] Today, in a post-Fordian moment this piece can speak to us from a place where, in Western Europe and the Anglophone world at least, factory work becomes obsolete in comparison to the twenty-first-century breakdown of workplace relationships. In the cultural imagination of the contemporary Deliveroo or even the silicon valley type of workforce that Andrew Ross discusses in his book *No Collar: The Humane Workforce and its Hidden Costs* (2004), the collectivity that the twentieth-century factory represents can be idealized as a site of fulfilment – that of the post-war dream of full employment and a workforce that draws power from unionized solidarity. To be clear, factory work is alienated; however, in a period beyond the factory, in a time of complete atomization, post-war factory work could be seen as a space of a cohesive and stable labour force. In the chapter, taken from the same book titled *Mass Ornament,* Kracauer describes the women who are the Tiller Girls who had lost their factory jobs in Lancashire, England, and took to the stage. These women, a cinematic sensation at the time, were working the stage in an effect reminiscent of the factory machines at work. *Mutiny,* I would argue, is in some ways a new iteration of the mass ornament – a post-Fordist, feminist iteration, as an effect of accelerationism. In the original Tiller Girls, the fragmentation of bodies was of density of limbs taken in as one image in time; in *Mutiny* the fragmentation is linear, of interruption and of incomplete bodily actions led by a quirky, scratchy soundscape that forms a spine of the film: the cut of the edit accentuating their quirky movements and the atonal sound that interrupts that are repeated again and again – all giving a mood to the film – and both referring back to the experiences of women's lives at work in their respective historical moment.[14] The mesmerizing limbs of the Tiller Girls that moved to crafted songs of their day now give way in *Mutiny* to an atonal, broken weave of sounds that become an aural collage of disjuncture. This offers a commentary on the working environment that drives a faster and faster working life at a time in the early 1980s when there was a dearth of jobs, a time when one person would be doing the job that previously two people had done. The alienated surface in this film is the representation of a seemingly myriad of people all taken out of any context.[15] This is a plethora of outtakes that has no establishment, denouement or resolution. It is an ongoing rhythmic flow of bodies – a lone woman dancing in an office setting, a violin being played by a toothbrush on the street, bits of discussions, a man dancing. The mass ornament is now translated into a different kind of surface of alienation: indifference as the sign of capitalism.

The kind of endgame that punk is associated with is analogous to the No Wave films in the United States, set out in the interplay between detritus, violence and desire by artists such as Steve Nares or the B's. However, these concerns or operations can be seen also in a range of other films, such as those by Abigail Child, Bette Gordon, Leslie Thornton in the United States and Anne Robinson and Sandra Lahire in the UK. The difference between the No Wave artists and the examples I explore is between, on the one hand, works that give some kind of redemptive response to the world and human relations and, on the other hand, the cynicism and nihilism of the No Wave artists. Vivienne Dick is an important artist here. She was associated with the No Wave, but her approach was distinct in its humanism, as picked out very early on by Jim Hoberman (1979). The underlying nihilism in much of the work in this period, even of the punk artists, can be attributed to the ongoing threat of nuclear war. The impact of this threat that pervaded the Cold War period until its end cannot be underestimated. The concrete contingency of this time that draws through the 1970s to the early 1990s is concerned with the double impact of this nuclear underbelly of cultural consciousness coupled with economic dissolution. These issues are configured in many ways through the artist films, but the fear of nuclear threat is palpable. However, in these works it is always foregrounded within and through human relations.

The British and US contexts are also very different and the works demonstrate this in a variety of ways. The British work tends to use documentary practices, either by working with mediated imagery or by using and disrupting documentary methodology. Sandra Lahire and Anne Robinson's works of this kind, while still very much art, are drawn from documentary practices. They focus on the industry itself and its effects on workers in a direct way, while the US artists such as Gordon and Thornton do not make the nuclear threat the core focus but a device that sets the mood and explains the outlook as wallpaper for the times the subjects inhabit. However, this is a false dichotomy as the works by Robinson and Lahire play with the imagery through colour, negativizing and tinting, while the American artists tend to stick to the documentary image while playing mainly with structure.

Some works by Anne Robinson, for example, *A Capital Adventure* (1986/1992), filmed at Bank, situated in London, offers a sense of apocalypse in a film ostensibly innocent of nuclear references. Bank in the city of London

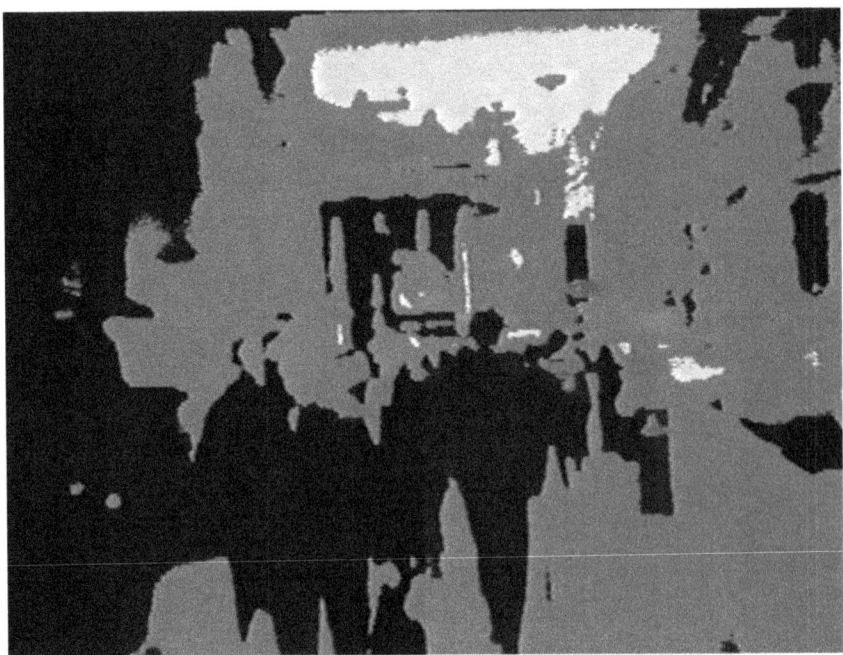

Figure 27. *A Capital Adventure* (1986–92, Anne Robinson). Courtesy of the artist.

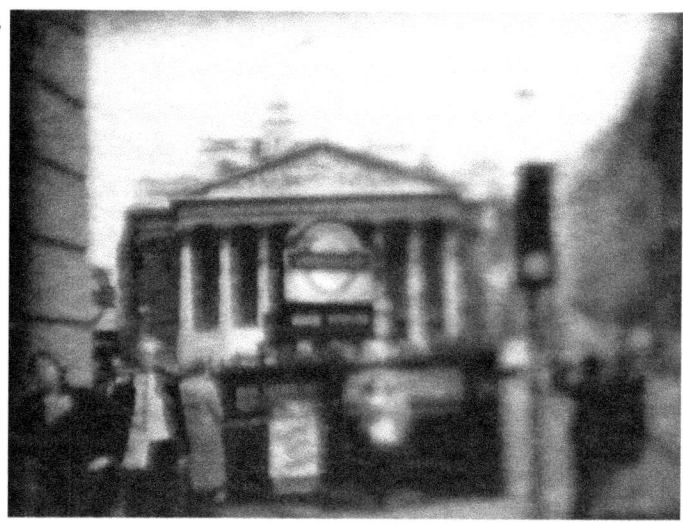

Figure 28. *A Capital Adventure* (1986–92, Anne Robinson). Courtesy of the artist.

is where the Bank of England and the underground station of the same name are sited. Arguably the Bank of England is one of the key seats of Britain's establishment power – the other being the monarchy – and in this film is figured prominently, siting the importance of the relationship between the seat of power in the UK that is represented in the seeming stability of the buildings and the lack of actual stability in the cinematic metaphor of the stormy orange sky. The sky, a force of nature that is juxtaposed with the imposing and static buildings, gets gloomier and more stormy throughout the film and acts as a metaphor for the lack of stability. Robinson took the sound from a freebie cassette of an audio adventure story that was included in a war magazine of the time. The play is of a cheesy story – typical of the time – of a group of secret service men with BBC RP accents, in the Savannah of Africa who get caught by poachers. The poachers, of course, have the usual stereotypical accent for criminals in British films of London working-class English accents. The footage is filmed by Robinson herself and then edited several years later. The image is slowed down, which distorts and eventually breaks down the fabric of the film, changing the colours into painterly blues, blacks and yellows. The film then returns to the slow-motion fuzzy clarity of the men in suits at Bank, now going down into the black hole of the underground, while the aural narrative talks of baboons, seen through the binoculars, drawing a direct parallel between animal life and the workers in the city. The images of city people walking along the streets of Mansion House and the tube at Bank disintegrate fully at one point: a metaphorical breakdown of society. At another point the sky becomes a cadmium orange, probably through using the saturation function on the analogue U-Matic edit desk.[16] The heavy skies are rendered heavier by the juxtaposition with the Radio 4 voice and the narrativizing of the slightly absurd story of MI6 agents in the jungle and the image of city workers walking backwards down into the hell of the underground. As the secret army in the narrativizing radio fiction gets caught, the imagery shifts to the buildings and the statues emerging from the building's arches. The stone statues, of semi-naked women trapped forever in their stone effigies, adorn these buildings and in this film represent establishment patriarchal power, that of women trapped, immobile. However, in this vision the men are equally trapped in their absurd commuting into the mouth of 'the tube'. A sequence of close-ups of the female figures in stone ensues until one minute before the end when it reverts back to the city scene. The film is ominous in the absurdity of the juxtaposition between the sound and imagery but also features an apocalyptic sky that associates capitalism and the city with our impending doom, both in terms of the seeming disintegration politically, of the social contract by Margaret Thatcher, but also the ongoing backdrop of a nuclear holocaust.

Robinson's *Four Minute Cut* (1986) is more explicit. The mediated imagery is all from documentaries with experts speaking about the safety of nuclear power and news announcements about the Chernobyl disaster. In the continuous snippets of various footage, the viewer sees a continuous roll of TV presenters derived from documentaries. Robinson edits a stream of men, man after man in her film, the talking heads who pronounce the safety of nuclear power. This is an accumulation of male politicians scoffing at those who fear it as a threat as a performance of masculine bravado. A female narrator of the film, Robinson herself, contradicts this media 'master' narrative being represented in the film with facts about percentages of populations suffering with leukaemia and the comparative increase of cancer in populations within a short radius of nuclear power stations. These devices in the film foreground the gendered nature of the debate, or at least the way the debate had been gendered – also by Greenham

Common of course – the voice of male authority versus the voice of woman as truth-teller. The film also positions the male as artifice in opposition to the woman as authenticity. Halfway through the film, the mediated imagery in a transition shocking for its sudden juxtaposition of register gives way to the image of two women kissing, locked into a hold – a doubling of blond spiky hair. The camera is circling the two women, in a park then in a hallway, then as fragments. The sound of sirens that accompanies the circling camera around these women adds to the alienation of the surveillance feel of the camerawork and the sense of impending danger – in this case to love. The text that runs across the bottom says, 'stabbed in the back' and posits a gendered betrayal, building on the dichotomy set up in the earlier part of the film. The opposition of men as warmongers and women as lovers is set up within the context of nuclear annihilation through a framework of human relations that the women represent: an intimate human relation that serves, in this film, to trump the ever-present mediated chatter of fear of nuclear holocaust, usually in the background of the 1980s. Even the narration amplifies the distance between the genders by elevating the authenticity of women through their amateurish lack of professional presence – as well as truth-tellers to the male media's lies. The woman's voice is stilted and amateurishly humane besides the mediated performances of male speeches, presented as threats. Most pertinent, however, is the way in which the film moves from the male talking heads in their public persona, carrying all the authority, to the simplicity of the females kissing with none of the pretensions of TV professionalism that brings to light the ethical conflict at the heart of the nuclear debates of the 1980s. All the amateur qualities are brought to bear here, the stumbling, humble voiceover, the figures in the hallway, badly framed with flat lighting. However, despite these 'amateurish' pretensions, there is an expertly edited breaking up of shots and an expressionist tendency to the sound, fragmentation and use of stills in close-up that lends meaning beyond the simple juxtaposition. In this way it can be said to utilize melodrama as a strategy of stereotypical ciphers, where 'the exaggerated gestures and expressions must be read for how they charge the narrative with an intensified significance, with meaning in excess of what the narrative depicts' (Petro 1989: 31). The move from the former set of images to the latter makes the point in a direct and simple way that loving relations are

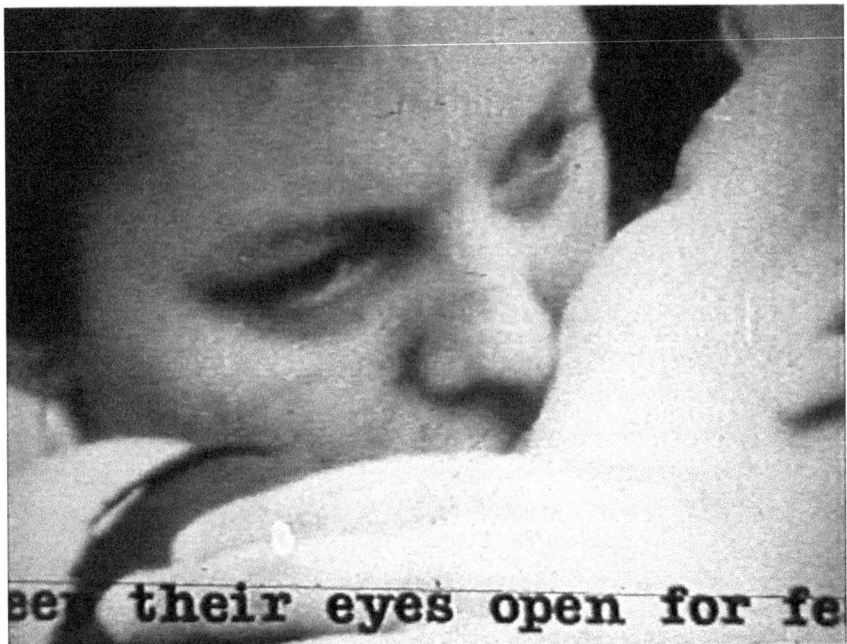

be their eyes open for fe

Figure 29. *Four Minute Cut* (1986, Anne Robinson). Courtesy of the artist.

at the core of all relations, that nothing comes without it: that the amateur, the authentic and the female are the only attributes to trust.

Sandra Lahire made a series of nuclear films between 1986 and 1989. *Serpent River* (1989) is the last of this series, the others being *Uranium Hex* (1988), *Plutonium Blonde* (1986) and *Terminals* (1986). *Serpent River* is a serious work, like Robinson's treatment, and focuses specifically on a damaged site of the landscape and its predominantly female workers. The damage is due to the nuclear industry and this narrative of ordinary workers is set against the denial of the corporate employers. Lahire's trilogy makes use of experimental documentary forms. What sets it apart is the use of colour tints, negativizing and montage to produce an experiential piece of work. The film is marked by repeated shots of X-rays and naked backs, her own body intermingling with the bodies of others. This is a repeated motif in all her films, but particularly those films that deal with nuclear power and its effects making for an understanding of the world that is always embodied. Women and children are also never far away in *Serpent River*, skating or going into the nursery in the snow. Throughout there is a woman's voiceover describing working in the town where uranium is mined. The blue that pervades the whole film and the constant sound of machines produce a sombre mood. Approximately ten minutes into the film there is an extraordinary passage. It is a still image that depicts women drilling underground. The still is black and white, which adds a sense of strangeness to the blue-toned moving images that it interrupts. The machine sounds are still constant. There is a flashing of light, like lightning or a flash bulb that together brings traces of science fiction into consciousness. Most of the film shows people working, drilling into rock, in a blue world and sometimes in purple, and throughout the film, water is depicted in various ways. The landscape is ever present, tinted in blues and yellows as a metaphor for the contamination of the mining being done. There is uranium in the drinking water. We are told about this halfway through the film, and for the first time we see children playing beach ball – untinted but in slow motion – by the beach, which drives home the impact of the information. Like Anne Robinson's film, this work asserts the central importance of values and ontologies of women in the political debates on nuclear power that were being fought by women and sidelined since.

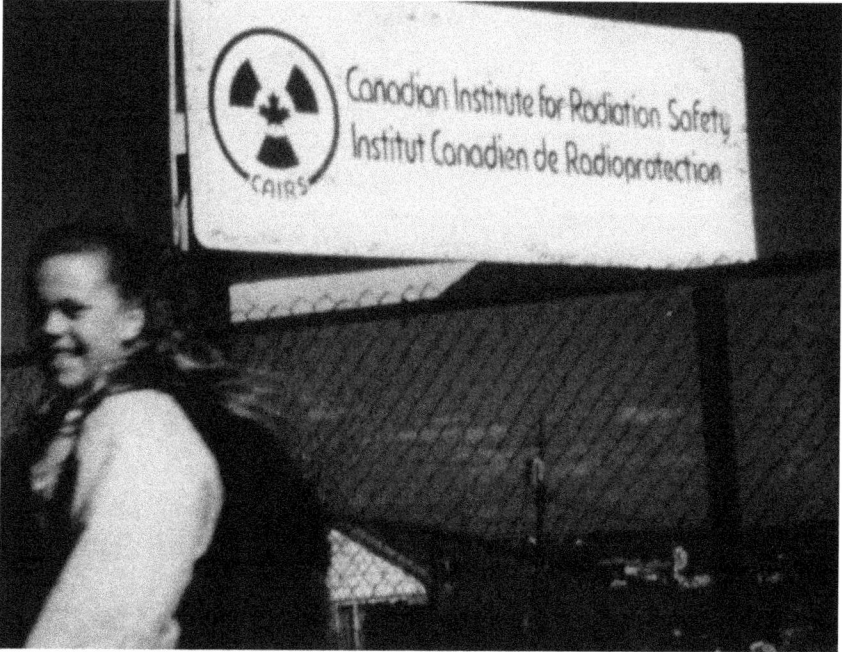

Figure 30. *Serpent River* (1989, Sandra Lahire). Courtesy of Sandra Lahire and the LUX, London.

The artists working in the United States, such as Leslie Thornton and Bette Gordon, have a different approach. In their work the subject of the nuclear holocaust and industry is embedded within wider interests rather than the effects of the nuclear industry being the main focus. The politics of Thornton and Gordon's films are more nebulous and accumulative. Thornton's film *Peggy and Fred in Hell* has been reworked by Thornton over several decades. The series is more about zeitgeist than establishment and foregrounds a specific political point of view. This may have something to do with Thornton growing up with a father and grandfather involved in the nuclear industry where the involvement and also the secrecy surrounding it were both normalized.[17] *Peggy and Fred in Hell* has the titular children as the main protagonists. The central conceit of the film is that these two children are in a post-apocalyptic space, the main site of which is a room full of cast-off objects that itself exists within a bubble of the contemporary, the nostalgic past and the nuclear past. These children, while living in extraordinary circumstances, focus on the ordinary, like children do. Thornton's *Peggy and Fred* is distinct from, say, the protagonists in Samuel Beckett's *Waiting for Godot* whose response was inertia – although there are some resemblances in the overarching mood of the film. These children carry on, and their engagement with their surroundings in the everyday is what keeps them going. The interruptions to their movements in the room, of other footage shot by Thornton supplemented in places by found footage, create a sense of 'outside' that is lacking in Beckett. As Thornton herself says, they 'approach this flattened spectacle like one would any desert – they keep moving' (Wees in Petrolle and Wexman 2005: 28).

The focus of the film is manifold and the abstraction is established by the opening shots, which is of found footage from Bell Laboratories, of the movement of singing vocal chords shot on silent film in the 1920s. The footage is overlaid with a section of Handel's opera *Rinaldo* interspersed with Yma Sucmac singing 'bom-ti-ti-bom'. This shifts to shots of the bottom of a TV screen with a voiceover repeating the terms of the optimum sound level of a female voice taken from an educational documentary. Only after this sequence do Peggy and Fred of the title appear in the guise of a boy singing, his voice emerging out of subsonic sound, casually singing to himself in a strange space that is not entirely familiar in its set-up but appears as forgotten somehow due to the proliferation of objects without reason or order. After some time with the boy singing, the film cuts to a TV screen buried in a pile of what can only be described as what seems discarded 'stuff'. The TV screen is showing two birds pecking at each other; again, opera is in the background, interspersed with sound from a TV programme. The TV screen then shows a desert-scape and a factory. The screen within a screen offers a distancing mechanism that is nonetheless emotive through the distancing, pushing the idea of the outside world further away from the viewer – into an anachronistic and nostalgic TV box – an imaginative leap away from the room depicted in the film. The TV screen is increasingly obscured by what could be wiring or it could be tree branches dumped in front of the screen, on the general pile of stuff, obscuring the moving images, burying all signs of life. There are no other people here beyond the two children – the last still alive? Reality is portrayed through screens and leftovers: the dislocation of subjectivity is purposefully alienating, but as the viewer cannot yet make out either context or forward moving trajectory in the absurdist and attenuated editing, the overloading of

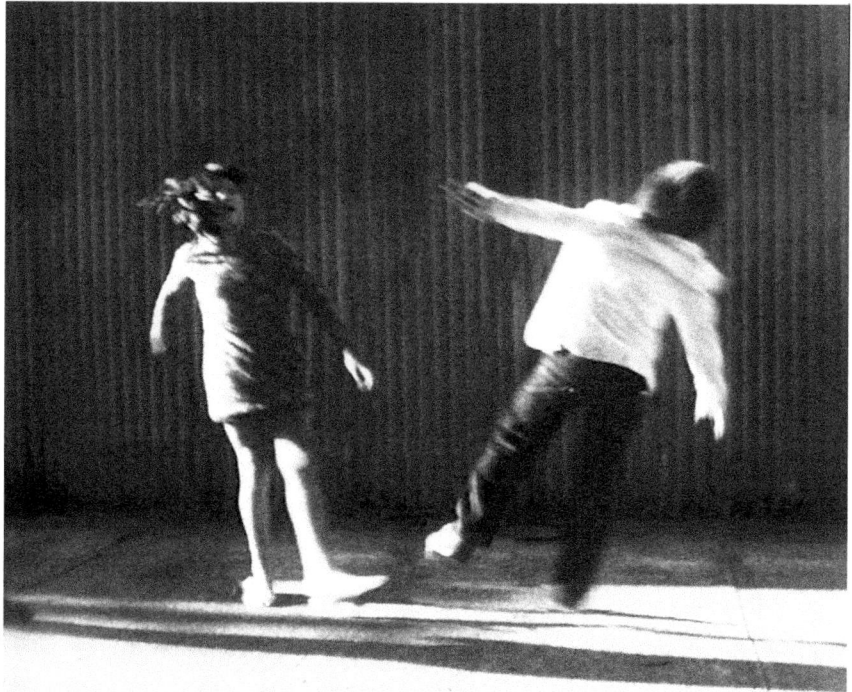

Figure 31. *Peggy and Fred in Hell* (1983–2015, Leslie Thornton). Courtesy of the artist.

absence is alienating and threatening. Yet Thornton also manages to capture and contrast an uplift created by the soundscaping with a deflationary sense of the everyday and the common ubiquitous needs of the children to simply live and keep on living.

The direct references to bomb culture are oblique – but knowing, such as the jump cut to an inverted film footage of a droplet falling into water by Harold Egerton, which invokes a nuclear explosion. These particular high-speed shots were employed in order to develop the technology to film the atom bomb.[18] This kind of documentary footage was hailed in the public eye as the new realism in the United States at the time of making but was actually in the service of nuclear science. Other images of war such as a nighttime aeroplane battle from the Second World War pepper the film in disjointed clips, in between the more prosaic shots of the children going about their everyday activities in the strange room. The juxtaposition between the humanism of the opera and the post-human, post-nuclear depopulation that these children inhabit by implication through these references to post-war images, sound and aesthetic, situated in the desert – all this sets up a powerful immanent critique and an incipient undertow of violence.

A similar undertow of violence can be found in Vivienne Dick's film *Staten Island* (1978) through the idea of a post-Holocaust dystopia that is never stated but merely implied in this short film that depicts Pat Place in a silver boiler suit and barefooted, picking through the detritus on Staten Island shore. It is as if this is her only existence. No one else is present. Place wades through the water in the opening scene to reach the rubbish-filled coast in this five-minute short. Throughout the film the camera is mostly focused on Pat Place picking up detritus to put in her plastic bag or close-up shots of her sitting, looking at her things. Halfway through the film Joe Meek's pop single *Telstar* (1978) starts playing, adding to the sense of dislocated strangeness. Suddenly the camera moves from close-up to establishment shot of the river and then a reverse zoom pulls away even further and pans to a cold winter sun that sparkles through the darkness. The natural lighting of the cold bleak day focused on the sky blacks out the screen, all the while the tremulous sci-fi music playing, finally zooming back in to the silhouetted figure of Place. It is unbelievably bleak, similar to Thornton, of isolated individuals marooned in a depopulated landscape with nothing but leftovers from the twentieth century.

Marasmus (1981), by Betzy Bromberg and Laura Ewig, is similarly enigmatic. Bromberg started making films in 1977 and now works in California. Her films have a rich and textured sensibility, both enigmatic and multi-layered. Her early films had a distinctively New York flavour, not unlike the films of Gordon and Dick from that same period, although Bromberg was not part of that scene. *Marasmus* is a twenty-minute film shot in California and structured through a wide range of imagery and textures such as the layering of footage from the California desert, tinted footage of the landscape, the many varied filmed portraits of women, and fragments of staged acted vignettes. Similarly to Novaczek, Bromberg's *Marasmus* intimately interweaves personal visual responses to the world with the politics of power. One such example is the way in which the abrasive soundscape incorporates voiceovers accounting angrily about the lack of control over the means of production of oil and the effect of this on pollution levels. The angry voice is interspersed with haunting vocalizations. The footage from New York of a woman walking along a modernist rotunda quickly gives way to lone female figures in a desert space. *Marasmus* is a bridging work from her earlier New York pieces to what are Bromberg's current interests and methodologies. The title refers to a state of acute malnutrition which is an obvious metaphor for the state of the world as accounted for in the film. The film gives visual language to entrapment, isolation and fear through the depiction of women's faces filmed in close-up or women in the desert, crying or staring, walking around oil pumps that dot the desert landscape. The threat of technology is also conveyed through colour and drive-by footage of refineries. Like Anne Robinson's film, the critique is highlighted by the juxtaposition between sound and image. In this case, the conflicting representation is conveyed by a man's voice telling how he is not worried, while the imagery of the oil fields in the desert gives a different message. Halfway through the film a woman in a gold-sequined skirt, her head covered in a scarf, is walking in circles in a ruin in the landscapes, with the hills in the distance. The sound is abrasively staccato: brass instruments making noises that squeak and shriek like a crazed form of jazz. The film here brings to mind the godmother of experimental film, Maya Deren, in its metaphysical allusions of women in the landscape. Then a sudden shift occurs of fading to black, which acts as a deflationary holding space. Then it shifts towards absurdist melodrama, footage of the modernist rotunda and a male voice overstating absurdly, 'It leads to exactly the same noi-oi-oi-oi situation situation'. The next shot is of a woman sliding down a slope, then a woman in a black costume with sound capture of the chattering of women 'oh my god … give it to me … ' again and again, all the while shots of close-ups of single female faces, several in succession parade past in the film. In this way, the fear and isolation give way to hysteria. These are repeated motifs: women in the landscape, women pressing their hands against the window, close-ups of women's heads, heightened colour. The camera is always moving, echoing the fast editing. The shrieking sound gives way to a melancholic piano with a montage of a woman's face pulling against plastic over a domestic interior in black and white and a woman peering through a branch she is holding. The film builds up to a visual kaleidoscope of blues and oranges depicting distorted single figures in

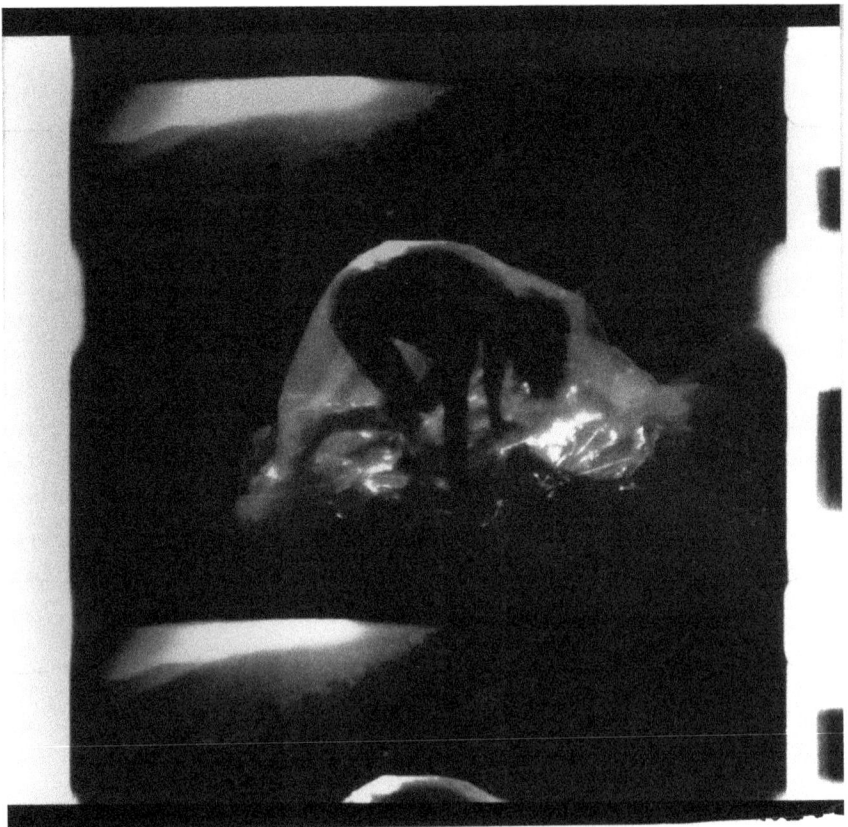

Figure 32. *Marasmus* (1981, Betzy Bromberg), frame enlargement. Courtesy of the artist.

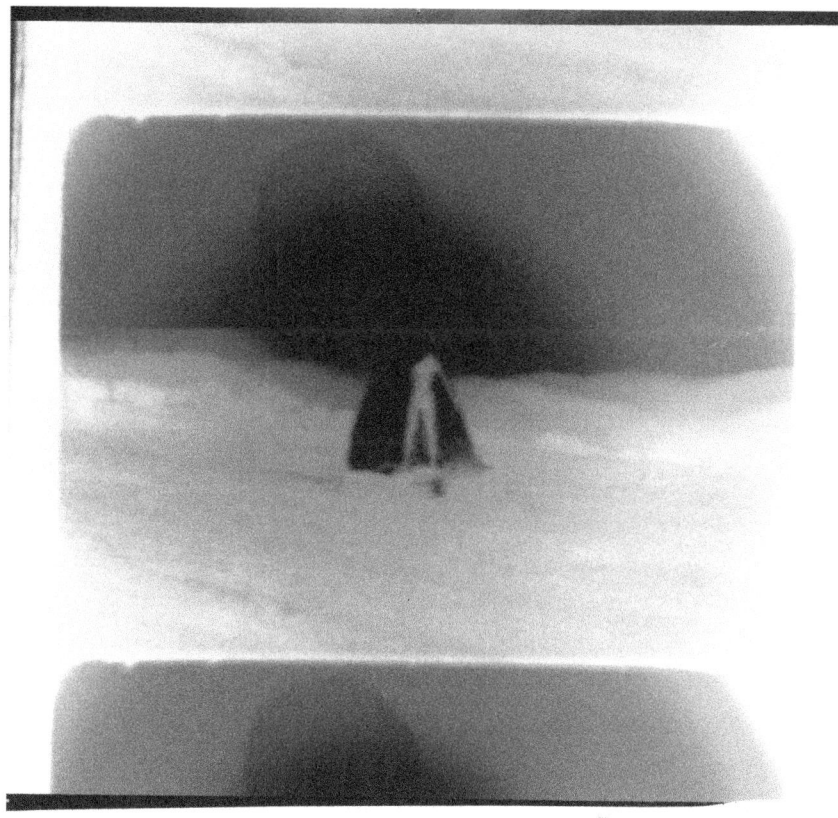

Figure 33. *Marasmus* (1981, Betzy Bromberg), frame enlargement. Courtesy of the artist.

the landscape, lending a sci-fi apocalyptic end – or almost end, as the last shot is of a woman rubbing the back of her head as if in weary exasperation.[19]

A backdrop of nuclear bomb culture is also pervasive in Bette Gordon's *Empty Suitcases* (1980), which begins with a woman's voiceover reciting airplane flight times through a telephone, with footage of downtown New York. Suddenly another female voice narrates, 'Uranium is the basic ingredient of the atomic bomb' and continues to describe the chain reaction set off by a nuclear blast. The camera during this new sequence shows a fixed shot urban scene over the roofs of downtown New York of the river. The camera shifts to another fixed shot of West 11th Street and the narrator starts to tell of a live bomb discovered there and the development of the investigators into the specific house which had been used as a bomb factory. It is ominous but again delivers a message of what could happen through the contradictions between the aural and the visual. This is not an unusual device, often used by Jean Luc-Godard for example, and one Gordon, formerly a structuralist filmmaker, would understand very well.[20] However, while this introduction to the narrative – fragmented and intentionally undercooked as it is – sets the tone, it is quickly left behind to offer a more prosaic vision of a woman depicted in a photographic still in the middle of nowhere beside a rundown clap-board building with a suitcase – a commuter between Chicago and New York. Her life in New York is then depicted: the everyday life of the woman artist in downtown NY in its messy provisionality. Gordon later widens her vision again to cite workers' struggles in the film, but generally the everyday chaos of personal attachments and circumstances of the life of an artist in those times is what is foregrounded. Violence keeps re-emerging, however, in this film in episodic fragments: the violence of regeneration, of abusive couples, of activists and artists. Guns appear in bags and safety regulations for explosives. In the film subjectivity, activism and violence are interconnected. The underplayed narrative draws to a close: the woman becomes an activist. Significantly the last shot of the film is a police mugshot of Bernadine Dohrn, a member of the radical group The Weather Underground.[21] The sprawling deliberations across geography and love triangles, university employment and artistic choices all end in the arm of the state. The end of the film is a series of fixed frame shots, rostrum camera shots, texts and newspaper cuttings: distancing, fragmented, static. The interconnecting of the personal messiness of everyday life and its negotiations that operate against a horizontal juxtaposition of concrete political and politicizing events is a marker of this film and is paradigmatic of all the filmmakers in this volume.

For these artists, the street was the site of disintegration. Fragmentation didn't come from the 'kitchen table' of the post-war generation of feminists. Instead it came from the street, always there, cheap and easy to use. The discomfort of an era in what Kracauer identified as double homelessness of the 1920s and 1930s could be argued through the artists in this chapter. The characterization of the 'sham of the bourgeois interior and the anonymous otherness of the modern street' (Hansen 2012: 11) took on a new hue for young people in the 1970s and 1980s of the UK and US who now saw little prospect of employment in the new economic downturn. Instead of the image of the single artist in their kitchen struggling with childcare and the needs of domesticity, we now have the image of the group of artists in the street making their film together with no money.

The way in which these films both tacitly accept the underlying existential threat may be another way to account for the lack of finesse, lack of completeness and the violence of the films in this book. The viewing experience offers the 'ability of film to work unexpectedly on the senses, to jolt, to lure the viewer into a different temporal or spatial paradigm through a sideways image-door, which gives the contingent a bodily relation' (Harbord 2007a: 91). All the artworks turn away from the impending catastrophe as they see it instead working with a life forged and the human factor of love, relationships and work – or their lack. Bette Gordon's work uses the interplay of the dramas of love and politics, whereas Ruth Novaczek's work operates at the interstices of the dramas of love and the politics of identity; Ann Robinson's work sets up both the women kissing and all pervasive media catastrophizing as equal foci; Sandra Lahire interspersing her own naked body with felt tip drawn on and documentary footage from Canada; Vivienne Dick's depiction of young people living amid junk and detritus who focus not on activism and change but on how to keep going, how to live. These are just some examples of this dialectic that is often absent elsewhere and the way in which the parallel editing as described in the previous chapter can offer a new experience that requires heterogeneity through the extremes of the worldwide threat of annihilation and the need for ordinary life to continue in the meantime.

The sheer enormity of the threat of annihilation with no recuperative economic compensation of the kind that their parents' generation had been able to expect is here coupled with the emptying out of meaning that this backdrop engenders. These two factors were a toxic mix that gave their actions a certain menace and malaise. The ubiquity of detritus, emptiness, lo-culture and the everyday in these works highlight the need to concern oneself with the mere basics of survival. The urgency offered by these films is not one of endless wastelands and horror that might be found in science fiction but of people incorporating the backdrop of dread and getting on with the lives they have amid a directionless *néant* with no intervention and no support. The wastelands and detritus-filled cities are populated, with people doing things. The question is what kind of life to have? The seeming extremity of the situation from the world's richest nations gave rise to a superficiality and melodrama that could be read as an appropriately hysterical reaction in its disassociation.

Notes

1   While from a different trajectory, of documentary and agitprop, The Hackney Flashers were also at the forefront of the intersection of class and gender with *Who's Holding the Baby* in 1978.

2   Although there were some post-punk bands like Crass, The Poison Girls or the Au Pairs, who had a more overt politics.

3   Kracauer was critical of Eisenstein, seeing him as mechanistic (1960: 47), believing that a single shot of a close-up in itself can reveal 'disclosures of new aspects of physical reality' rather than merely a 'montage unit', a connector in a chain of signifiers.

4   Although Janet Harbord argues that that is a misreading of Eisenstein (2007b: 76).

5   *The Musketeers of Pig Alley* features Lillian and Dorothy Gish, who are young impoverished musicians struggling to stay alive in the back alleys of New York which ends in a shoot out.

6   This was part of a personal conversation, August 2017.

7   1970s glam rock also questioned masculinity but was arguably much less adopted by fans than the New Romantic look.

8   New Romantic is a music movement that grew out of punk and was a reaction to it in its excesses of fashion, its genderqueer approach to masculinity and its obsession with the inter-war years German culture.

9   In the Weimar period women were often represented as androgynous or bisexual (Petro 1989: 23).

10 I am not here aiming to make crass comparison between the Nazis and Margaret Thatcher or Ronald Reagan. There is, however, some scholarship on this matter: Jon Stratton wrote that punk was a belated effect of the Holocaust. See Stratton (2008).

11 Part 1: (1981); Part 2: Mutiny (1983); Part 3: Both (1988); Part 4: Perils (1986); Part 5: Covert Action (1984); Part 6: Mayhem (1987); Part 7: Mercy (1989), https://www.abigailchild.com/films/films.htm (Accessed: 21 March 2021).

12 These are outtakes from her own documentaries (MacDonald 1988: 198).

13 The Tiller girls were a dance troupe: https://tillergirls.com/.

14 'I think it is the SOUNDTRACK which reflects on itself and also speaks to the moment and adolescence of the women. You do not discuss sound (strangely) yet, it is the *sense* of the work for me. Or as I describe elsewhere, it is the "line" of the film – a kind of poetry of young women speaking to the state of being female... ' (Child, unpublished email to the author, 9 August 2020).

15 In fact *Mutiny* was a composite of outtakes from *Between Times*, *Game* and *Savage Streets*, as well as three local performers, Sally Silvers, Shelley Hirsch, Polly Bradfield, that Child shot (MacDonald 2005: 212). Although according to Child 'most of Mutiny was shot for a film *(BETWEEN TIMES)* that I directed in Minneapolis, with only about 3% found images from other "popular" [or not] sources' (Child, unpublished email to the author, 9 August 2020).

16 Processes explained by Anne Robinson in an email to the author, 10 April 2020.

17 This is not to say that Thornton does not have views; just that they are not presented as a critique in the film itself.

18 This might also have been a shot of a nuclear bomb. It was often hard to tell the difference – thanks to John Timberlake for these insights. Thornton had access to this kind of footage through her father, who was a physicist in the atomic industry.

19 'Instead of using a normal camera emulsion, I used what is known as a "print" stock which is not intended to be shot through a normal film camera. Its intended use is for duplication at a laboratory (in order to make a print from a normal film stock which was shot through a camera). This particular film stock has a very very low ASA, which means it needs an abundant amount of light for proper exposure. Thus it was a great stock to experiment with out in the desert. The orange/red image is the original camera negative which ran through my camera, and the cyan/blue is the subsequent print made from the negative.' From email correspondence by Bromberg to the author dated 26 February 2020.

20 The disjunction of sound and image is a common trope of these punk filmmakers and established arguably by Amos Poe in *The Blank Generation* (1976) (Hawkins 2015: 47).

21 The name Marion Delgado signifies this, as they adopted this name as a protest. The Weather Underground Organization was a radical left militant organization who planted bombs in their campaigns. They were defunct by 1977, three years before the making of this film.

5

Representation and the inability to situate: The undecidability of women's punk

Hysteria in the modern sense emerged at the same time as first wave feminism and was taken up and discussed again within second wave feminist discourse. In the text *Hysteria, Feminism and Gender Revisited*, Cecily Devereux (2014: 38) argued that feminism could be described as an active response to – or symptom of – conditions of the time, whereas hysteria is a negative response, or at best a passive response. I would suggest a less binary or maybe performative interaction between feminism and hysteria. If we take hysteria to be an excessive response, in the form of a pre-verbal unreasoned outpouring, then this can be a legitimate way to find the voice and language previously denied. I would therefore argue that it was through an hysterical response that a new definition and form of art was worked through.

In a live version of the song *Man Next Door* (1980), Ari Up of The Slits descends into babble with the band before starting the song. Seeing The Slits live in the 1970s, I witnessed the band descend into babble on several occasions. This is in part an affectation and an embarrassment of the young Ari Up setting herself up as free spirit, fetishizing what she would have seen as the pre-language, pre-civilization 'savage' in a way that is not – or should not be – possible today. The B side to the EP of *Man Next Door* is the song *In The Beginning*, where Ari sings about a visceral pre-verbal rhythmic silence that exists outside of coherent language. I would like to bracket at this point the naïveté of privilege or outright racism that a postcolonial reading would take us to and – just for this point – to posit an approach to this emerging musical form that punk forged for women: that of the hysterical as an emergent feminist form. I suggest that here is a struggle to find a language for women, one that celebrated a pre-verbal form and tried to actively suppress the symbolic order, which, although an impossible aim, could be an understandable process of becoming. The Slits, I could argue, are providing in their songs a space for developing outside of language, as women, in order to create their new and different form of music, even if it is through a racist stereotypical lens.

Having discussed collage and its possibilities from the point of view of disintegration in the filmwork of these women, I now turn towards another strategy that is a useful framework to think through the way in which the artists I am writing about develop their work and what is at stake in the forms they use. Siegfried Kracauer has been a key touchstone in the previous chapter. Here, I would like to return to another feature that was introduced in Chapter 3 that has relevance to the kind of filmmaking being discussed here, that of temporal dissonance, which is opened up by the possibilities of parallel editing. I will reflect on temporal dissonance through the mechanics of this kind of editing. I will argue that this mechanism of parallel editing is a core building block that gives life to the experience of incoherence borne out of the lived experience of exclusion. It is a re-animation of that exclusion through a demand to be taken seriously. There is something of the incoherent about being institutionally and structurally excluded: it can make no sense – as sexism and misogyny, indeed racism, are not rational. To be not taken seriously or to be systematically marginalized despite intellect and talent must go against everything that does make sense. Therefore, to make no sense is, in fact, a way of making sense to those outside of the order of the sensible. It is my proposition that the language of incoherence is an appropriate response to patriarchal capitalism for women under a system that gives language to men to create and command.[1]

In mainstream cinema, temporal play has been used and developed in a number of ways, such as in flashback or dream sequences. It has also been used in explorations of the material or as a diaristic device in some experimental film. However, temporal play is used by the women in this volume in particular ways that foreground the tensions between self-understanding and stability in the world. This way of working foregrounds the very instability of not having an adequate place of engagement with public life.[2] Not only does this form distress temporal norms of cinema, it is also a way of bridging interior and exterior worlds, the psychological with the real. In art terms, it could be said to bridge the interiority of surrealism and the exteriority of, say, cinema vérité, or to use Kracauer's taxonomy, fusing the cinematic traditions of Méliès and Lumière. However, there is traction in invoking the interior and exterior specifically within a history of feminist discourse. Works such as *Uranium Hex* (1987), discussed later in the chapter, illuminate specific ways in which the fusion of interior and exterior worlds gives rise to a political voice that is uniquely expressed. Through the learned strategy of explicitly stating one's subject position or stake in the narrative, this makes for a new perspective on the politics that broadens out what is required of the viewer and of the situation focused on within the film itself.

All these tensions, of time, space and responses to the world, give rise to an experience of discombobulation commensurate with the times of change and reconfiguration of women's thinking in relation to patriarchy. Importantly much of this work and cinematic methodologies were developed through second wave feminism as questions were asked as to how to be a woman. While feminism was a liberation, it also required a complete reinvention of self in a world that the women themselves were having to construct from scratch. The only model – apart from a few pioneers, such as Maya Deren, a much celebrated 'grandmother' of feminist cinema – was one exemplified through the patriarchal force of male subjectivity, which most women did not want to adopt. Thus, an aesthetic of defiance, one of refusal to situate subjectivity or fix experience within a coherent landscape, is not a surprising outcome and it is significant that many of these artists use this strategy in their work. Moreover, I would suggest that parallel editing is in itself a feature of these works as a marker of a female subjectivity in the making. What has now become commonplace, the idea, following Judith Butler *avant la lettre*, that there is no essential self – that we perform our selves, formed through the violence of heteronormative patriarchy – was arguably being explored by feminists who were involved in the making of themselves as feminists and documenting this process through art.

Ruth Novaczek's *Cheap Philosophy* (1992) is an example of one way of representing such a shifting subjectivity that does not know itself or at least a sense of self that does not settle on any singular explanation or experience. This work consists of a series of vignettes of different selves posited alongside each other of what we might now describe as 'selfies'. At the time the direct address was not so ubiquitous as it is now in the age of *YouTube* performers and

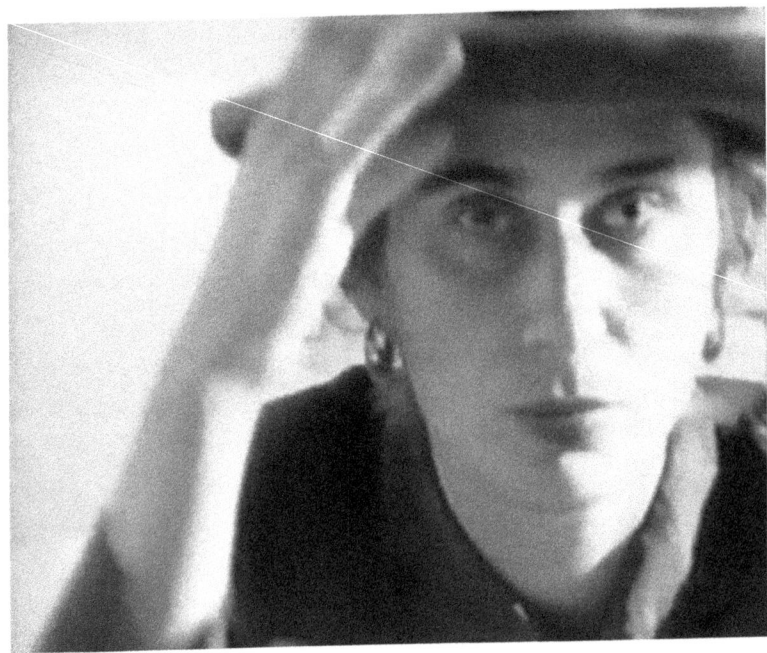

Figure 34. *Cheap Philosophy* (1992, Ruth Novaczek). Courtesy of the artist.

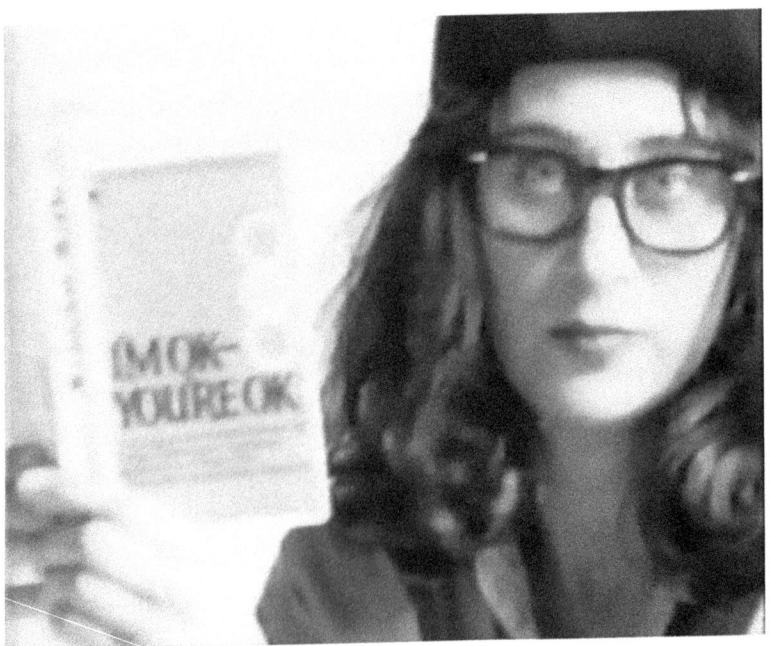

Figure 35. *Cheap Philosophy* (1992, Ruth Novaczek). Courtesy of the artist.

vloggers. Novaczek's film is constructed like a variety show, jumping between snippets. Some of these fragments are only two or three seconds, others longer, but none really longer than ten seconds, of the artist dressed and acting in different personas: as a JAP – Jewish American Princess – with a fedora, almost as orthodox gender bender, as a nerd with a self-help book, sometimes just clicking her fingers to music or telling a range of phrases depending on the costume such as: 'Don't you call me neurotic', 'She said, you know you look like Cher' or *I'm Ok, You're OK* after the famous self-help manual of the time. This film shares some similarities with Lynn Hershman Leeson's diary films, of fragmentation of form, of narrativizing experience, of lo-fi, such as *First Person Plural* (1984–96). Like Leeson, who also desired to make herself anew and who produced many works performing this desire, Novaczek's film enacts or even can be said to celebrate incoherence through repetition, excess and differencing. However, while much of the intention is similar, Leeson's work aims to explain her motives and to give some coherence to history in a way that Novaczek does not even seem to try.[3] Leeson describes in her trilogy of video tapes a mental and physical state that happened in the past and allows the viewer to see the unfolding of her sense of self. The state of unfolding is similar to Novaczek and certainly the Roberta Breitmore work of Leeson has the sense of experimental investigation; however, Leeson's video work is narrated from the position of analysing her motives and sense of being in the world, which in the end offers a singular autobiographical explanation, despite the multivalent devices used. Novaczek takes a step further, if such a linear adjective can be used. In *Cheap Philosophy* she neither tries to explain nor tries to make sense of 'herself'. Here she merely presents each fragment without a suturing motif such as the overarching voiceover that Leeson and others habitually employ.[4] The audience is never given any totalizing understanding or conclusion. Moreover *Cheap Philosophy* is witty and deflationary, rather than just self-reflexive. It both takes itself too seriously – in its hysteria – and not seriously enough, in its formal incompleteness. *Cheap Philosophy* remains in edgy incompleteness, a composite portrait formed from different voices, mostly coming out of Novaczek's own mouth with different wigs on. But beyond that even, the opening sequence is in a completely different register: it is of a woman – Vicky Klein, who is later singing in the film – running down a path in the distance of a landscaped garden at Dartington

Hall, a medieval country estate and at the time, also an Art School. The colour is heightened to a sickly green fluorescence, the woman tiny in the extreme distance. There is no explicit reason for what this sequence means, although possibly a lover running away from a relationship that might precipitate the main protagonist's flight into self-help and fragmentation. However, there are no clues; the shot does not establish a place where the rest of the film happens nor does any sequence or narrative develop but instead merely jumps from this silent vision of a woman running into the distance to the series of direct address vignettes of Novaczek speaking as other. These are snippets that call judgement of her on herself, others on her, her speaking to an imagined other, speaking different parts of herself. One persona says, 'Don't call me neurotic' with a faux-American accent,[5] sunglasses and a vintage black 1950s cocktail dress and bright-red lipstick. Another writes, 'I wish I was dead, I wish you were dead, I wish my parents were dead'. Before that she splutters, 'I hate you so much': childishly emphatic. Another calls for revolution. There is a man that appears in two shots, again without explanation, in one saying, 'Boy you should have seen the chicks in there'. Cliché sits on top of cliché. The American

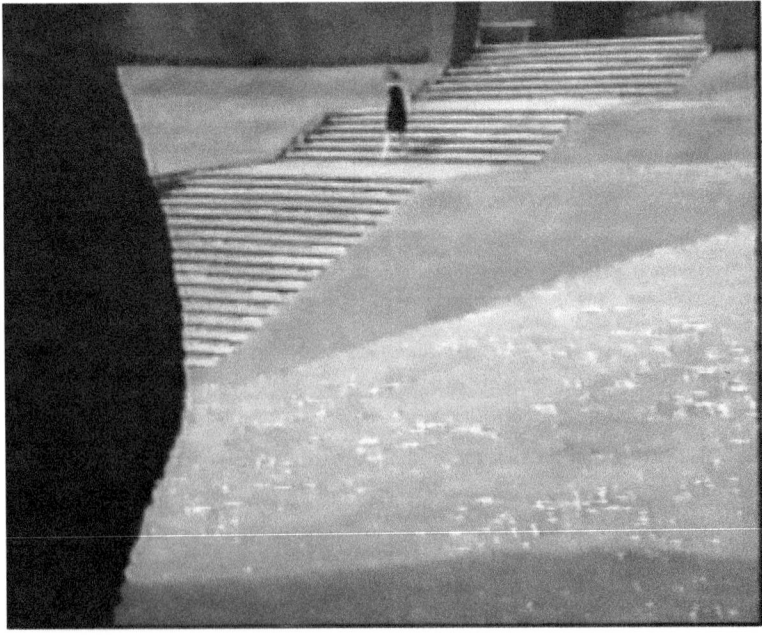

Figure 36. *Cheap Philosophy* (1992, Ruth Novaczek). Courtesy of the artist.

accent is a cliché, all the while a twentieth-century formative backdrop to the Anglophone world, particularly the Jewish Anglophone communities. The film switches from persona to persona, some with repeated moments. There is very little sense of time, and little sense of place as most of the shots are in a claustrophobic close-up with just a wall for backdrop. The shots are tinted and have the effect of looking like no white balance was used, although in true punk fashion white balance was used and it was colourised later for a cartoon-like effect.[6] It is an uncompromising work about the failures of trying to be a woman, and the even more extreme failures of trying to be a Jewish woman. The film is as degraded and fragmented as the construction of her subject. Time does not matter here because the film is parading a subjectivity in process and in a process that never ceases throughout one's life. Place doesn't matter because it is a diasporic identity with no place of home, so the film parades an hysterical floating subjectivity that does not have its place. The gaps in editing produce a new place to be: the jumping back and forth and the repetition, the shifts from black and white to colour, the tinting and heightening posit a passing of time that has no linearity and so is ever in the present: parallel editing par excellence.

As a form, parallel editing privileges heterogeneity as an equalizing force rather than proffer a singularity. Parallel editing therefore works as a powerful metaphor for undecidability as the ways in which the breakdown of narrative and narrativizing sequencing creates an inability to prioritize. It is in this way, of undecidability, that the discombobulated subject is thrown into disarray; like *Cheap Philosophy*, the subject does not know who they are except that they are in a process of continually searching and inconclusive finding, to search again.

Parallel editing, according to Doane, and as similarly described in Chapter 3, is one of three types of editing established in early cinema, each of which creates its own drama but allows the viewer to make sense, through visual means, of a narrative storyline. The first is shot followed by reverse shot, as described earlier, using repetition to create narrative coherence. The second is the chase, popularized through comedy and thrillers, which serves to re-inscribe linear time. The third is parallel editing, which creates a jump in space and time, implying that two events occur simultaneously. While the chase edit builds a linear movement that creates the semblance of normality, parallel editing creates suspense through desire and fear. Classically it has been used to create tension by showing what two characters might be doing simultaneously unbeknownst to each other. Parallel editing is essentially a kind of extreme montage that brings discontinuity through introducing elements happening in different spaces at the same time. In the films I discuss how parallel editing is used to accentuate the lack of time difference as an 'out of time moment' or a composite that defies linear time completely creating a sense of anxiety or heightened gratification or discombobulation from the visual and temporal disjunctions that are foregrounded in this methodology of editing, as opposed to the delayed gratification of the slow look. In *Cheap Philosophy* (1992) for example, even without the Hollywood narrative form, the parallel edit creates tension and anxiety by the weight of its use throughout the film. Each image is cut into another parallel image of the self as persona without hierarchy. The composite that these multiple parallel edits build up creates an extreme incoherent montage that through the intensity of its relentlessness perpetrates an hysterical effect.

Doane explains the classic parallel editing as an edit that replaces spectatorial time with cinematic time (2002: 193). This form of parallel editing used by Novaczek, Child and others pushes cinematic time into the realms of incoherent time – or out of time – as a more extreme version of cinema that confounds the idea of a forward movement by adding a spatial dimension. As suggested by Harbord by way of introducing what is at stake in this form of editing, 'it was a function of early cinema to make time legible, for Kracauer it is to confuse the so-called legible categories through which we experience the world' (Harbord 2007a: 99). It does this through an immanent contingency of producing chance encounters in the cinematic image that makes for 'imaginative analogy' (99). Through the 'imaginative analogy' this kind of work venerates the chance encounter to produce a new kind of reality that defies the logics of representation through the illogic of chance.

Montage in any form venerates contingency like no other cinematic form. At its most basic, montage is an edit. Any edit offers a gap in meaning; however, when done as a parallel edit and even more as multiple parallel edits with no establishing shots, reverse shots or chase shots, it creates an obvious fissure through its contingent narrative incoherence. It is thus seen and noted by the viewer, through its incongruity. In other words parallel editing makes explicit what is usually merely implicit – the passage of time and the traversing of place – but the extreme and repetitive parallel edit both marks and confounds an acceptable bridging of time and place. Through making the jumps explicit and incongruous to viewers' expectations of narrative, filmmaking highlights the ways in which our sense of reality can so easily be undone by cinema. A form of parallel editing in extremis not only undoes a sense of reality through playing with time in unusual ways but throws questions of stability back onto the subject who cannot orientate themselves through it in ways that I will further explore through the examples that follow. So the form of parallel editing that I will be looking at propagates incoherence or what could be called undecidability in the viewer. I propose that in the dearth of precursors to what might be an aesthetic language forged by women, incoherence may be a strategic step towards finding new language. In incoherence it may be, as I suggested with the band The Slits at the beginning of this chapter, a proto-language that accounts for women trying to find a sense of self unfettered by the patriarchal expectations of the old femininities. In turn this represents a renegotiation of what seems to be the legacies of an aesthetic language that was born, fostered and given meaning through patriarchal interpretive systems. Instead of a proscriptive embargo on self-representation, a propositional incoherent formation can amplify the distracted gaze, so revealing both the operations of patriarchy and capitalism. 'When significant components of reality become invisible in our world, art must make do with what is left, for an aesthetic presentation is all the more real the less it dispenses with the reality outside of the aesthetic sphere' (Kracauer 1995: 79),

If Kracauer argues that film offers a distracted gaze that reveals the operations of capitalism – and Paul Virilio suggests that contingency is now built into the operations of capitalism – what does it mean to offer the distracted gaze itself in its incoherence as in itself integral to the operations of a film or, even more, as integral to the agency of a viewer rather than presenting it as a problem for the viewer: an absurdist – and dialectical – manoeuvre? One might suggest that Guy Debord's film *The Society of the Spectacle* (1974) does just this and in some ways it does. However, I am proposing the films in this book as distinct.

The films I am proposing do not bury the tension between desire and anxiety by aiming to excise all desire from the spectator's vision but by embracing that tension. This framework of distraction and incoherence does not berate the viewer by repeatedly suggesting the viewer is part of the problem and distinguishing the 'ignorant' viewer from the artist who exists in this schema as the problem solver: the construct offered by Debord through his objective to save us from capitalism through his art. While Debord offers fragmentation as in the service of capitalism stating that 'fragmented views of reality regroup themselves into a new unity as a separate *pseudoworld*' (1994: 10), I would argue that artists such as Novaczek and Child are inviting the viewer to reframe the world offering alternatives through agency, not as spectacle but as affect. A *pseudoworld* it may be – a strategic and temporary interim holding position, but Novaczek and Child are not offering a new unity, for unity is an anathema to them; they are instead keeping the viewer enfolded within the fragmentation as a way of drawing them into the artists' own experience through the visibility of the awkward jump cuts suturing different modes of address. Different spaces and time together also give rise to a rupture that lends agency even within the experiential that these films engender. What I mean to say here is that the bringing together of the Brechtian rupture and the experiential through this mode of making the film enriches in a way that is both immersive and distancing at the same time. In his landmark film *Society of the Spectacle*, Debord offers an asymmetrical relationship between viewer and film. The position of the filmmaker as set up by the narration offers a critique of the world and a manifesto for the viewer to learn how the world works in the eyes of the artist/ filmmaker. This role of the artist as seer and teacher is in some ways akin to the criticism of Andy Warhol, in Chapter 1, who, while having a nuanced and deflationary approach to image-making, is still situating himself as the one who knows, as opposed to the viewer, who learns: this is a conservative self-positioning derived from a positivist model, that of the narrator being the static and certain holder of knowledge despite the dialectically structured opposition between the image and text. Instead, the filmmakers I discuss here such as Abigail Child, Vivienne Dick or Bette Gordon make films as a channel for their own distracted subjectivity, offering their experience in humility, through the contingent form of parallel editing. In this way the works operate as a marker for the problems of capitalism while, at the same time, embracing the viewer through the celebration of the element of desire in the films.

The forms of art that I describe here are ones that constellate around the Brechtian debates of art and of critique. Brecht argued for a critical complexity that would make active agents of those interrogating the image and, by the same token, required an image construction that required its interrogation. The attenuated relationship with that aim has been in effect to excise desire from the logics and lexicon of art practice, as a force of alienation, as Laura Mulvey states: 'It is said that analysing pleasure destroys it ... that is the aim of this article' (Pollock 2003: 245, fn 55). Desire was the shadows on Plato's cave mesmerizing the public into the subjection of capitalism. In this scenario distanciation had become the orthodoxy for critical practices in the 1970s that intervened in the false consciousness of Plato's cave. This orthodoxy has evolved into artworks that could be seen as a mannered evolution of this orthodoxy. The prevalence of this methodological mode for critical lens-based practices is a testament to its hegemony in art schools, rather than the more complex yielding through sensuous knowledge the Frankfurt School advocated. This is the difference between the multi-sensory nature of a haptic vision that brings in the viewer's experience and celebrates the yielding that desire brings rather than the positivist all-seeing – i.e. godlike – nature of the enlightenment that requires the disinterestedness in the Kantian trajectory. What is at stake is the relationship between desire and the politics of situatedness, which in Brechtian terms are incompatible. What was taken up of Brecht was to do with the division between formal strategies such as fragmentation in order to interrogate the image that 'any revolutionary strategy must challenge the depiction of reality' as opposed to, say, fragmentation 'as juxtaposition of disparate elements to bring about emotional reverberations', which Claire Johnston sees as reactionary and merely propping up the ideological problems of patriarchy and capitalism (1979 in Thornham 1999: 37). She likens it to surrealist automatic writing, which she considers the ultimate logic of this intention, and merely romanticism, which will not 'provide for the tools to construct a women's cinema. Such a strategy would be recuperable by the dominant ideology: indeed in that it depends on emotionality and mystery, it invites the ideology .... Our objectification ... can only be overcome by developing the means to interrogate the male, bourgeois cinema' (Thornham 1999: 39–40). In sum, however, despite her seeming proscription on romanticism, she advocates an entryist approach:

> At this point in time, a strategy should be developed which embraces both the notion of films as a political tool and film as entertainment. For too long these have been regarded as two opposing poles with little common ground.

In order to counter our objectification in the cinema, our collective fantasies must be released: women's cinema must embody the working through of desire: such an objective demands the use of the entertainment film. Ideas derived from the entertainment film, then, should inform the political film, and political ideas should inform the entertainment cinema: a two-way process.

(1999: 39–40)

Desire can be seen in another way through the discussion of Miriam Hansen that Colin Perry identified (2016: 69). Through her interest in the Frankfurt School, Hansen brings the idea of experience and the 'oppositional counter publics' using her formulation of excluded audiences who 'mediate individual perception with social meaning' (Perry 2016: 70) and according to Perry allows the audience to navigate 'the shock of modernity' through desire. This thinking is a way of fusing the psychic with the social, and Perry draws this together by invoking some key British 1970s feminist films such as *Nightcleaners* (1975), *Riddles of the Sphinx* (1977) and *Song of the Shirt* (1979).

My own interpretation of the ways in which desire can function to navigate patriarchal modernity is through a different kind of disjunction than that which Perry draws from and that I foreground in part due to its elision in the British feminist canon as cited in the previous paragraph. Here I would like to describe how parallel editing and a heterogeneous, distracted viewer enables a new subject through desire. Mary Anne Doane states that 'parallel editing eroticises time, injects it with desire, expectation, anticipation and displaces the spectatorial time of viewing by contributing to the instruction of a "lived" imaginary temporality' (2003: 193).

Amplifying the desire injected into cinema through the vertigo of disjunction as described by Doane, desire, in a literal sense, is inhabited in a conscious way to upend dominant expectations, through the subject matter of personal relations with the world. This can be seen in *Liberty's Booty* (1980), where the subject is the relationship between prostitution and women's working conditions. The title implies that the liberty of women is at the cost of her dignity; however, the film complicates this through its devices and the multi-layering of heterogeneous experience bringing together the experience of sex workers, with McDonald's workers on strike for better working conditions, with friends out in the landscape, enjoying themselves.

The film opens with the artist Greer Langton sitting on a sofa. She handles a large cloth 'doll', a sculpture she has made, stuffed with several fabricated foetuses that she is prizing out of the doll's womb, while she describes the process of extricating them. After this task is completed Langton proceeds to hug this oversize, but not quite human-sized doll. This section is a surreal preface to what is essentially an experimental mockumentary drama. The moment with the doll both situates the rest of the film in the body and introduces the idea of the abject or absurdity of childbearing. It also acts as a foil to the function of the female body as receptacle for male desire, or male need. Through the abject strangeness it critiques the ubiquitous association between woman, the body and motherhood. Given the title of the film and its subject matter – that of prostitution – it also speaks to the notion of the lost object of desire in human relations.

Using the preface of the doll as a kind of *ostranenie*, it also offers an antimony to the kinds of womanhood presented in the rest of the film. The tempo then shifts to the filming of a biker through the streets of New York with the sound of a rock and roll song called *B Gas Rickshaw* by a band whom Dick knew, called The Raybeats. The first short scene after the credits zooms in on a woman's face, in colour, wearing sunglasses. It zooms out in black and white to the same woman sitting in a lower east side apartment with some musical fragments from the 1960s in the background. This cuts to a shot of a woman – we do not see who she is as the shot is from the neck down – panning down to the woman's crossed legs, in pink leggings, sitting on a red sofa, the edge of the frame is at her neck, brutally cutting off her head. This is an unusual shot which would normally be a head shot with the feet off frame instead of the leg and body shot with the head off frame. A woman's voice is narrating – possibly the woman sitting – the choices of becoming a sex worker; she says, 'most people, if it comes to not having any money and having money or having very limited amount will choose doing something they never thought they'd do'. The depersonalization of the person talking with their head out of frame adds to the estrangement that is further bolstered by the music and the camerawork. The camera is hovering around her disembodied voice and fragmented body, slowly roving around the room, moving its focus to a retro, kitsch lampshade, 1960s glasses, pictures: every object is particular, is trashy, but voluptuous and excessive. The environment that the woman talking inhabits is bold in colour and the materials glossy. There is an intimacy to the close-up and a texture to the image. The visual gorgeousness of the red sofa, against the pink leggings of the woman and black of the walls of the room, highlights the tension in the voice, the anxiety in the camera movement; the voice and the fragmentation of the body are juxtaposed with the desirability of the rich pinks and oranges in this passage. The objects filmed are also objects of desire and excess: a cocktail glass with silhouettes of naked women as decoration, a lamp with a silver glitter-covered platformed sandal on the base, a leopard skin covered chair. The film then cuts to a very different scene, in black and white, of women in an apartment talking about how they would furnish it. Then again the camera returns to a bedroom with 1950s classics playing on the portable record player, and in colour, back to the roving scrutinization of interior space, 'retro' objects on a dressing table, a record player and an unmade futon. Songs play, again some Motown which, even then in the 1970s was a cool retro, followed by some MOD music, also retro, in their interrupted succession. Halfway through the third song, the scene abruptly cuts to an apartment, that is a brothel, with a woman speaking to a client on the phone introducing the 'girls' and their prices, 'a rate of fifty dollars for the half hour, eighty dollars for the hour'. And on it goes. While there is some overarching presentation of narrative, it is continually undermined by the disconnected and inexplicable links between scenes that burst into the narrative. There is an accumulative effect of being on the edge of chaos that is the result of a sustained set of sequences that do not fit. Although this could be said to be an extreme version of Brecht's distanciation, it is so absolute that it defies that explanation, particularly through the visual excess of the imagery generally both in terms of the visual imagery being for the most part inexplicable in relation to the narrative and also to do with the inexplicability of the relationship between scenes. Although the film attempts to ground the viewer in the material conditions of sex workers, it is not to do with a rationalist approach to the politics of the situation but more to do with being swept along with it. Contrary to Brecht there is no structural spine to situate the subject, just an ongoing heterogeneous interruption of experience that undermines the division of major and minor narrative to discombobulate the viewer.

In all these films there is an ethics of embodiment, albeit estranged and alienated through patriarchy and capitalism. There is also a belief in the redemptive tension between the body, the world, politics and the intensity of relationships. All the films deal with desire and the anxiety, existential and political, of being a woman in the particular world in which the artists find themselves. The social construction of the artist and also the material conditions of living are entwined with an excessive love of the image which both distances and pulls the viewer in. So, while fulfilment is always thwarted in the text, the image is full of desire that is not undercut or excised but, in fact, is amplified by the excesses of parallel editing. One example is the famous scene in *Liberty's Booty* where a group of women sex workers are eating in a McDonald's – the women desiring food, the women as objects of men's desire in their profession as sex workers – and the voiceover comes into the film of the Irish workers at McDonald's who strike for decent working conditions – desire for a decent living wage – describing the event of the strike. The effect on the viewer is of different forms of need and desire colliding in one space.

In a later sequence the analogies of desire are reversed: some of the women acting as sex workers are filmed walking in the hills of Bun Glas in Donegal, Ireland.[7] The wind is blowing in their hair and they are wearing functional clothing for the wind and cold. The soundtrack at this point is The Doors' *She's Not There*. This is a moment of liberation – the air and the space so different to the claustrophobia of the lower east side walk up that was the brothel, with all the women waiting for men. Suddenly into this moment comes the voiceover of a woman describing what she will do for men, over the song in the background with the vista of Ireland in the shot. Again, one reality interrupts another in this parallel shot. In the spaces between these shots and soundtracks a woman may have the space to ruminate on difference, but as Doane states, 'the gap between shots mimics the gap constitutive of desire' (2003: 194). Thus reason, as taken from Brecht, and desire, as taken from Doane, are constitutive of one another in the invisibility of the space between shots that is opened up by parallel editing.

So, if incoherence reveals the distractedness of cinema through disassociation that 'allows us to see how the unconscious moves between memory and perception, between affects and language and between the individual and society' (Campbell 2007: 134),[8] it is in the traversing of these different states that agency is derived from a film. These states are to do with traversing being and doing, as well as thinking and feeling. The oscillation between being and doing, between these states of certainty, between embodiment and disassociation is an hysterical retreat that happens when one cannot square the circle. When your only language is the language of patriarchy – the Law of the Father – that unwittingly – arguably – excises the woman, you need to find a new language of how to be a woman, even in its very impossibility. Impossible because we cannot truly go back to an unsymbolized moment. Maybe, as Kristeva believes, 'we can change the social structure by changing representation' (Oliver 1993: 103) and women can embrace the symbolic in their own way, by forging a new form of representation through parallel editing. If this produces an hysterical space, it is an hysteria that is, in film, a strategic essentialism that will in time give way to a new language of female écriture.[9]

'When I began making *Petit Mal*, I was trying to understand my and other women artists' place in society and in the world' (Siegel 2020: 80). Betzy Bromberg made a series of three films in New York in the 1970s that she now refers to as a trilogy, although it may not have been intended so in the making. There is a loose connection in terms of the backdrop of New York, often the East Village and desire. The first film, *Petit Mal* (1977), is ostensibly about the tensions in a relationship between the woman who narrates and considers herself to be a feminist and the boyfriend's expectations of her, although it is ultimately about the tensions that women, especially young women, felt at that time – the gap between their feminist views and society's expectations of them. The second film, *Ciao Bella or Fuck Me Dead* (1978), describes itself as a love story in three parts, and the final film, *Soothing the Bruise* (1980), is a longer film that intersperses the politics of oil, masculinity and again, desire. What brings these films into a close dialogue is not only the preoccupation with life on the street, in the apartment, of love and the desired subject but also their treatment in the film, formally and stylistically. Each film is constituted through fast edits and jump cuts that are soundscapes through cult songs. Although the artists did not know each other, the editing style of these early Bromberg films are not unlike others of her generation making work in New York and London such as Vivienne Dick, Sandra Lahire and Ruth Novaczek. The love of seduction of the image and the abstraction of constant interruption are ever present in all, as is the manipulation of the documentary form to unashamedly tell an incoherent story of a life lived in the moment. *Ciao Bella* opens for example with a black-and-white image of a washing line over a yard in the lower east side of New York, the washing swaying in the breeze. The view is from the sixth floor of a room in the Hell's Angels' Clubhouse in New York.[10] Over this shot is the voice of a man shouting, 'So I don't give a fuck, you know, I'm doing alright now. Some day I might need some bread, I'll ask you for it, you know, and I told him someday might not never come pal' and we hear a woman's voice laughing in response. The film then cuts to a photograph of a biker sitting on his bike with a woman's voice stating, 'then all the Angels gathered 'round and they each took turns throwing dirt on the grave'. After the opening titles the establishing shots are in a club, women are serving in the bar, probably the topless bar Bromberg herself worked in, The Fiddle and Bow in Queens, New York. Bromberg herself is behind the bar. The disco is playing and we see a mixture of women dancing behind the bar, pouring drinks. This is all shot in situ, some in colour and some in black and white. The images are dark and fuzzy. Despite the early shots in the bar, the film is constructed through seeming non-sequiturs and interruptions. It is ostensibly a story of a relationship embedded in a life's moment. From the bar the film suddenly cuts, using a jump cut, to a momentary shot of a woman walking away on the sidewalk, then an elderly woman in daylight in the street, standing by a parked car showing a photograph, seemingly of her younger self, then a series of reverse zooms of a group of women sitting on rocks beside the sea, then back to the woman with the photo and the woman walking away, back and forth between these shots – all the while another male voiceover talking about the acidity of orange juice. A few moments later we see a woman, topless, at home, absorbed in putting on a skirt, intercut with a sweaty female naked dancer working in the club. There is a conscious contrast between the self-absorption of the woman putting on her skirt in a matter-of-fact way, in front of a mirror, without parading her body, despite the viewer's gaze, and the flash of the gyrating woman dancing sexily to the notional hungry gaze of the assumed, off-camera male looks. The film alternates between footage of street scenes, club scenes and bikers and young women, building up a fast pace of jumps between these different disconnected sites, each beautiful moments in themselves with no explanation – just strands to be drawn together by the viewer. There are a series of black-and-white shots of a walk-up apartment, the street, views out of the window and more washing lines. A woman, again a voiceover, says, 'So one night I was working in the Fiddle, right. I quit. This is about the time I said fuck it. Fuck everything ok. And it was the week of note and I said Fuck everything as soon as I start up with JC'. At one point we see a cat, filmed in muted colour with an echo laid over the meow adding an air of menace. About six minutes in after a poignant stretch of the Brian Eno song *By The River* over shots of Manhattan's east river, a woman states over the grainy colour shots of one of the club dancers: 'This is not a love letter, it's a wolf ticket'. A snake appears and a screeching sound is introduced over the colour footage of a woman dancing in the club; central to the frame is her gyrating topless body. The camera zooms into the crotch. That scene is then intercut with a shot of a man and a boy in an apartment. The man is washing the boy's ears with a flannel and then we again see a snake slinking around a pole against a gold backdrop, the same shot as at the beginning of the film. As earlier in the film the edits ricochet between a series of shots of the dancing woman, the man and boy in the apartment, the snake and the man driving away on his bike. The end of the film is near and the camera pans the apartment in a wistful sweep, with a woman's voice explaining how 'he's

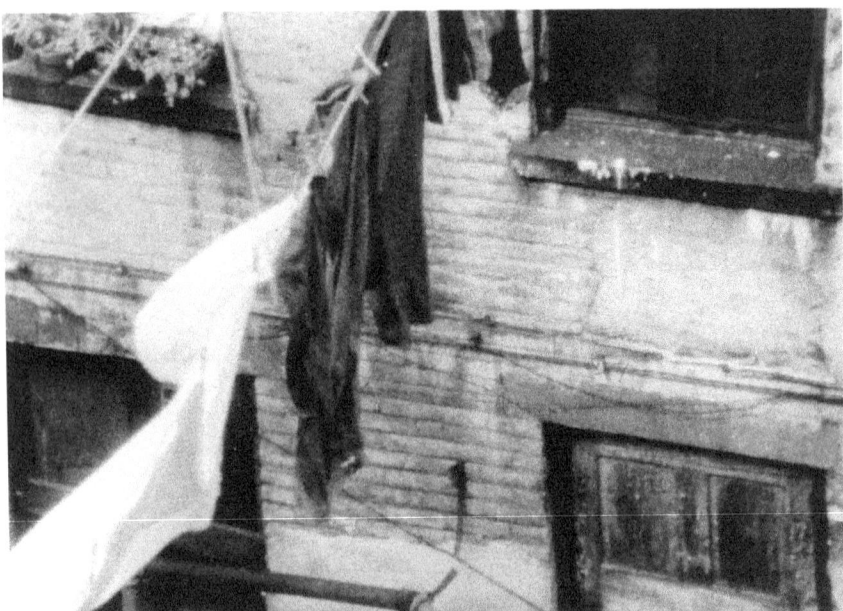

Figure 37. *Ciao Bella or Fuck Me Dead* (1978, Betzy Bromberg), frame enlargement. Courtesy of the artist.

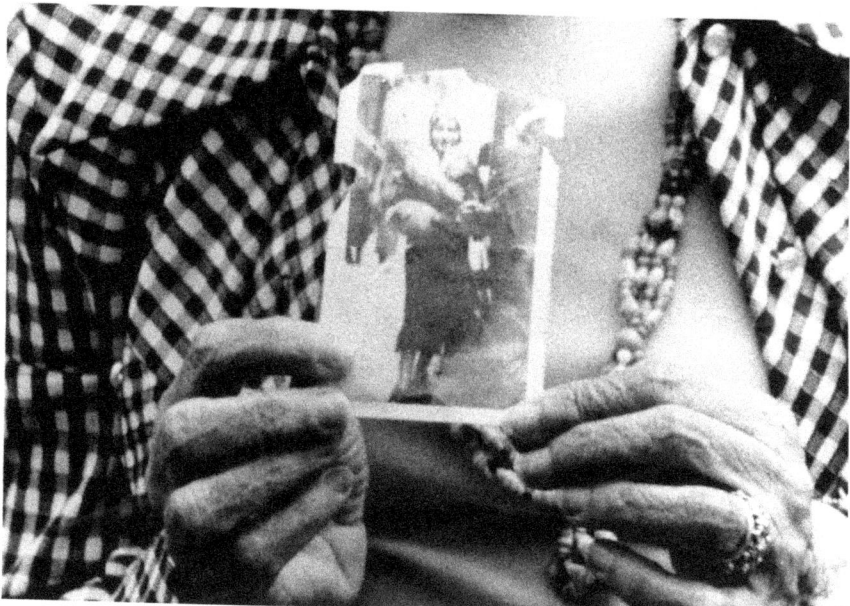

Figure 38. *Ciao Bella or Fuck Me Dead* (1978, Betzy Bromberg), frame enlargement. Courtesy of the artist.

gone and dead'. There is another abrupt cut to a shot of a woman's face – and finally the disco song 'It's so hot, hot, I'm burning up, up' is playing to the final image of the same shot of the woman we saw dancing earlier, naked except for panties, squatting down, feeling her breasts then clutching her crotch while jumping up and down. This film, like the others in the Bromberg trilogy, builds the sense of a lived relationship to a moment in the life of a woman. It shows details without filling in the circumstantial narrative, which is left to our imagination. The desire to know what is going on is thwarted, but instead, the gaps are important in delivering an impression rather than a story, grounded in experience as lived relationships with all its range, from the day-to-day love to the alienated fantasy of unfettered libidinous freedom in the go-go club. In this film both situations are fantasies and both grounded in real life.

So desire is also inhabited in terms of the methodology through parallel editing that puts to the fore an experiential understanding of the world, in its lack of linearity and without the safety net of an obvious forward-thrusting narrative drive. Each of these instances described situates the women differently and establishes a life of disconnectedness and distraction. The lack of connection is only countered by the viewer's insistent desire to make connections. It is difficult to work out which aspect of this heterogeneous vision is the primary driver of the narrative, such as it is. In the swirl of images, however, are beauty, visual excess and pleasure.

To use parallel editing routinely as the main form in work is to reject the notion of a totalizing gaze, a singular vision of the world or a reasoned argument. This does not even offer an incommensurate argument in the way that the essay film often claims to: it goes further. This kind of work, while not being incoherent even while the intention of the artist may be coherent, does not ever entirely cohere and gives up ownership of meaning. In its 'flood of images … apparent staging of oppositions, repetitive reproduction versus endlessness' (Harbord 2007a: 94) it is the absolute antinomy of the long look that champions a singular minimalist vision. The long look hopes to find the real through the intensity of the gaze that is normally missed in the speed of real life. Parallel editing finds the real in the speed of life.

This is also another way in which the deflationary is at work: despite the claims of finding more in the long take, the knowingness of slowing down the image sets up its own hierarchy between the artist and viewer as the artist here becomes the seer, offering a secret mystery that only they can reveal. By contrast, parallel editing offers no claims to an authentic or singular truth in the gaze of the lens, instead a constant set of questions posed by juxtapositions that do not make external sense but yet build up into an experiential imposition. In some ways similar to the dialectical shock discussed by the Frankfurt School, parallel editing, however, does not transform in quite the same way. It does not wake us up to the problem of what to do to make a better world. New deductions – as per the dialectic – are not made; instead, it puts the spectator in the position of dissociative undecidability through the 'flood' of images that sweep away the 'dams of memory' (Harbord 2007a: 94). This notion of the dissociative is one that repeats again and again in so many of the films discussed, not only in the interplay of genre but also in the juxtaposition of seemingly random images or transitions of direct visual imagery – from the bright oversaturated yellow flowers in *Uranium Hex* (1987) or the dance of the frighteningly thin semi-clothed body in *Terminals* (1986), both made by Sandra Lahire, to the fast pacing of montage in Ruth Novaczek's *Tea Leaf* (1988) and *Cheap Philosophy* (1992), to the non-sequiturs in *London Suite (Getting Sucked In)* (1990); the list could go on and on. From this range I will give some in-depth examples to draw out more nuance on the issue of disassociation. Each of these artists emerged out of a structuralist approach but embraced a punk aesthetic: Bette Gordon, Anne Robinson and Abigail Child. Each of these artists offers a different take on this tendency, beginning with *Empty Suitcases* by Bette Gordon.

Bette Gordon taught at the University of Wisconsin-Madison, working at times with James Benning, an experimental filmmaker, known for his structuralist films, who also taught in the film department. In 1979 Gordon moved to New York, where she made *Empty Suitcases* in 1980. Earlier films such as *Exchanges* (1979) or *Still Life* (1975) consisted of repetitious reframing of film forms and materials. In these early films the attention to the changes of colour and form through the repetitions of the film time and spatial arrangements – through optical printing which created repetitions and overlaps – were engaging and accomplished. By contrast, while the previous films were abstracted and non-narrative – or semi-narrative (from Gordon to author, 15 February 2021) – in construction, *Empty Suitcases* sets up a narrative form in the shooting only to unravel the expectations that are introduced, through a series of dissociative layers sutured together with black space between each scene. Gordon's trajectory was from structuralism towards mainstream film. However, somewhere between these two ends of filmmaking, when she first moved to New York, her work begins to sit within the framework of AV Punk. Films like *Anybody's Woman* (1981) have a slacker vibe, with some insertions that stand out. In some ways it echoes Vivienne Dick's *Liberty's Booty* (1980) or Tessa Hughes-Freeland's shorter *Baby Doll* (1982) in subject matter and also in approach. However, *Empty Suitcases* (1980) is a work that particularly stands out through its range of disjointed motifs.

Empty Suitcases (1980) is a film with a loose narrative of a woman who cannot choose between her life in New York and her life in the mid-west. Even this nomadic indecision is prescient of today,[11] although in this film it appears without aim or context. The film opens with an operator's recorded voice repeating the departure times of Pan Am airline flights from a phone recording, while the image is of the Hudson river. In the film there is a further unexplained parallel narrative that speaks to the epoch of its making and acts as a scenic backdrop of nuclear threat and armed militant activism. This is again a voiceover account over fixed shot scenes of downbeat Manhattan that continue for five minutes – then a photograph of a woman with a suitcase followed by a scene of her packing the suitcase and then footage of moving trains. These can be explained, albeit in their disjointed way. It is a narrative of sorts built up through self-contained but disjunctive vignettes. And like Bromberg's earlier *Ciao Bella*, these layers hold together, just about by the conditions of the processes of cinema itself which forces the viewer to continue looking in a linear way. As with any encounter, the brain tries to form patterns wherever it can. However, it is as if the connecting web of shots that would explain the narrative has been excised, leaving the viewer to make any connections they can with this fragmented information – reminiscent of Abigail Child when she says, 'I had long conceived of a film composed only of reaction shots in which all causality was erased. The isolation and dramatisation of emotions through the isolation (camera) and dramatisation (editing) of gesture. What would be left would be the resonant voluptuous suggestion of history and the human face' (Sitney 2008: 256).

To cite one example, from *Empty Suitcases*, of a sequence that stands out above all in the film: this scene is of a fixed shot of Vivienne Dick's apartment, a walk-up on the lower east side. We can only see the windows, two windows that thus act as the facade. It takes place in the ninth street walk-up belonging to Vivienne Dick in the lower east side of New York.[12] Nan Goldin and Vivienne Dick repeatedly parade into the frame and out, always in time to the X-Ray Spex song *ART I FICIAL*. Goldin and Dick walk to the windows; one takes a picture of the other with a 35-mm camera. The other poses for the shot. They both walk towards the camera and out of shot again. Each time they come into the frame and pose beside the windows of the tenement apartment, they are wearing different clothes and they alternately take photos of the other. All the while the soundtrack *ART I FICIAL* is booming out. The scene starts at the beginning of the song and ends at the end of the song. The foregrounding of this visual motif through the song itself enhances the estrangement of this scene. One could surmise, for example, that it is all about location and a supposition of what the character might do in New York. However, this is such a stylized operation that cannot assimilate within the language of the rest of the film or the expectations that have been set up previously. There is no explanation within the film as to why this is happening, and the shift in language and setting at both ends of the sequence makes it stand out as a moment outside the film. Towards the end of the film a rationale of sorts is manufactured when these photos taken earlier in the film are presented as a sequence of black-and-white stills. There is no explanation within the film about what this sequence or its sequel is. It is a denouement of sorts, one of memory for the character and the passage of time in one's life – a stand-out moment – or it could merely allude to the affect of different materialities. One may assume that this sequence and its later evidence imply a social

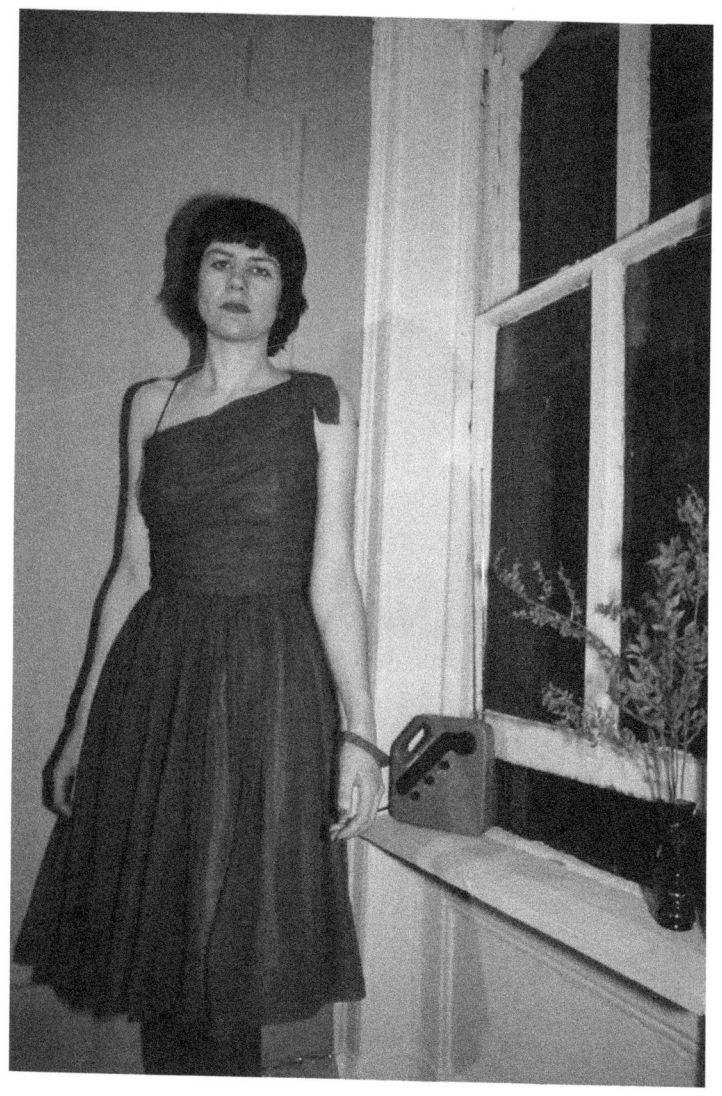

Figure 39. Vivienne Dick in *Empty Suitcases* (1980, Bette Gordon). Courtesy of Nan Goldin.

milieu in New York, left behind when the protagonist went back to live in the mid-west. However, no explanation exists within the logic of the film for the shift in the cinematic language, across a range of cinematic registers. It is as if the essay form has been stretched, leaving the gaps wider so that the narrative voice cannot explain the gaps nor offer a coherence or meaningful explanation.

Another example of the withdrawal from an associative vision is Anne Robinson's *Corridors* (1986). This is a film that in some ways draws from structuralist films. The repetitive abstractions and use of colour lend a look of those processes and methodology of the previous generation who taught her, but offer a counterpoint to some of the more robustly structuralist tendencies. In this way it can be brought into dialogue with, say, some of the work of Lis Rhodes, which has an experiential effect in the viewing, such as *Light Music* (1975) or *Dresden Dynamo* (1971). Similar to Rhodes' work from the 1980s that drifted away from the earlier purity of methodology, *Corridors* has references within the film that lay clearly outside of the film itself and through the subjectivity of women. It explores the life lived of the artist and her milieu. The difference between the two may be to do with the focus on formal finesse and visual relationships that are by intention less coherent in Robinson's work. *Corridors* is a two-screened film shot on super 8 and then edited on analogue, low-band U-Matic edit suite. All of the still/text material was made by silkscreen printing, and the process darkroom work for these images involved use of super 8 film stills and film strips slightly moving images in some cases, which are combined in the proofs with drawings, text etc. The prints were re-photographed and fragmented to vary image-viewing distance at the later stage of remaking this two-screen, digital version of the installation.[13] There are four sections titled *Love, Work, Money* and *Fear*. Robinson herself describes it as 'moving in and out of consciousness in saturated colour'.[14] The right-hand panel is an ongoing abstract formation of colour rectangles derived directly from the screen prints in bright-reds, blues and browns that continues throughout and inevitably impacts on the sister panel. The left-hand panel is filmed and distorted. The first section begins with a corridor in the first chapter, distorted and fuzzy. It is entitled *Fear* and is intensely claustrophobic. Definitions and pronouncements of the state of agoraphobia waft in, as narrations intervening into the sound from time to time.

Sometimes some snippets from Deleuze and Guattari's *Anti-Oedipus* (1972) form part of this narrated disjointed insertion. The intensity of the ongoing sound was made by synthesizing a response from looking at the film itself and then remixed. The second section, entitled *Work*, consists of a repetitive shot of a floor being mopped to the sounds of a vacuum cleaner. The third section, *Money*, is constructed through the sounds of a cash machine in a supermarket and a woman climbing up a drainpipe. The sound here is insistent through the high-pitched noise of the punching of the keys in this now-defunct piece of supermarket machinery. The final section, *Love*, has a very different feel, and depicts two women, joshing and kissing against the wall of a building, with an eerie over-echoed *a capella* rendition sung by Viv Acious of *Me and My Gal* in a clearly identified working-class London accent. The whole film is constructed around a mix of normally incompatible languages and formed through the splitting between the abstract imaging of the screen prints on one panel and the filmed 'documentary' imagery on the other, presented side by side. 'I would maybe say a way of using altered technologies – "queered" film technologies to create a sense of distanced perception.'[15]

The disassociation here arises from the mix of abstraction and everyday images on a dual screen – itself a dissociative mechanism. There is category breakdown of imagery even while there is an imposed taxonomy of 'fear', 'work' 'money', 'love'. Each category is dealt with in broadly the same way of splitting, abstraction and noise. Robinson's formal device fuses the universal experience of women with the specificity of particular subjectivities but does not fill in any gaps with regard to character or subject. Instead, this is the work imposed on

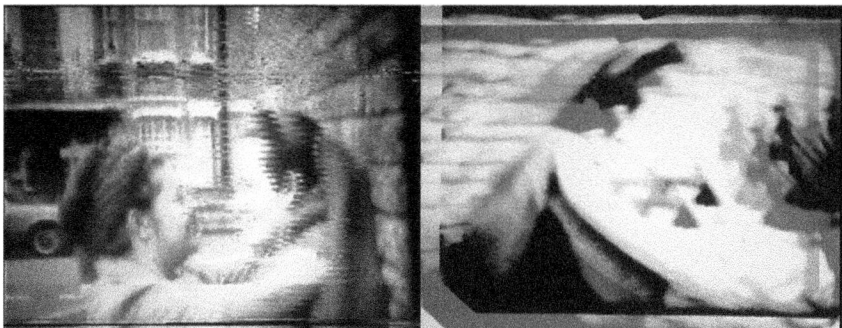

Figure 40. *Corridors* (1986, Anne Robinson). Courtesy of the artist.

the viewer: 'disassociation is also a creative movement of contingent time which moves between the conscious and the unconscious ... connecting defensive dualisms between life and death, memory and perception and transforming anxiety into a new experience with the object' (Campbell 2007: 137).

Both Bette Gordon and Anne Robinson, each in their own way, worked through structuralist film to reverse out of it, commenting on the materiality of film towards a sensorial exploration of subjectivity. One can almost work up a dialectic gloss in looking at the work that incorporates some of the look of structuralism without any embargo on the depiction and representation of the subject. While acknowledging the lessons of materialist film in terms of interruption and discombobulation of the viewer, what ensues is a rich, complex interface that defies the kind of narrative structures of stability while still holding on to the idea of an engagement with concrete concerns in the world.

Hysteria is to do with asking questions of the feminine, about being caught between being and doing where the association with being is toxic and requires disassociation which goes to the heart of being a woman in patriarchy. Patriarchy has prevented women from fully exploring what a woman can be and from knowing what a woman can be. I would propose that these films exemplify the struggle to find out what the possibilities might be. However, these films do not represent a refusal, as proposed by Judith Halberstam, of 'radical passivity' (2011: 140) or of sacrifice, but instead working with a myriad of possibilities, like multiple personalities held together only by the subject that cannot know itself.

Sandra Lahire would probably not recognize that definition of her work which, on the face of it, is focused, political and utilizing documentary forms to publicize the atrocities perpetrated in the name of the nuclear industry. Yet her film *Uranium Hex* (1987), part of a loose series on this theme, fuses together the toxicity of uranium with the toxicity of the effects of patriarchy on the body. These different languages make sense only through the logic of the film itself by dint of this correlation being in the film. In many of her works, the body acts as a ghost emerging out of other imagery for a moment of reflection, to disappear again. Lahire overlays imagery to abstract, making space for an experiential and visceral relationship to the subject. Forms emerge and situations are hinted at. This film is no exception: it opens into darkness with only a hard-hat headlight shining out of the screen; grunge noises that imply factory sounds, abrasive to the ear, accompany the imagery of blackness with lights; hard-hats and pieces of machinery depicted in close-up out of the darkness, in movement. It is hard, when first viewing the film, to make out what the viewer is being shown here. It becomes apparent when after about twenty seconds, a head and shoulders shot of a woman from behind appears. The woman is in white overalls, giving a visibility and explanation to the previous shots. However, the imagery is interrupted the whole time with an overlay of an orange light rotating as from the local fire department rescue truck. Then we have the coming together of the imagery of the lights with the sound of a police vehicle that fills the screen, giving way to a woman in white overalls on hands and knees and the title credit *Uranium Hex*. The film, for the most part, is shot in close-up, in the mines, going down the shaft and in the lift, also drilling. The imagery alternates between negativized and close-up that creates an effect of colour saturation and slo-mo documentary footage of diggers and drilling repeated for effect. Incidental sound and incidental conversation pass through the work, sometimes floating, as in the dialogue such as 'the only thing that frightens me about going down into the underground is going down in the cage', which enriches the incidental emergent imagery that floats in and out of the blackness. Sometimes the sound is abrasive and intrusive, when it is drilling and industrial sounds. Lahire uses the incidental lighting of the helmets, vehicles and mineshaft as a heightened eerie contrast to the blackness. Montage is used to great effect here. Suddenly a young girl's voice sings 'in a cabin, in a canyon, excavating for a mine … ' from the famous folk song *Clementine* over yellow-tinted footage, then purple-tinted footage with abrasive machinery sounds, followed by a voiceover of a woman stating, for example, 'on average one uranium miner gets killed a month by cavings' with the next shot of a yellow-tinted helmeted man over purple-tinted machinery all emerging out of blackness. We are two minutes in and so far there is no establishment or shots that give explanations of what is being looked at. At three minutes and twenty seconds in, a woman's back comes into the shot – a back of extreme thinness, with ribs and spine sticking out. It is the back of the filmmaker one might assume, who battled against anorexia most of her life, which was ultimately the cause of her premature death. This naked back shot filling the screen is then repeated several times in fairly close succession – introducing the notion of being an embodied being in this film about labour conditions – however, due to the thinness it is a body in struggle, an estranged body, not a body of desire.[16] Another such moment of interruptive agency is further into the film at eight minutes and forty-three seconds when the camera pans over some trees and in an arch and down to a field of daisies. The yellow daisies fill the screen in a heightened moment of colour that is not constructed through the industrial or technological but through nature, in its particular formation of circles and curves. For a moment it is silent movement; then an industrial sound breaks the spell and the camera pans back over the trees into a jump cut back to the machinery. Later a connective moment of voiceover that explains the daisy shot: 'they are destroying the beauty of the country and everything else, even the drinking water'. However, the daisy shot and the back shots when viewed on a large screen are still a mesmeric intervention that takes the viewer out of the experience of mining and labour, for a brief moment, into another experience of being – the allusion to toxicity of the yellow daisies both shimmering and urgent in their yellowness and the emaciated back with the prominently knobbled spine that also becomes the end shot.

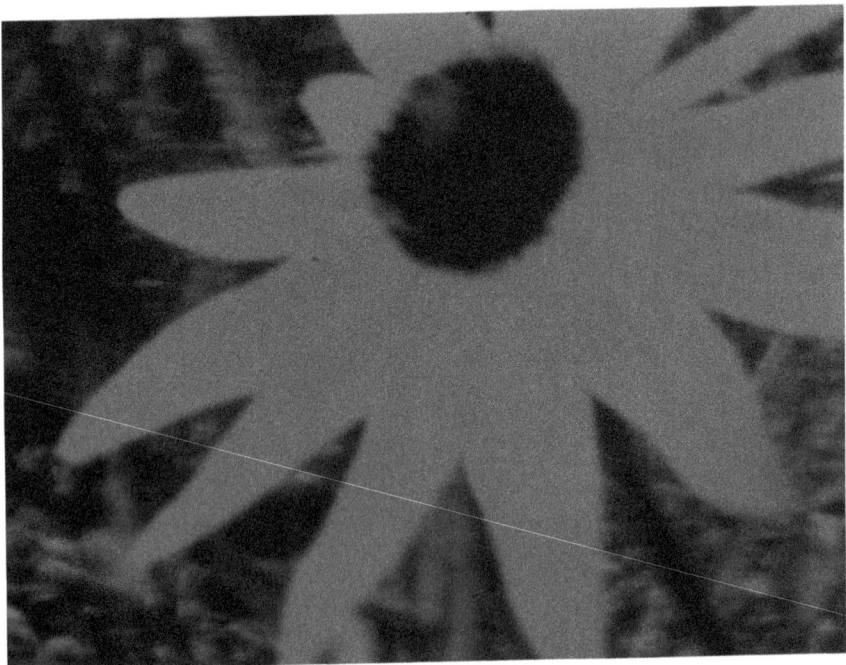

Figure 41. *Uranium Hex* (1987, Sandra Lahire). Courtesy of Sandra Lahire and LUX, London.

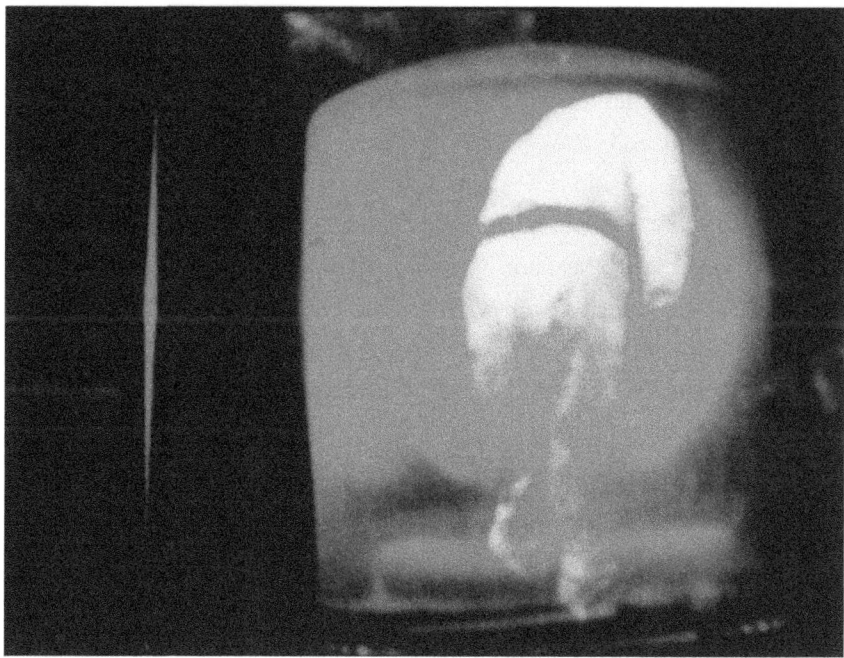

Figure 42. *Uranium Hex* (1987, Sandra Lahire). Courtesy of Sandra Lahire and LUX, London.

Impurity is the nodal point of all the works. These films thrive on erasing and repositioning while at the same time affirming categories through juxtaposition, and heterogeneous clashes within a film. The original impulse towards repetition and working the film that is a marker of experimental film continues. The repetition of structuralism that aimed to bring the viewer back to reality by demonstrating the materiality of the film instead becomes a marker of random contingency that sets out to dislocate, discombobulate and unnerve.

Erasing, repositioning as well as affirming is taken to the next level by Abigail Child, whose whole oeuvre has been marked by what Derek Bovier calls an 'ontologically impure approach' and of 'responding to a process of discontinuous synthesis' (2011: 9). In his analysis of Child's work, he continues that she 'undermines the logical structures of cinema from the inside, directly addressing the theatricality of film representation and the techniques of framing, lighting, staging and cutting shots' (2011: 9). It is this impurity of the film genre that is central to the idea of a language being formed through its very breakdown of coherence – of not squaring the circle.

Child's series *Is This What You Were Born For?*, as described in the previous chapter, is heterogeneous – the films working through several different genres – while within each film different methodologies are represented in her approach. Child, who trained in documentary practice, demonstrates above all the way in which the films in this book straddle the classic cinematic taxonomy of Kracauer between Méliès and the Lumière brothers, between fantasy or theatre and documentary, boldly rejecting even a semblance of orthodoxy or allegiance to any particular cinematic ethos. That Child writes poetry and makes collages adds to the notions of excess and intermediality, allowing for an experience where the visual world is accessible and useable in all its forms: everything is up for grabs in a non-hierarchical way – not only making meaning in new ways of clashing and heterogeneous references but being led by seemingly nonsensical imagery and connections that are tied to an emotional landscape of autobiography. Moreover, despite the linkage to autobiography, as I describe below with Abigail Child's more recent *The Suburban Trilogy* (2011), coherence is constantly challenged and the works move easily between genres and references within each work, as well as between the different films in the 2011 trilogy.

The progenitors Méliès and the Lumière Brothers represent signifiers of the movement between being and doing, between the imaginary (narrative) and the real (documentary) – or the virtual and the real – a place of hysterical dissociation in capitalism. These dichotomies are represented often as simple binaries. The films in this book, however, are attempting to bridge this dichotomy – while also acknowledging in the work itself, through its unreadability, its very unbridgeability – of the narrative and documentary as presented while also bridging the dichotomy between formalism and its elevation and the relegation of the personal and the domestic. Thus through the impossibility of this bridging, the feminine is rendered hysterical in capitalism, that is patriarchy as the site of trauma mired in the dissociative, of the state of being and the state of doing that the films have to re-visit again and again. What I would like to emphasize is the disjunction between what women are supposed to be interested in and what they often are – the imposition of patriarchal formalism as detached from subject matter. Alienated abstraction – distanced – can engender an hysterical disassociation. *The Suburban Trilogy* offers us a vision of what this might mean in cinematic terms.

The Suburban Trilogy, a twenty-first-century trilogy, is made of three films: *Cake and Steak* (2002) is the first, *The Future is Behind You* (2004) is the second and *Surf and Turf* (2011) is the third. The first, *Cake and Steak*, uses a mélange of found footage, shot by Child; the second uses black-and-white historical found footage from the 1930s, and the third is shot and filmed by the filmmaker as a documentary. The usage of found footage and sound which is brought together in a variety of ways forces an overarching reading within a wall of clashing and seemingly random associations which is set up by the first film but also sparks an uneasy relationship between these films that look like they were conceptualized separately but now stand as a trilogy. The device of incoherence through repetition, jump cuts, sound and image clashes confound legibility of the work in any other way than a visceral and affective accumulation.

Cake and Steak is a film that, according to Child, is about 'the education of the girl child'.[17] Of the three this film particularly, both in formal terms and within a narrative structural drive, is distinctive and performs, if not invents, a language where unintelligibility holds its own knowability. The film's structure and visuality posit making sense through nonsense that is nonetheless necessarily tied to the signifiers of the family, unlike Dada, which is a nonsense of floating signifiers. The proposition here is that there is no sense to the coherence of the world presented for a girl except that it is constructed by the world she inhabits. Outside of that world it makes no sense. The film opens with a dual-screen repetition of shot footage of fragments of suburban buildings – trees, houses, hedges, walls, garages and a film noir soundtrack. The footage presents a doubling with a vertical line down the middle. Using a device of *ostranenie*, what would normally be the establishing shot, sets up an irreconcilability through the vertical doubling: normality is put on the back foot. The cinematic language is not unlike Warren Sonbert, whose films were of everyday footage with seemingly no connective tissue beyond the circle of daily experience. However, Child's footage, at least in *Cake and Steak*, is worked up, repeated, pulled close up, stretched and rendered abstract, albeit anchored through words that appear on occasion throughout the film. These are the words of girl training, such as Kleenex, deodorant, Jewish Rye Bread. The film moves from these suburban shots to a repeated pan of a café looking over San Francisco Bay. The camera is fixed on the daylight outside, rendering the people inside in silhouette, gestures repeated, again rendering everyone strange and the sound moves to an advert, repeating the word 'discontinued' again and again. The film moves through different stages of a girl's life – starting in chapter two with footage from a girl's confirmation, intercut with a fairground big wheel and related sound of 'God had his angels all around her' repeated again and again in fragmented sections of the phrase at times as well as the whole phrase at times, in the same absurdist way as the previous found sound. There is also degraded footage interspersed. Over one of the instances of the degraded, grisailled footage are the words 'good girl', drawing a contrast between the normality of life and the expectations of a young woman that sucks the life out of her. Then follows the word 'tomboy' over the girls in their white wedding frocks of confirmation. Then 'second best friend'. The repetition of the children builds up into shorter and shorter sections, with sound reverberating through its aural repetitions to a crescendo of abstracted montage with the words 'nanny', 'maid', 'au pair' and 'help' appearing in succession over the montage of children from this bygone post-war age. Then after the second section comes chapter four, a short chapter of a family assembling in the garden to lunch: close-ups of people moving in a front garden, women carrying bowls of food. Again, the

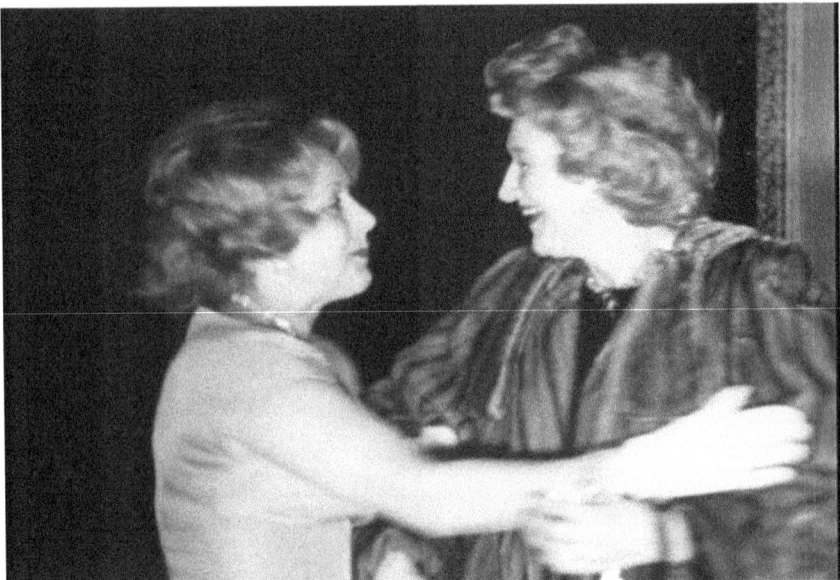

Figure 43. Two women from *Cake and Steak* (2004, Abigail Child). © Abigail Child.

words come in 'domestic', 'cook', 'princess'. For no apparent reason the numbers attributed to each section do not follow consecutively. There is a short section, followed by chapter seven of a girl practising her majorette moves in a garden, trebled, doubled, angled, slowed down and repeated. This is interspersed with the military parades of its probable emergence and a man in a checked jacket shooting off screen, children running around and a woman in a fur coat.

Chapter eight contains a section where two women with perm hairdos in fur coats from the 1950s pass each other. Child repeats the footage so that they bob past again and again; it starts to look as if one woman is yanking the other across the screen. The frame zooms in so that only the heads are visible. The repetition speeds up, slows down and speeds up again, moving from a jaunty 1960s whistle of a pop song to a slower cinematic soundtrack as the image becomes more abstracted through scale and disintegration to extrapolate the humour in the movements and the ridiculousness of people. The word 'bombshell' comes on the screen; then 'baby doll', 'femme fatale', 'lolita' appear amid young teenagers practising ballroom dancing with each other. Between the ridiculous we then see the coercion, the interpellation that forms female

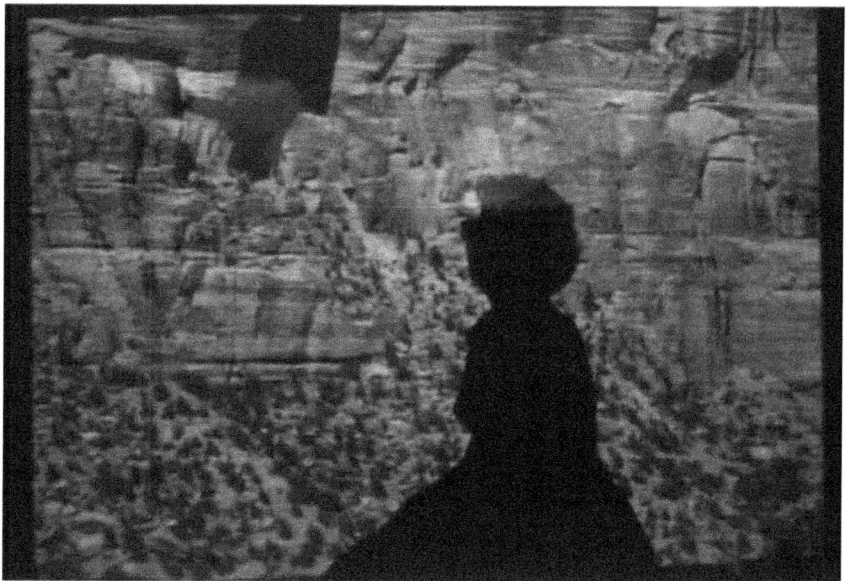

Figure 44. Woman silhouette from *Cake and Steak* (2004, Abigail Child). © Abigail Child.

subjectivity and behaviour, ridiculous and ridiculed without the context that situates the sympathy of the viewer. On and on it goes, footage of swimming pools, and bathers, playgrounds and mad domestic dogs running distractedly to the sound of ping pong balls. The usual episodic divisions break up the seemingly random structural devices into bitesize pieces that have a dream-like quality while being anchored in the everyday documentary. The images bombard the senses as analogous to the way in which imagery bombards in daily life, through one's life.

Cake and Steak is an exemplar of what Jan Campbell suggests is Kracauer's account of dissociation as a 'notion of distracted experience as both hysterical dissociation and a more embodied and historical active dreaming' (Campbell 2007: 133). What is at stake here is, as Campbell describes, 'placing dissociation rather than repression as the centre; mechanism of the psyche allows us to see how the unconscious moves between memory and perception, between affects and a language and between the individual and society' (134). What these films do is foreground this tendency within film and, in so doing, help us accept those interstices as the building blocks towards agency, not through a rationalist approach but through an experiential one that seizes on contingency and elevates the seeming but not actual randomness of the unconscious as its own drive towards agency.

Although Kracauer was clearly thinking not about art films but about the Tiller Girl musicals of the 1930s in his thinking of the mass ornament, I would argue that punk film deals with the everyday experience of life in its deflations and desires analogous to the popular culture that Kracauer wrote about. He was not so interested in the primacy of the aesthetic of the image that is often the focus and preoccupation in writing about artists' film – in fact, he did not particularly like film that was art any more than photography that was art. His interests were to do with popular culture, capitalism and the masses. In some ways the point of the *Mass Ornament* for Kracauer was the way it described film's propensity to ignore the interior life of the women – showing it as a lack of interiority. The aim was to read the way the surface look tells us about the interior workings of society, through its superficial formations – not to tell us of the timeless needs of the individual. The films described in this chapter also tell the viewer about interiority through a focus on the superficial workings of the world and their cultural formations. While noting that the film is made by a woman, we do not need to hear the woman speak as the filmmaker uses the mechanisms of her formation to speak through her in the juxtapositions, the devices and the very radical disjunctions that create the discombobulating effect through the disjunctive core of the films.

If we take it that the focus on the machine-ing of the body through its surface in the mass ornament is hysterical, it is so in the subsumption of the human into a nonverbal entity and an interiority that has no visibility but performs instead as a cipher. Punk film operates through a collapse of interiority in the very moment of its presentation. When a conscious interiority is presented it is deflationary. As well as *Cake and Steak*, this can be seen in other examples such as *Cheap Philosophy* (1992) by Ruth Novaczek and *Anybody's Woman* (1981) by Bette Gordon. In *Cheap Philosophy* (1992), it is through an ironic gesture. The self-deprecating humour and ironic title are part of a visual language where there is no self beyond the very propositions of self and where none of these selves are believed or believable. Novaczek in *Cheap Philosophy* (1992) offers a kind of hypervisibility masking the lack of selfhood beneath – or the fear of lack below. All is constructed through the structures of representation and is critiqued not through a counter-text but through an over-identification, as Kracauer suggests: 'The mass ornament performs as a disguise as a kind of formulaic but hysterical masquerade' (Campbell 2007: 140).

Another expression of hysterical exteriority is Gordon's film *Anybody's Woman* (1981), which, as one example, has several passages where sexual acts are narrated as an extreme state of dispassion. In one, the woman spends five minutes – out of a sixteen-minute film – slowly and passionately narrating an intimate moment of sexual fulfilment to a man who is clearly bored, looking out of the window. After this extended moment of non-sexy sexual narration, the man asks the woman if she has paid the phone bill. When she responds in the negative, he leaves the café and walks off camera. According to Gordon the man cannot cope with her voicing her sexuality and being a strong, liberated woman (16 February 2021). She composes this scene in such a way that it appears to be a deflationary gesture which does not explain but merely presents. Gordon here exposes and highlights not what is at stake for the man and woman as particular individuals but the exchange value of marriage through its inversion of a sexually vocal woman and a silent man, where the protagonists not only become ciphers but perform the disconnect: mass ornament is a legitimate mode of experience for people because it reflects the reality of the economic system, and is therefore more true than artistic productions 'which cultivate outdated noble sentiment in obsolete form' (Kracauer 1995: 79).

It seems that Abigail Child also follows this approach. In her book *Motive for Mayhem*, part theory, part prose, she states, 'It's the surface and the unassimilated parts that give us a grasp on the world. They provide the stage for our imagination and what the author can do with absolutely ordinary people' (1989: 8). Her films *Perils* (1986) and *Mayhem* (1987) are a case in point that uses the language of slapstick and noir, both classic Hollywood genres and popular forms. Child takes these outdated but popular forms and has fun with them. By taking the gestures and movements, she turns the genre signs into anachronistic ciphers: in her aim to make a film with just 'reaction shots' where 'all causality was erased' (1989: 11), she enters into the realm of the hysterical. In these works there is no way to develop a position as a viewer. None of the images can be held on to long enough to interrogate the logic of an argument and the connections across the images slip and slide. There is clearly something going on – and in this sense it is different from an abstract piece of work like Len Lye that creates an internal logic of shape and form – but with no clues as to why anyone is in the frame or what they are doing with the other protagonist. Some examples are images of startled faces and shadows looming, staccato sounds breaking through as non-sequiturs to the images that are brought together with sequences of a women sitting with her legs exposed, a telephone handset sat between her open thighs or of couples joshing. Through evocations of different genres, the emotions conjured are the same in both films where desire and fear are intertwined. However, without the signifying tropes that give meaning to gestures, the overall effect is of an absurdist lack of coherence. With merely ongoing sequences of reaction and movement, with no narrative, verbal exchange or connection between one shot or another, the films are both abstracted from life and distracted in terms of form. *Mayhem* plays with the drama of the tableau and abstracts the constellation of tension that is the hallmark of noir; *Perils*, in its narrative refusal, is abstract but wholly embedded in life by way of the stream of faces and bodies turned towards the camera, looking, entreating. It is a distracted gaze, however, that allows the viewer to reanimate their engagement with the world through it. The accumulation of this is that the viewer has to renounce rational understanding, instead giving herself to the flow of experience where she cannot place herself in any specific way. We can see the experience that Child delivers here described in Kracauer's introduction to the *Mass Ornament*: 'Here, in pure externality the audience encounters itself; its own reality is revealed in the fragmented sequence of splendid sense impressions. Were this reality to remain hidden from the viewers, they could neither attack nor change it; its disclosure in distraction is therefore of moral significance' (Kracauer 1995: 26).

Furthermore, whereas the classical Hollywood that Child draws from 'is a narrative mode which represses melodrama in a pre-Oedipal arena, as bodily textual excess' (Campbell 2004: 31), Child explores the 'bodily textual excess' as central to her oeuvre. By focusing on the outtake, the interstices rather than the narrative drive or characterization, she becomes focused on the body, in *Perils*, the glance, the look. In *Mayhem* it is the tableau-esque arrangements of bodies across the screen. According to Tom Gunning, Child works the deferred desire of a narrative falling apart. Gunning states that 'Child explores the disintegration of narrative, breaking it up into fragments which nonetheless still bears the trace of narrative desire' (Gunning in Bovier 2011: 22). He continues that we are not talking about a narrative that does not resolve itself,

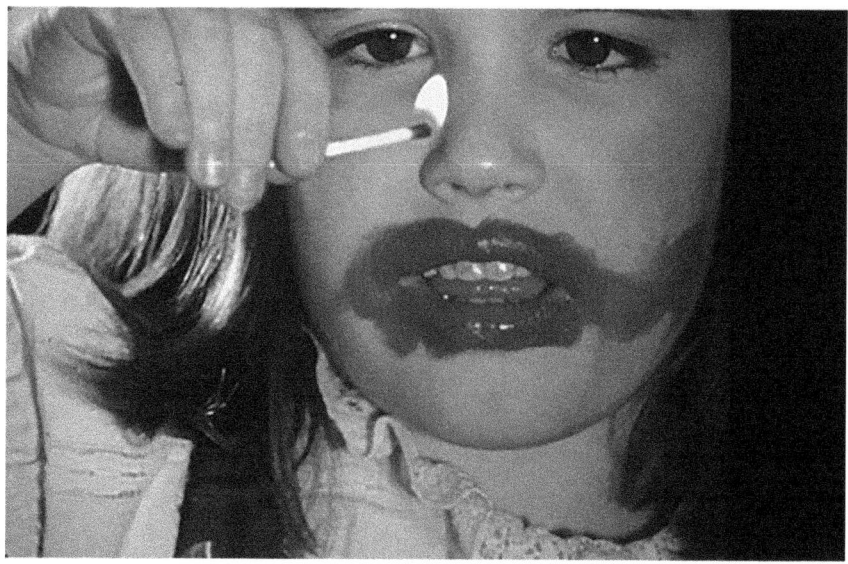

Figure 45. *Jennifer, Where Are You?* (1981, Leslie Thornton). Courtesy of the artist.

as with Antonioni's film *Blow Up* (1966), but instead Child constructs the films around the idea of a narrative that does not even get started. The film becomes a deferral of desire through the starting and stopping of the interstices. Between a narrative drive and the cutaways, the film creates an extreme lack that both heightens and reveals the mechanisms of desire that are bound to narrative, threatening its nonfulfilment while holding it up as a tantalizing offer. Caught between these states is an hysterical hovering.

Hovering between desire and threat, these themes are played out in a very different way in Leslie Thornton's *Jennifer, Where Are You?* (1981), where a girl, in close-up, is putting lipstick on. She is doing it 'badly', a piano is playing and a male voice repeatedly shouts, 'Jennifer, where are you?' In this film there is an establishing shot of a suburban residence, a middle-class setting upside-down; this appears again in the middle of the film. The upside-down-ness of the home, and later of several figures, alludes to the aversion to the apparently normal run of things, a critique of the aspiration of middle-class mores that we see in *Cake and Steak,* but as a darker reverie to the pregnant and seething underbelly of that normative appearance. The films then cuts to black, the piano still playing, which leaves space for the viewer's imagination and their speculation to soar on what this might be about. Suddenly a red-tinted stingray ray swims past – a piece of appropriated footage – which then cuts back to the girl: this is an obvious metaphor for the place of girls in society. A second piece of red-tinted fish footage is inserted later in this short ten-minute film. In the first half of the film, the girl holds a hand mirror that accentuates her childlike state while also accentuating the gulf in age between her and the man who is clearly agitated. 'Jennifer, where are you?' Is he looking out for her safety, or is he threatening? The ambiguity of both the threat and desire of incest hangs over the film but is never stated. The girl smiles in the film, but her eyes look uncertain, and this continues again and again. In the second half of the film, the girl, still with red lipstick smeared over her face, is given matches to blow out, another allusion to danger and desire – playing with fire. That she is given the matches by an adult hand diminishes her agency even further. Like *Cake and Steak,* this is a piece bound by evocations of American suburban post-war life, but the ways in which this is evoked foreground the ways in which women are at the centre and have the most to lose. The use of the hysterical mode is a cinematic translation of the patriarchal construction of femininity. Hysteria was a common mode of employ in the 1980s as a force to reconstitute womanhood through its very language of oppression, drawn from the writings of Cixous, Irigaray and Kristeva (Devereux 2014: 29). Whereas Mary Kelly, who is cited in Devereux's *Hysteria, Gender and Feminism*, uses the notion and discourse in order to deconstruct its meaning and therefore its effects, the punk motif uses it as a distinctive methodology of affect. It is not a romantic engagement, as Kelly suggests, but more of a modus operandi. As Cecily Devereux points out, feminism and interest by women in hysteria are closely connected in that they are both responses to patriarchy. The punk work is both hysterically engaged and critical. The irreducibility of these films to any singular or unambiguous narrative forms their power.

Notes

1   R D Laing's experiments in the UK that posited schizophrenia and other mental health problems to be a sane response to an insane world was popular reading in art schools in the early 1980s.

2   It is to be remembered that in the 1970s and 1980s there were very few women teaching in art schools and showing in galleries. This is evidenced by the report conducted by Pam Skelton titled, 'Women and Art Education' (National Association of Teachers in Further and Higher Education) *NATFHE Journal* May/June 1985 pp. 18–21. Also worth noting is the overview of the relationship between women teachers and women students in art schools: *Women Working in the Arts* (London: Arts Council of England document, 1992).

3   Although Novaczek's first degree was in the history of art at the Courtauld, so the naïveté in *Cheap Philosophy* was an obvious ironic device.

4   Even when Novaczek brings a narration into a film, it is a fictionalized narrator. These were initially sketches for performances she did at the time, at the LFMC and at the Krakow Jewish Arts festival and in Cologne at a women's film festival … these were site specific (paraphrased from email to author August 2020).

5   Novaczek often adopts an American accent to signal a certain and hegemonic kind of Hollywood representation of Jewish women (from email to author August 2020).

6   Email to the author (Novaczek August 2020).

7   They went there 'to escape the razzmatazz' of the pope visit (from email to author 31 July 2018).

8   Which Jan Campbell puts at the heart of the psyche, instead of repression, he argues.

9   This term is taken from Hélène Cixous (1976).

10   Email to the author (Bromberg 18 August 2020).

11   So many artists live 'between' London and Berlin or LA for example. Also the artist as nomad has been theorized by the art historian Marsha Meskimmon in her Routledge book *Contemporary Art and the Cosmopolitan Imagination*, although it is likely it has always been thus for some artists.

12   'The lower east Side walk up was my apartment in 9th street – the camera facing the windows where I shot *She Had Her Gun All Ready*. I never really understood that scene and I am not sure if Nan did either' (email from Vivienne Dick to the author, 16 August 2020).

13   From email to author (Robinson 25 April 2020).

14   From email to author (Robinson 25 April 2020)

15   Email to the author (Robinson 1 March 2018).

16   Email to the author from Sarah Pucill, who was Sandra Lahire's partner 'when you speak of Sandra's body not being desirable … you could emphasise that (maybe) this was a deliberate strategy (ie how she showed her body) in order to disrupt conventional representations of a woman's body on screen as desirable. (for some readers who could misinterpret that Sandra's body was just simply undesirable … of course it was a punk strategy also.' (10 February 2021).

17   Email to the author (Child 10 August 2020).

Conclusion

In the introduction I discussed *Interior Scroll* (1975) by Carolee Schneemann. This work is one of the foundational works by a key pioneer in feminist practices of her generation in the United States. *Interior Scroll* is also axiomatic of the issues highlighted in this book because the text that is written on the titular scroll that Schneemann pulls out from her vagina is one that harbours a conversation encapsulating what is considered wrong with women's work by the arbiters of the 'then hegemonic formalism' (Jones 1998: 2). The 'hegemonic formalism' that Jones is referring to, and one that is highlighted in the performance, is a conversation by a structuralist filmmaker about art made by women in general and Schneemann in particular. That conversation and the relationship between the scroll text and the performance go to the heart of the problematic that this book deals with: the relationship between the artwork by women filmmakers and the rules by which women have had to play in order to be visible as artists.

Schneemann's brave performance, that was a liberatory roar of anger at the strictures put on women artists, was a response to the dictates of these structuralist filmmakers. As a performance it articulated 'a "passionate and convulsive" relationship to her audience that dynamically enacts the dislocation of the conventional structures of gendered subjectivity of this explosive period' (Jones 1998: 3). In so doing it performed the change it engendered. At a key point in American art history this work disrupted and changed the audience's expectations of art. Feminism also had an impact on the world of experimental film and Laura Mulvey's text *Visual Pleasure and Narrative Cinema* (1975) is still the foundational guide to the thinking of much feminist work in film.

Amelia Jones argues that Schneemann presents an intersubjective relationship and is a statement of female – and genital – presence rather than absence – that destabilizes the male gaze (Jones 1998). Jones rightly points out the importance of this work that speaks so clearly to the core argument of my book. However, forty-five years later, it can be argued that the performance of *Interior Scroll* has become an image – the image of the performance – that in many ways is now subsumed into the dominant male gaze of the focus on the female body that links it to the histories of the nude in art. The image of Schneemann standing legs akimbo on the table unwittingly reinforces the argument on the scroll that is not so clearly remembered 'You are charming, but don't ask me to look at your films' (Jones 1998: 3). The title *Interior Scroll* – not to mention the text that critiques the male focus on structuralist film – is easily lost in the visual impact of the image of her strong naked body with a long thin penis-like column of paper coming out of her vagina: the work becomes the negation of the negation.

As I describe in the introduction, the text that is written on the scroll of *Interior Scroll* that activates Schneemann's genital power in the performance is the voice of men. It functions to represent the super-egotic voice that imputes women's work as lacking in clear vision and intelligence. It functions to highlight the way that patriarchy condemns women to doubt their own work, their own methodologies, interests and processes, in its specificity – as not structuralist enough and not – in their view – great art.

Schneemann, born in 1939, in *Interior Scroll* (1975) and her film *Fuses* (1965) set the stage for the next generation to rework and rethink the language of art that derived from the late Greenbergian diktat of purity of form and truth to material that was still the touchstone of art school education, in my experience, even in the 1980s. The structuralists as represented in *Interior Scroll* – in their devaluing of women's art practices, at least those practices that were not mirroring their own desire for purity – were merely ventriloquizing what was the pervasive attitude towards art that 'Purists make extravagant claims for art because usually they value it more than anyone else does' (Greenberg 1940 in Harrison and Wood 1993: 554). In that statement they were implying that they were more serious about art and made deeper art than women who chose to work in other ways. This nascent cry of rage for a language of her own was heard loud and clear by the next generation of artists that I discuss in this book.

The younger women such as Vivienne Dick, Bette Gordon, Ruth Novaczek and others set out a provisional language distinct from the Kantian model of disinterested agency or the Victorian Arnoldian standards of art in the service of edification that has beset the dominant narratives in art in the twentieth century. Importantly Schneemann set out her position as 'physical, visceral **and conceptual**' [my emphasis] (quoted in Jones 1998: 160), thereby rejecting the aspirations of a purely intellectual approach. Bringing together the three elements, as she states it, confounds the Cartesian split as well as acts as a rebuttal to the opposition between depth and superficiality that is implied in the Greenbergian statement cited above. In her bringing together of the intellectual and emotional spheres, she was an important precursor for what I am arguing. Not only this but unusually Schneemann straddled the art world and the experimental film world. Her film *Fuses* (1965), a cinematic piece, is an erotic and rich evocation of desire and sexual gratification. It is filmed by her and her partner during sex, as if seen by her cat. It is colourful, and enigmatic, offering an affective abstraction interspersed with images of the couple having sex, including Schneemann performing fellatio. This film exudes sexiness and desire without objectifying the female body. The collaging of imagery, the dense colouration and the fragmentation takes it away from the objectivization of the body into a somatic activation for the viewer in her experience as a sexual being. It has some of the hallmarks of the slightly later punk work: the collage, the fragmentation and the representation of the body and desire as a lived experience. The film is wonderful, and it is this wonder that differentiates it from the later generation of punk artists that I set out in this book who did not possess the optimism to revel in the visual in this life-enhancing way of visual excess. If they talked about sex, as many did, it was through strip joints, sex workers and porn. If they talked about the body, it was not the 'natural woman' or the 'body beautiful' but the body inhabiting the urban site or subculture, the mass ornament of the surface revealing the tensions in alienation.

Throughout this book in several different ways across the chapters I have set out how women challenge notions of what great art might constitute that has been formed through patriarchal structures. In some ways following in the footsteps of Lauren Rabinovitz, who discussed the challenges facing the previous generation, I analyse the working processes of artist filmmakers operating as young women in the late 1970s to the 1990s – and many still working now – who have been working through the methodologies of collage, heterogeneity, provisionality, DIY and the kitchen table aesthetic. I present the ways in which these offer a new aesthetic that confound normative values in the hierarchies of art production and reception. The artists in this book all work with the lived experiences of desire, community, fragmentation and the politics of human relations and they in turn eschew a cool, intellectual distancing mode of production. The artists of this generation learned from the generation of Deren, Wieland and Clarke, who 'lived in the avant-garde that attempted to contain and recuperate them' and lived the same effects 'the results of such attempts were more a series of conflicts over the meanings of their work and power roles ... their lives, lab and artistic production were crisscrossed by circumstances that necessitated they oppose contemporary avant-garde practices' (Rabinovitz 1991: 223). Robinson, Novaczek, Thornton and others have also been subject to these processes, navigating through the avant garde and the underground. However, through the approaches of a deflationary, intermedial heterogeneity of image production, these particular women discussed in this book build a distinctive filmic language from which to speak as artists. This language differs from prevalent modes of address within the cultures of Anglo-American lens-based artworks that favours the long-look work requiring high production values and large teams. They drew instead from the more libertarian underground and worked it to suit their own conditions of making and interests. Despite this there are some distinctive younger voices that have reached prominence in contemporary art that require close attention to the ways in which they develop the legacy of these artists.

Sadie Benning (b. 1973) has incorporated many of the elements discussed in this book into their working practice with great confidence and continued to make work that is awkward, lo-fi, discombobulating, but humane. They started making films very young after a tragic accident, where their friend was killed. At that time, Benning's father, an experimental filmmaker, gave Sadie a toy PXL-2000 PixelVision camera as a present, which they then used to make films. These works, begun when the artist was just fourteen, explore themes of isolation, emotions and narratives of love and death. The imagery in their films was initially very blurry and awkward, because of the camera's capabilities. Although their filmwork has changed since these early works, much of their approach and methodology remains. Now Benning works mainly with paintings, made from layers of resin and paint that depict bold abstract imagery developed on their phone as well as installations. Their work has, however, moved between many different heterogeneous iterations that include animation and sound work as well as film and painting.

Benning was a founder member of the post-punk band Tigre in 1998 and worked with them until 2001[1] – so the close links between punk music and the attitudes of a punk aesthetic in film and video continue. *A Place Called Lovely* (1991), one of Benning's early works, was filmed from the bedroom, like many of the early films, and has an autobiographical feel to the work that is structured through a disjointed narrative of short statements disconnected by images and appropriated pop music that builds up the mood of the film. It is typically constituted through the pixel camera, found footage and drawings, and sometimes all of these elements are caught within the same frame. Of course, we are not sure if it is autobiography or fiction, taking on a kind of mockumentary form. In any case, the film is slightly threatening and a bit sad. It builds up a dark picture of violence, both connected and disconnected. The pixels from their camera make for a blurred image that is the spine of the film with found footage peppering the narrative of abuse. The opening shots are taken looking out of the window at the road and houses opposite. It is of a typical American working-class neighbourhood with clapboard housing and dishevelled front lawns. The mood is decidedly downbeat. There is a child's drawing fixed to the window that obscures part of this view, immediately setting up a layering of the image visually and signals a familial home. Despite what we know, of Benning being a child of a university lecturer[2] the imagery and the structure of the film is constructed as *their* world, that is Benning's, of everyday working-class life that is a life of difficulty. Although this initial pan of the camera acts as an establishing shot, we are soon lost in detail and excerpts of narrative that do not easily correlate. Again, there is the difficulty to situate oneself as the viewer. At one point early in the film we hear a little boy's voice saying 'I love you I love you … God dammit you fucker I wanted to be alone'. The camera at this point pans over some black marker writing on chip wallpaper And/I/Wanted/To/Be/Alone! Each shot shows one word at a time. This cuts to a shot of a pixelated, out of focus photograph shot from the side. There is no explanation at this point and what is most noticeable is the range of textures in the work heightened by the staccato editing. As the camera pans to the music of an ice cream van we see a poster with a sequence of photographic headshots, akin to the headshots in a high school yearbook. The camera sweeps up and across still out of focus, all the while to this tinkling sound. One of the images has been torn out but the camera does not linger on this. It is just caught in passing. The camera pulls out slowly and the rectangle that is the poster made up of smaller rectangles of portraits becomes a floating rectangle hovering momentarily in a black void. From this abstracted photograph of portraits the film shifts to a close-up head shot from below of a woman – the artist? – beating her fists into the camera. The light bulb from above and behind casts a dramatic shadow of lights and darks over the body. The voiceover says 'One day when we were older, I beat Ricky with a telephone cord in an alley … this time he was crying and I still felt helpless'. There is an obvious disjunction between the voice telling and the body acting and the mood of the film is in some ways a reflection on film noir although in a very different way from Abigail Child's own in *Mayhem* (1987) which was a more playful homage to film noir. Then a momentary open mouth screaming gives way to the famous footage of the shower scene in the Hitchcock film *Psycho*, appropriated from the TV, then cutting to a sheet of paper on which, 'I was scared a lot' is written. Each passage is juxtaposed by a different mood, so to follow is a voice saying 'of Ricky' over some upbeat jazzy music and the flicking through of a magazine, from hairdos to guns, in 1950s style illustration adverts. At one point later in this short film, the image is of a photograph of a man that she has held up to her face. The edge of the photograph cuts the screen into a third and two-thirds, highlighting the rectangle and the image as image. In the smaller third is a fragment of Benning's face that aligns with the face in the image, creating a collage of imagery even within the one shot. Then the film shifts registers and the narrator recounts a series of child murders. Newspaper images of Black children are paraded along the while and the narrator stating how she felt implicated by the world but alienated from it. To drive it home the next passage is of the song 'America' with a woman's head in front acting self-conscious then faux glorifying, her facial features grimacing in fake joy. Then back to the grunge and the writing 'that scared me too'. Each passage in the film has to be there, each one making a point and building the experiential meaning, albeit in a disjunctive way. Thus the imagery veers across a myriad of different shots and forms, between close-up of the self and mid-range shot of a room or kids' playground and written words shot by Benning to magazines or appropriated film footage.

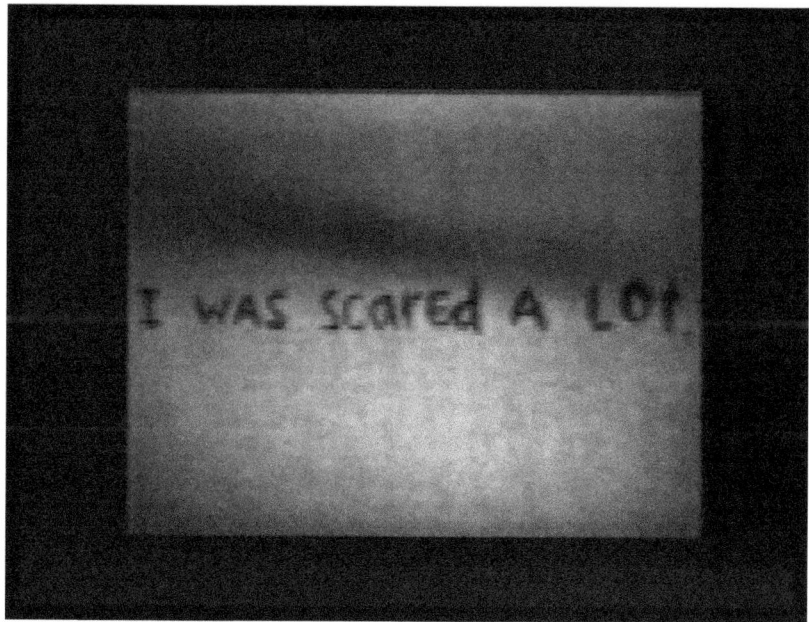

Figure 46. *A Place Called Lovely* (1991, Sadie Benning). Image copyright of the artist. Courtesy of Video Data Bank

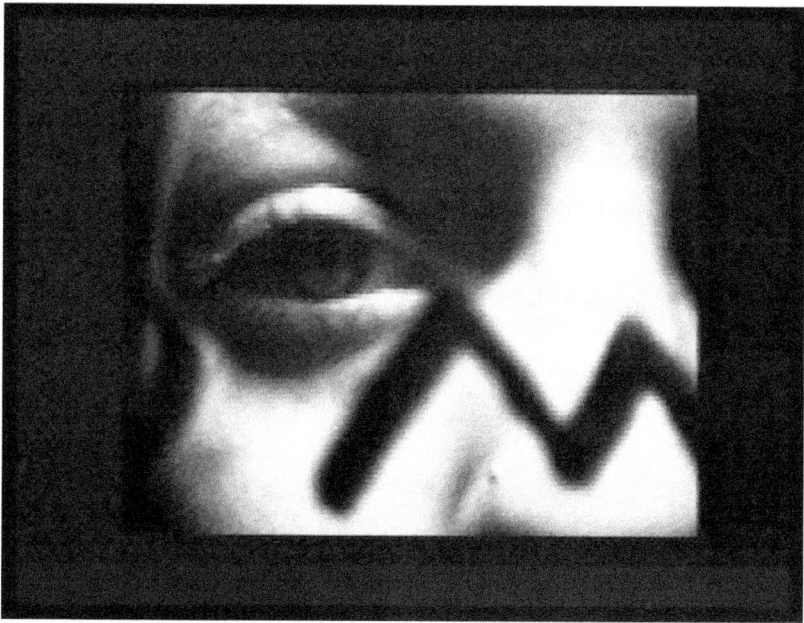

Figure 47. *A Place Called Lovely* (1991, Sadie Benning). Image copyright of the artist. Courtesy of Video Data Bank

This film encapsulates all of the processes and strategies that populate this book. The film disorientates, so the viewer cannot easily situate themselves; it uses collage strategies of a heterogeneous range of imagery that is mixed together both sequentially and within the same shots. It is homemade, in the bedroom – as opposed to the kitchen – eschewing high production values. It uses hand-held lo-fi cameras, footage shot from the TV, marker pen writing on paper and walls, sparse rooms with bare lightbulbs. The sound is either a voiceover or found sound from films, retro pop songs being about building up mood and experience to comment on human relations and lived experience. It is fragmented and knowingly melodramatic but all these devices coalesce into an overarching deflationary work. These works are not unlike Novaczek's later poetic narratives and there is a similar intensity of emotion, visual claustrophobia and the interweaving of poetry and politics.

Martine Syms (b. 1988) is also based in the United States. Her work exhibits extensively and incorporates video into installations that also consist of wall drawings, sculptural forms, apps and photographs. She also distributes her films through Video Data Bank as single screen versions. Like Benning, her work often incorporates words on walls. Sym's texts are painted on exhibition walls, theoretically informed, like slogans, covering the walls in carefully painted bold purple-and-white blocks that are interrupted by the video screens. She also writes and incorporates her studies of the history of Black filmmakers and subjects into her work. The staging within her exhibitions is important as the artist requires an embodied relationship to the works where the viewer is forced to consider their viewing conditions and the relationship to power and experience. Many of the video works are seen as fragments. Like many installations the viewer is not required to be there at the beginning but to pass through and imbibe the effect of the multiple sources and textures in the video and installations. However even if viewed in a linear way there is a carefully orchestrated look of randomness, provisionality and contingency in this work that brings it into the trajectory of this book as well as the multivalent visuality and the sense of the lo-fi[3] – even as the works are anything but. Syms would originally put her work on *YouTube* and she talks about that culture of DIY immediacy that formed her – making independent records, self-publishing and making videos at the Echo Park Film Centre co-op. For Syms the accumulation of different platforms is interesting and part of the culture of a Black woman. So the contradictions of production that this represents are also paralleled in the heterogeneity of language, form and source material that draws widely. As with many other of these artists described, breadth is depth and many of the works are fast-moving, engaged with popular culture and the histories of cinema. She is an African American and her work deals with the 'gulf between lived experience and its representation' (Jones 2018). In a Du Boisian sense Syms is completely engaged with the requirement to shift registers at will and this is embedded in her methodology of making the work. She talks about twoness and the slight differences in the shots and her choices, in the cut, that she derives from Fred Moten and his analysis of music and African American consciousness (Syms and Marks 2016). Her work demonstrates all this through the relationship between the footage she shoots and the footage she appropriates, between the snippets of conversations and the music recorded from the repertoire of Black music: like all the other artists in this book, she presents the world as she experiences it around her, through the conditions as she sees it, of living in the United States today. Syms is interested in the ways in which the public sphere creates a backdrop of consciousness that we all engage in and how it forms our sense of self, history and culture.

In the video interview from her exhibition at the ICA in 2017 she describes how she makes a collage in real time by taking images from the internet (Syms 2017). This can be seen in her most recent film installation also, from 2020 called *Ugly Plymouths*. The film is a short three-channel installation. Each screen is portrait shape, long and narrow, and can be seen online as a single screen piece. It is shot in LA we are told and shows an interplay between voices trying to hook up amid imagery of the city. There is a constant interplay between coherence and its opposite as the viewer follows the voices that are stripped of all adjacencies, reminiscent of Abigail Child wanting to make a film only of outtakes, thereby forcing the viewer to fill the gaps. The visuals, like the 'narrative', are snippets that look like they are mined from Syms's own archive of filmed footage, everyday images of car parks, the ocean, singers on stage, people performing on the side streets. The voices of the three characters do meet up, and at that point, the visuals converge and three screens simultaneously show fireworks for a few shots before disassembling again. We hear several aural excuses: 'how do you know I'm bougie', 'last week was a lot of fun but I feel we should slow things down for a bit', and 'I had a really lovely time hanging out on

Sunday'. The film ends with a mutual distancing and night fireworks. The film is a collage of place, like an impressionistic poem of alienation. We are told in the press release that the starting point was Bob Kaufman's poem *Hollywood*: 'the city is sick, without leave. Actors, artists, pimps, sale clerks, and poets are selling delusions whole-heartedly, where there is always a catch and never a foundation'. The poem is a critique of all the sleaze of LA. This film is not such a clear critique but an update of a slick alienation of noncommittal singles living 'the life'. The high production values and slickness of the exhibition lend glamour to the imagery that is juxtaposed and challenged by the reference to the disgust of the Black Jewish beat poet of an earlier generation. In the juxtaposition is the undecidability of the work. Syms is interested in gesture

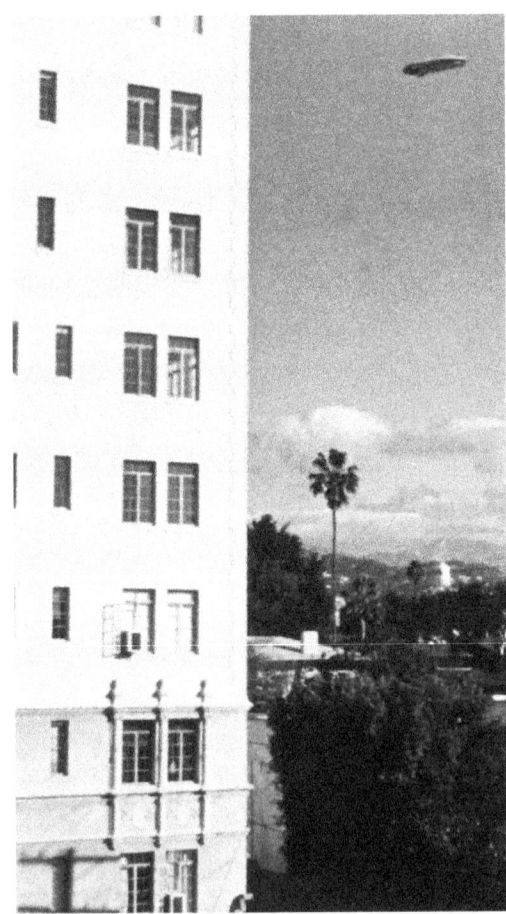

Figure 48. *Ugly Plymouths* (2020, Martine Syms), [still], 3 channel video. © Martine Syms. Courtesy of Sadie Coles HQ, London and Bridget Donahue, New York.

and uses repetition habitually. This work, as many of her others, currently has the high production values required of international galleries; however, the visual language is one of making connections through visual disconnections that jar and collide. It is a language full of a visual understanding of the lo-fi appropriation that has developed through the internet and its accessibility. And it is a world seen by a confident woman at the peak of her career.

In this book I have discussed works that were an integral part of the emergence of a new cinematic female subjectivity. The works that I have written about are from a period when film and video were not an established part of the art world but a margin of the experimental film world – in itself a margin. While there were a few precursors in this milieu who were role models

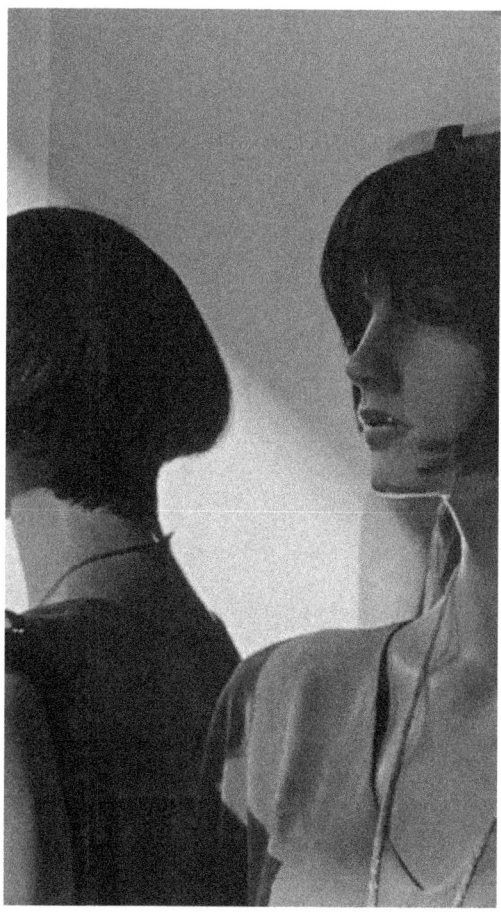

Figure 49. *Ugly Plymouths* (2020, Martine Syms), [still], 3 channel video. © Martine Syms. Courtesy of Sadie Coles HQ, London and Bridget Donahue, New York.

to this generation, such as Shirley Clarke or Maya Deren, they were still – from the vantage point of the 1980s – the exceptions, working in an overwhelmingly male-dominated world (Rabinovitz 1991: 222).

This book has endeavoured to delineate an approach to artists' video and film that is generative and enabling by using extensive case studies to celebrate an approach to filmmaking that is not often noticed. I have presented these artists as part of an important historical moment of change. This moment of the late 1970s and 1980s is one that is worth recuperating. These artists are a link between second wave feminism, video practice and emergent subjectivities. It offers a pre-history that is currently missing for young artists. It is also important to look again at what it is possible to make without publicly funded budgets, production teams and fancy buildings to exhibit in. As I write, I wonder what will happen to artists now in these uncertain times of economic precarity. How will they make work, exhibit, gather together in mutually supporting milieu? Punk arose in a similar period of uncertainty and precarity and found its own answers that may serve to inspire those in the contemporary moment. For this reason, as much as the amazing aesthetic invention, the work of these women demands careful scrutiny once more.

Notes

1   This band was set up with Kathryn Hanna, who had been the lead singer in Bikini Kill, one of the key Riot grrrl feminist post-punk bands.
2   Benning's parents separated and she grew up with her mother.
3   The work has high production values embedded in the filming and the installations.

Filmography

1912
The Musketeers of Pig Alley – D. W. Griffith

1929
Man with a Movie Camera – Dziga Vertov
Un Chien Andalou – Luis Buñuel

1930
Borderline – Kenneth Macpherson

1943
Meshes of the Afternoon – Maya Deren and Alexander Hammid

1948
In the Street – Helen Levitt

1959
Pull My Daisy – Robert Frank/Alfred Leslie

1960
Psycho – Alfred Hitchcock

1961
The Connection – Shirley Clarke

1963
The Cool World – Shirley Clarke

1964–6
Screen Tests – Andy Warhol

1965
Fuses – Carolee Schneemann

1966
Chelsea Girls – Andy Warhol

Blow Up – Michelangelo Antonioni
Unsere Afrikareise – Peter Kubelka

1967
Portrait of Jason – Shirley Clarke
David Holzman's Diary – Jim McBride

1968
High School – Fred Wiseman
Funny Girl – William Wyler

1970
Performance – Nick Roeg

1971
Klute – Alan J. Pakula
Dresden Dynamo – Lis Rhodes

1974
The Society of the Spectacle – Guy Debord

1975
Nightcleaners – Berwick Street Collective
Still Life – Bette Gordon
Light Music – Lis Rhodes

1976
Pressure – Horace Ové
Lost, Lost, Lost – Jonas Mekas

1977
Riddles of the Sphinx – Laura Mulvey, Peter Wollen
Petit Mal – Betzy Bromberg

1978
Guerillere Talks – Vivienne Dick
She Had her Gun All Ready – Vivienne Dick
Staten Island – Vivienne Dick
Ciao Bella or Fuck Me Dead – Betzy Bromberg
Jubilee – Derek Jarman

1979

Beauty Becomes the Beast – Vivienne Dick
Scar Tissue – Su Friedrich
Song of the Shirt – Sue Clayton
Exchanges – Bette Gordon

1980

Liberty's Booty – Vivienne Dick
Empty Suitcases – Bette Gordon
Soothing the Bruise – Betzy Bromberg

1981

Anybody's Woman – Bette Gordon
Visibility Moderate – Vivienne Dick
Gently Down the Stream – Su Friedrich
Marasmus – Betzy Bromberg
Prefaces. Part 1 of *Is This What You Were Born For?* – Abigail Child
Jennifer, Where Are You? – Leslie Thornton

1982

She Said – Susan Stein
Baby Doll – Tessa Hughes-Freeland

1983

Variety – Bette Gordon
Born In Flames – Lizzie Borden
Peggy and Fred in Hell – Leslie Thornton (1983–2015)
Mutiny. Part 2 of *Is This What You Were Born For?* – Abigail Child

1984

Covert Action. Part 4 of *Is This What You Were Born For?* – Abigail Child
Territories – Isaac Julien
Real Woman – Anne Robinson
First Person Plural – Lynn Hershman Leeson

1985

From Romance to Ritual – Peggy Ahwesh
The Fragments Project – Peggy Ahwesh (1985–95)

1986
Passion of Remembrance – Sankofa
A Capital Adventure – Anne Robinson (1986–92)
Tea Leaf – Ruth Novaczek
Four Minute Cut – Anne Robinson
Perils. Part 5 of *Is This What You Were Born For?* – Abigail Child
Working Girls – Lizzie Borden
Ballet Black – Stephen Dwoskin
Handsworth Songs – John Akomfrah
Terminals – Sandra Lahire
Corridors – Anne Robinson

1987
Uranium Hex – Sandra Lahire
Mayhem. Part 6 of *Is This What You Were Born For?* – Abigail Child
The Last of England – Derek Jarman
Plutonium Blonde – Sandra Lahire

1988
Measures of Distance – Mona Hatoum
Both. Part 3 of *Is This What You Were Born For?* – Abigail Child

1989
Tracks – Susan Stein
Mercy. Part 7 of *Is This What You Were Born For?* – Abigail Child
Serpent River – Sandra Lahire

1990
Rootless Cosmopolitans – Ruth Novaczek
London Suite (Getting Sucked In) – Vivienne Dick

1991
Young Soul Rebels – Isaac Julien
A Place Called Lovely – Sadie Benning

1992
Eerie – Sandra Lahire
The Crying Game – Neil Jordan
Cheap Philosophy – Ruth Novaczek

2002
Cake and Steak – Abigail Child

2004
The Future Is Behind You – Abigail Child

2010
Robinson in Ruins – Patrick Keiller

2011
Surf and Turf – Abigail Child

2020
Ugly Plymouths – Martine Syms

Bibliography

Adams, R. (2008) 'The Englishness of English Punk: Sex Pistols, Subcultures, and Nostalgia', *Popular Music and Society*, 31(4), pp. 469–88.

Agamben, G. (2007) 'Notes on Gesture', in *Infancy and History*. London New York: Verso, pp. 135–40.

Albertine, V. (2015) *Clothes, Clothes, Clothes. Music, Music, Music. Boys, Boys, Boys*. Main edition. London: Faber & Faber.

Althusser, L. (1971) *Lenin and Philosophy and Other Essays*. New York: Monthly Review Press.

Anarchy in the UK – The New Underground Cinema (DOCUMENTARY) – YouTube (no date). Available at: https://www.youtube.com/watch?v=lpNA75b2hCw (Accessed: 20 October 2020).

Anonymous (2015) *30 YEARS LIVE AID – The Great Disillusionment | eclipsed Rock Magazin, eclipsed.de*. Available at: https://www.eclipsed.de/en/current/30-years-live-aid-great-disillusionment (Accessed: 29 September 2020).

Anonymous (2020) *One Work / Ugly Plymouths, Tank Magazine*. Available at: https://tankmagazine.com/tank/2020/02/ugly-plymouths/ (Accessed: 21 August 2020).

Araeen, R. (1987) *The Other Story*. London: Southbank Centre.

Arnold, M. (2009) *Culture and Anarchy*. Oxford New York: Oxford University Press.

Art & Language (1999) *Art & Language in Practice Vol. 1: Illustrated Handbook*. Barcelona, Spain: Foundation Tàpies.

Arthur, P. (2005) *A Line of Sight: American Avant Garde Film since 1965*. Minneapolis; London: University of Minnesota Press.

Augé, M. (1995) *Non-places: Introduction to an Anthropology of Supermodernity*. London: Verso Books.

Baal, I. (2005) *Poly Styrene: Plastic Fantastic, Dazed*. Available at: https://www.dazeddigital.com/music/article/24454/1/poly-styrene-plastic-fantastic (Accessed: 20 October 2020).

Badiou, A. (2007) *The Century*. Cambridge: Polity Press.

Baldwin, M. Ramsden and M. Harrison, C. "We Aimed To Be Amateurs," *Art-Language* (new series) 2 (June 1997): pp. 40–9.

Balsom, E. (2017) 'No Masters: The Cinema of Peggy Ahwesh | Frieze', *Frieze*. Available at: https://www.frieze.com/article/no-masters-cinema-peggy-ahwesh (Accessed: 31 January 2021).

Basciano, O. (2017) 'Whitney Biennial: Emmett Till Casket Painting by White Artist Sparks Anger | Art and Design | The Guardian', *The Guardian*, 21 March. Available at: https://www.theguardian.com/artanddesign/2017/mar/21/whitney-biennial-emmett-till-painting-dana-schutz (Accessed: 3 October 2020).

Batchelor, D. (2000) *Chromophobia*. London: Reaktion.

Bauman, Z. (1988) 'Exit Visas and Entry Tickets: Paradoxes of Jewish Assimilation', *Telos*, 77, pp. 45–77.

Bazin, H. (2004) *What Is Cinema? Vol 1*. Berkeley, CA: University of California Press.

Beckett, A. (2009) *When the Lights Went Out: Britain in the Seventies* London: Faber & Faber.

Beech, D. and Roberts, J. (2002) *The Philistine Controversy*. London: Verso Books.

Bell, C. and Howe, Z. (2019) *Dayglo: The Poly Styrene Story*. London: Omnibus Press.

Benjamin, W. (1972) 'A Short History of Photography', *Screen*, 13(1), pp. 5–26.

Benjamin, W. *et al.* (2016) *One-Way Street*. Cambridge, MA: Harvard University Press.

Benjamin, W. (2019) *Illuminations: Essays and Reflections*. Harcourt; NY: Mariner Books.

Berardi, F. 'Bifo' (2017) *Futurability: The Age of Impotence and the Horizon of Possibility*. London: Verso.

Black, H. (2017) 'Hannah Black's Letter to the Whitney Biennial's Curators: Dana Schutz painting "Must Go" – Frontpage – e-flux conversations', March. Available at: https://conversations.e-flux.com/t/hannah-blacks-letter-to-the-whitney-biennials-curators-dana-schutz-painting-must-go/6287 (Accessed: 8 February 2021).

Bovier, F. (ed.) (2011) 'Strategies of Appropriation in *Is This What You Were Born For?*', in *Is This What You Were Born For? Strategies of Appropriation and Audio Visual Collage*. Geneva: METIS, pp. 7–12.

Bovier, L. (2006) *Linder: Works 1976–2006*. Zurich: Jrp/Ringier.

Brodkin, K. (1999) *How Jews Became White Folks and What That Says about Race in America*. New Brunswick, NJ: Rutgers University Press.

Brooks, P. (1976) *The Melodramatic Imagination: Balzac Henry James, Melodrama, and the Mode of Excess*. New Haven; London: Yale University Press.

Buchloh, B. (1991) 'From Detail to Fragment: Décollage Affichiste', *October*, 56, pp. 98–110.

Burger, P. (1984) *Theory of the Avant-Garde (Theory and History of Literature)*. Minneapolis: University of Minnesota Press.

Butler, A. (2011) *Women's Cinema: The Contested Screen*. London; New York: Wallflower.

Butler, J. (1990) *Gender Trouble: Feminism and the Subversion of Identity*. New York; London: Routledge.

Butler, J. (1993) *Bodies That Matter : On the Discursive Limits of "Sex"*. London: Routledge.

Butt, G. (2007) 'Stop That Acting! Performance and Authenticity in Shirley Clarke's Portrait of Jason', in Mercer, K. (ed.) *Pop Art and Vernacular Culture*. London: MIT Press/InIVA, pp. 36–55.

Butt, G., Fisher, M. and Eshun, K. (eds) (2016) *Post Punk Then and Now*. London: Repeater.

Campbell, J. (2004) *Film and Cinema Spectatorship: Melodrama and Mimesis*. 1st ed. Oxford: Polity Press.

Campbell, J. (2007) 'Are Your Dreams Wishes or Desires? Hysteria as Distraction and Character in the Work of Siegfried Kracauer', *New Formations Lawrence & Wishart*, 61, pp. 132–48.

Carter, M. (1998) 'Cross-Cultural Autobiographic Performance in the Video Works of Sadie Benning', *Signs*, 23(3), pp. 745–69.

Cavasola, R. (2015) 'A Reading of Contemporary Hysteria from Lacan's teachings'. *European Journal of Psychoanalysis*, (3/1).

Chambers, E. (2014) *Black Artists in British Art: A History from 1950 to the Present*. London: I.B.Tauris.

Child, A. (1989) *Motive for Mayhem*. Elmwood, CT: Pressed Wafer Pr.

Child, A. (2005) *This Is Called Moving: A Critical Poetics of Film (Modern & Contemporary Poetics)*. Tuscaloosa, AL: University Alabama Press.

Child, A. (2012) *Is This What You Were Born For? + Dvd: Strategie d'Appropriation et Collage …* 1st ed. Geneva: S.l.: METIS.

Cixous, H., Cohen, K. and Cohen, P. (1976) 'The Laugh of the Medusa', *Signs*, 1(4), pp. 875–93.

Clarke, A. (2019) *Ugly Duckling? 1961 Plymouth Custom Suburban Wagon, Barn Finds*. Available at: https://barnfinds.com/ugly-duckling-1961-plymouth-custom-suburban-wagon/ (Accessed: 23 August 2020).

Clarke, T., Greenberg, C. and Fried, M. (1985) 'The Critical Debate and Its Origins', in Frascina, F. (ed.) *Pollock and After: The Critical Debate*. London: Paul Chapman Publishing, pp. 21–88.

Clarke, T. J. (1985) 'Clement Greenberg's Theory of Art', in Clarke, T. and Frascina, F. (eds) *Pollock and After: The Critical Debate*. 2nd ed. London: Routledge.

Connolly, M. (2004) 'From No Wave to National Cinema: The Cultural Landscape of Vivienne Dick's Early Films (1978–1985)'. Available at: http://www.luxonline. uk/articles/from_no_wave_to_national_cinema(1).html.

Cottingham, L. (2000) *Seeing through the Seventies: Essays on Feminism and Art*. Amsterdam: Routledge.

Court, B. (2019) 'Racializing Amateurism: Punk and Rap', *Third Text*, 34(1), pp. 49–61.

Cowie, E. (2011) *Recording Reality, Desiring the Real*. Minneapolis, MN: University of Minnesota Press.

Crangle, S. (2010) 'Dada Is Bathos! Or of the Hobbyhorse Endlessly Rocking', in C. Crangle and P. Nicholls. (eds) *On Bathos Literature Art Music*. London: Continuum.

Dalal-Clayton, A. (2015) 'Coming into View: Black British Artists and Exhibition Cultures 1976–2010', PhD thesis unpublished.

Damon, M. (1997) 'Jazz-Jews, Jive, and Gender: The Ethnic Politics of Jazz Argot', in Boyarin, J. and Boyarin, D. (eds) *Jews and Other Differences: The New Jewish Cultural Studies*, Minneapolis; London: University of Minnesota Press. 161, pp. 150–75.

Debord, G. (1994) *Society of the Spectacle*. London: Rebel Press.

Deepwell, K. (2014) 'Felicity Sparrow - Forming Circles', *n.paradoxa*, 34, pp. 86–95.

Devereux, C. (2014) 'Hysteria, Feminism, and Gender Revisited: The Case of the Second Wave', *ESC*, 40(1), pp. 19–45.

Dick, V. (2020) 'New York Our Time -Vivienne Dick Revisits a City Then and Now', *RTE* https://www.rte.ie/culture/2020/0224/1117331-new-york-our-time-vivienne-dick-revisits-a-city-then-and-now/ (Accessed: 1 June 2021).

Dika, V. (2012) *The (Moving) Pictures Generation: The Cinematic Impulse in Downton New York Art and Film*. New York: Palgrave.

Diskie, J. (2009) *The Sixties*. London: Profile Books.

Dixon, W. W. (1995) 'The Practice of Theory, The Theory of Practice: The Post-Colonial Cinema of Maureen Blackwood and The Sankofa Collective', *Film Criticism*, 20(1/2), pp. 131–43.

Dixon, W. W. (1998) *The Transparency of the Spectacle: Meditations on the Moving Image*. New York: State University of New York Press.

Dixon, W. W. and Foster, G. A. (eds) (2002) *Experimental Cinema: The Film Reader*. London: Routledge.

Doane, M. A. (1982) 'Film and the Masquerade: Theorising the Female Spectator', *Screen*, 23(3–4), pp. 74–88.

Doane, M. A. (2003) *The Emergence of Cinematic Time: Modernity, Contingency, the Archive*. 1st ed. Cambridge, MA: Harvard University Press.

Doane, M. A. (2010) 'Film and The Masquerade', in Jones, A. (ed) *Feminism and Visual Culture Reader*. London: Routledge.

Drucker, J. (2006) *Sweet Dreams: Contemporary Art and Complicity*. Chicago: University of Chicago Press.

Dworkin, A. (1988) *Letters from a War Zone: Writings 1976–1987*. New edition. Brooklyn, NY: Martin Secker and Warburg.

Dwoskin, S. (1976) *Film Is…: The International Free Cinema* Woodstock, NY: Overlook Press.

Echols, A. (1983) 'Feminist Capitalism and the Anti-Pornography Movement', *Social Text*, 7, pp. 34–53.

Edmond, M. (2016) 'Deracination, Disembowelling and Scorched Earth Aesthetics: Feminist Cinemas, No Wave and the Punk Avant Garde', *Senses of Cinema*, 80, pp. 1–23.

Eisenstein, S. (1969) *Film Form: Essays in Film Theory*. New York: Harcourt Books.

Elwes, C. (2004) *Video Art: A Guided Tour*. London; New York: I.B. Tauris.

Eshun, K. and Sagar, A. (2007) *The Ghosts of Songs: The Film Art of Black Audio Film Collective*. Liverpool: Liverpool University Press: Foundation for Art and Creative Technology.

Etgar, Y. (2017), 'The Ends of Collage', in Etgar, Y. (ed.) *The Ends of Collage*. London: Luxembourg and Dayan.

Everett, A. (1995) 'The Other Pleasures: The Narrative Function of Race in the Cinema', *Film Criticism*, 20(1/2), pp. 26–38.

Everleth, M. (2007) 'The First Statement of the New American Cinema Group: September 30, 1962', *Underground Film Journal*. Available at: https://www.undergroundfilmjournal.com/the-first-statement-of-the-new-american-cinema-group-september-30-1962/ (Accessed: 17 August 2020).

Everleth, M. (2018) 'Anybody's Woman – Bette Gordon', *Underground Film Journal*. Available at: https://www.undergroundfilmjournal.com/anybodys-woman-bette-gordon/ (Accessed: 18 August 2020).

Firestone, S. (1979) *The Dialectics of Sex: The Case for Feminist Revolution*. London: The Women's Press.

Frascina, F. (ed.) (2009) *Modern Art Culture: A Reader*. London: Routledge.

Freud, S, Breuer, J. (2004) *Studies in Hysteria*. London: Penguin.

Friedrich, S. (1980) 'Bette Gordon's Empty Suitcases', *The Downtown Review*, 2(3), Fall, pp. 16–17.

Frisby, D. (1985) *Fragments of modernity: theories of modernity in the work of Simmel, Kracauer and Benjamin*. Cambridge: Polity Press.

Fusco, C. (1986) *Young British and Black: A Monograph on the Work of Sankofa Film/Video Collective and Black Audio Film Collective*. Buffalo, NY: Hallwalls Contemporary Arts Centre.

Fusco, C. (2017) *Censorship, Not the Painting, Must Go: On Dana Schutz's Image of Emmett Till, Hyperallergic*. Available at: https://hyperallergic.com/368290/censorship-not-the-painting-must-go-on-dana-schutzs-image-of-emmett-till/ (Accessed: 8 February 2021).

Gaines, J. (1995) 'Feminist Heterosexuality and Its Politically Incorrect Pleasures', *Critical Enquiry*, 21(2), pp. 382–410.

Gambaudo, S. A. (2007) 'French Feminism vs Anglo-American Feminism: A Reconstruction', *European Journal of Women's Studies*, 14(2), pp. 93–108.

Gangitano, L. (2016) 'Sadie Benning', *Bomb*, 135, pp. 33–43.

Benning, S. and Gangitano, L. (2016) 'Sadie Benning', *Bomb*, 135, pp. 33–43.

Garfield, R. (2001) 'Ali G: Just Who Does He Think He Is', *Third Text*, 54, Spring.

Garfield, R. (2008) *Keith Piper: Speaking with a Forked Tongue*. Luxonline. Available at: https://www.luxonline.org.uk/artists/keith_piper/essay(1).html (Accessed: 3 October 2020).

Garfield, R. (2009) 'A Particular Incoherence: Some Works of Vivienne Dick', in O'Brian, T. (ed.) *A Particular Incoherence: Some Works of Vivienne Dick*. London: Crawford/Lux, pp. 36–53.

Garfield, R. (2013) 'Parallel Editing, Multi-Positionality and Maximalism: Cosmopolitan Effects as Explored in Some Art Works by Melanie Jackson and Vivienne Dick', *Open Arts Journal*. Edited by B. Schoene and B. Eleanor, 1, pp. 46–59.

Garfield, R. (2015) 'Anwar Shemza: Negotiating the British Landscape', in Dadi, I. (ed.) *Anwar Jalal Shemza*. London: Ridinghouse, pp. 19–25.

Garfield, R. (2017) 'Valences of Subjectivity: The Politics of Personal Narrative in Video Art', in *Art and The Politics of Visibility*. London: I.B. Tauris, pp. 137–66.

Garfield, R. (2019) 'Prescient Intersectionality: Women, Film: Moving Image and Identity Politics in 1980s Britain', in Reynolds, L. (ed.) *Women Artists, Feminism and the Moving Image: Contexts and Practices*. London: Bloomsbury, pp. 99–113.

Garnett, R. (1999) 'Too Low to Be Low: Art Pop and the Sex Pistols', in Sabin, R. (ed.) *Punk Rock So What? The Cultural Legacy of Punk*. London: Routledge, pp. 17–30.

Gessert, A. (2014) *Introductory Lectures on Lacan*. London: Karnac Press.

Gidal, P. (1996) 'Theory and Definition on Structuralist/Materials Film', in O'Pray, M. (ed.) *Avant-Garde Film 1926–1995*. Luton: University of Luton Press, pp. 145–70.

Giles, P. (2007) 'Historicizing the Transnational: Robert Coover, Kathy Acker and the Rewriting of British Cultural History, 1970–1997', *Journal of American Studies*, 41(1), pp. 3–30.

Gilloch, G. (2012) 'Fragments. Cityscapes. Modernity. Kracauer on the Cannebière', *Journal of Classical Sociology*, 1, pp. 1–10.

Gilroy, P. (1991) *There Ain't No Black in The Union Jack: The Cultural Politics of Race and Gender*. London: Routledge.

Gilroy, P. and Lawrence, E. (1988) 'Two-Tone Britain: White and Black Youth and the Politics of Anti-Racism', in Cohen, P. and Bains, H. S. (eds) *Multi-Racist Britain*. London: Palgrave Macmillan UK, pp. 121–55.

Goddard, M. (2013). 'No Wave Film and the Music Documentary: From "Documents" to Retrospective Documentaries', in Halligan, B., Edgar, R. and Fairclough-Isaacs, K. (eds) *The Music Documentary: Acid Rock to Electropop*. New York; London: Routledge, pp. 115–30.

Gordon, B. (2018) 'Voyeurism and Half-Lit Streets: Bette Gordon on Variety', *Talkhouse*. Available at: https://www.talkhouse.com/voyeurism-and-half-lit-streets-bette-gordon-on-variety/ (Accessed: 20 October 2020). email to the author, 15 February 2021.

Gordon, B. and Hawkins, J. (2015) 'Interview with Bette Gordon', in Hawkins (ed.) *Downtown Film and TV Culture 1975–2001*. Bristol: Intellect, pp. 131–46.

Granath, O. (2007) 'Andy Warhol, A Guide to 706 Items in 2 Hours 56 Minutes', in Meyer-Hermann, E. (ed.) *Andy Warhol, A Guide to 706 Items in 2 Hours 56 Minutes*. Rotterdam: NAI, Stedelijk Museum, Moderna Museet.

Grant, C. and Love, K. R. (eds) (2019) *Fandom as Methodology: A Sourcebook for Artists and Writers*. London: Goldsmiths Press.

Greenberg, C. (1961) 'Avant-Garde and Kitsch', in *Art and Culture: Critical Essays*. Boston: Beacon Press, pp. 3–21.

Greenberg, C. (1993) 'Towards a Newer Laocoon', in Harrison, C. and Wood, P. (eds) *Art in Theory 1900–1999*. Oxford: Blackwells, pp. 554–60.

Greenberger, A. (2017) '"The Painting Must Go": Hannah Black Pens Open Letter to the Whitney about Controversial Biennial Work', *ARTnews.com*, 21 March. Available at: https://www.artnews.com/artnews/news/the-painting-must-go-hannah-black-pens-open-letter-to-the-whitney-about-controversial-biennial-work-7992/ (Accessed: 3 October 2020).

Grierson, J. (1976) 'First Principles of Deocumentary (1932–1934)' in *Non Fiction Film: Theory and Criticism*, Barsam, R. (ed.), New York: EP Dutton and Co, pp. 19–30.

Grosse, A. (ed.) (2016) *Hysteria Today*. London: Karnak Press.

Groys, B. (2008) *Art Power*. Cambridge, MA: MIT Press.

Gunning, T. (1989) 'Towards a Minor Cinema: Fonoroff, Herwitz, Ahwesh, Klahr and Solomon', *Tom Gunning Motion Picturee*, 3(1/2), pp. 2–5.

Gunning, T. (2011) 'Abigail Child: The Pulse of the Last Machine', in Bovier, F. (ed.) *Is This What You Were Born For? Strategies of Appropriation and Audio Visual Collage*. Geneva: Metis Presses, pp. 13–34.

Gurkan, H. and Ozan, R. (2015) 'Feminist Cinema as Counter Cinema: Is Feminist Cinema Counter Cinema?', *Online Journal of Communication and Media Technologies*, 5(3), pp. 73–90.

Halberstam, J. (1998) *Female Masculinity*. Durham, NC: Duke University Press.

Halberstam, J. (1999) 'Oh Bondage up Yours! Female Masculinity and the Tomboy', in *Sissies and Tomboys: Gender Nonconformity and Homosexual Childhood*. New York; London: NYU Press, pp. 153–79.

Halberstam, J. (2011) *The Queer Art of Failure*. Durham, NC; London: Duke University Press.

Hall, S. et al. (1978) *Policing the Crisis: Mugging, the State, and Law and Order*. 1978 edition. London: Macmillan.

Hall, S. (2006) 'Black Diaspora Artists in Britain: Three "Moments" in Post-War History', *History Workshop Journal*, 61(1), pp. 1–24.

Halter, E. (2012) 'Close-Up: Hell Is for Children, Ed Halter on Leslie Thornton etc', *Artforum,* 51(1), pp. 514–21.

Hansen, M. (1993) '"With Skin and Hair": Kracauer's Theory of Film, Marseille 1940', *Critical Enquiry*, 19(3), pp. 437–69.

Hansen, M. (2012) *Cinema and Experience: Siegfried Kracauer, Walter Benjamin, and Theodor W. Adorno*, Berkeley, CA; London: University of California Press.

Hansen, Mi. (1991) 'Decentric Perspectives: Kracauer's Early Writing on Film and Mass Culture', *New German Critique*, 54, pp. 47–76.

Harbord, J. (August 2007a) 'Contingency's Work: Kracauer's Theory of Film and the Trope of the Accidental', *New Formations*. London: Lawrence & Wishart, 61, pp. 90–103.

Harbord, J. (1 October 2007b) *The Evolution of Film: Rethinking Film Studies*. Cambridge, UK; Malden, MA: Polity Press.

Harvey, S. (1982) 'Whose Brecht Memories for the Eighties', *Screen*, 23(1), pp. 45–59.

Hawkins, J. (ed.) (2015) *Downtown Film and TV Culture: 1975–2001*. Bristol: Intellect.

Heath, S. (1981) *Questions of Cinema*. London: Macmillan.

Hebdige, D. (1979) *Subcultures: The Meaning of Style*. London: Routledge.

Hewison, R. (1986) *Too Much: Art and Society in the Sixties 1960–75*. London: Methuen.

Hoberman, J. No Wavelength: The Para-Punk Underground by Jim Hoberman (1979), Copyright Jim Hoberman and Village Voice. Available at https://www.luxonline.org.uk/articles/no_wavelength(1).html.

Holdsworth, C. M. (2017) 'In Search of Lost Time: Cordelia Swann, the 1980s and the Use of History', *The Moving Image Review & Art Journal (MIRAJ)*, 6(1–2), pp. 68–78.

Home, S. (2005) 'Pressure Directed by Horace Ové review', *Pressure*. Available at: https://www.stewarthomesociety.org/luv/pressure.htm (Accessed: 7 May 2017).

Huddle, R. and Saunders, R. (eds) (2016) *Reminiscences of RAR: Rocking against Racism 1976–182*. London: Redwords.

'Interior Scroll', Carolee Schneemann, 1975, Tate. Available at: https://www.tate.org.uk/art/artworks/schneemann-interior-scroll-p13282 (Accessed: 14 July 2020).

Jeffries, S. (2016) *The Grand Hotel Abyss: The Lives of the Frankfurt School*. London; New York: Verso.

Johnston, C. (1999) 'Women's Cinema as Counter-Cinema', in Thornham, S. (ed.) *Feminist Film Theory: A Reader*. Edinburgh: Edinburgh University Press, pp. 31–40.

Jones, A. (1998) *Body Art, Performing the Subject*. Minneapolis; London: University of Minnesota Press.

Jones, A. (2012) *Seeing Differently: A History and Theory Identification and the Visual Arts*. Abingdon, Oxon [England]; New York: Routledge.

Jones, D. (2018) *Martine Syms: 'Don't Be Afraid to Be Narcissistic'*, British GQ. Available at: https://www.gq-magazine.co.uk/article/martine-syms-artist-interview-2018 (Accessed: 29 March 2021).

Judd, S. (2001) 'Making a Living in Art Education: A Woman's Experience'. Cheltenham and Gloucester College of Higher Education.

Kase, J. C. (2015) 'The Centre Cannot Hold: Blank City (2010) and the Problems with Historicizing New York's Independent Cinema of the Late 1970s and Early 1980s', in Hawkins, J. (ed.) *Downtown Film and TV Culture 1975–2001*. Bristol: Intellect, pp. 315–30.

Kathryn, S. (2020) 'My Own Lens and Skin: Betzy Bromberg on Personal Filmmaking', *Another Gaze*, 4, pp. 78–89.

Keshvani, R. (2018) 'Tom McPhillips Speaks to Rozemin Keshvani about His Film "A Lay in the Dife"', 2 March. Available at: https://thelockedroom-stmartins.blogspot.com/2018/03/tom-mcphillips-speaks-to-rozemin.html (Accessed: 24 February 2020).

Khan, N. (1976) *The Arts Britain Ignores: The Arts of Ethnic Minorities in Britain*. London: Community Relations Commission.

Khan, N. (1980) 'The Arts of Ethnic Minorities in Britain', *Journal of the Royal Society of Arts*, 128(5290), pp. 676–88.

Khan, N. (2005) 'Choices for Black Arts in Britain over Thirty Years', in Boyce, S., Baucom, I., and Bailey, D. (eds) *Shades of Black*. Durham, NC: Duke University Press, pp. 115–22.

Kidner, D. (2019)."'The Hoxton Mob Are Coming": The Lux Centre and the Merging of Cultures of Experimental Film and Video Art in the 1990s', in *Artists' Moving Image in Britain After 1989*, ed. Erika Balsom. New Haven: Yale University Press.

Kidner, D., and Sainsbury, A. (eds) (2018) *Nightcleaners and '36 to '77*. Raven Row: Koenig Books and LUX.

Kokoli, A. (2017) 'Pre-Emptive Mourning against the Bomb: Exploded Domesticities in Art Informed by Feminism and Anti-Nuclear Activism', *Oxford Art Journal*, 40(1), pp. 153–68.

Kracauer, S. (1960) *Theory of Film: The Redemption of Physical Reality*. Princeton, NJ: Princeton University Press.

Kracauer, S. (1995) *The Mass Ornament: Weimar Essays*. Cambridge, MA; London: Harvard University Press.

Krauss, R. (Spring 1976) 'Video: The Aesthetics of Narcissism', *October*, 1, pp. 50–64.

Krauss, R. (1979) 'Grids', *October*, 9, pp. 51–64.

Krauss, R. (1985) 'Photography in the Service of Surrealism', in *L'Amour Fou: Photography and Surrealism*. New York: Abbeville Press, pp. 15–56.

Krauss, R. (1991) 'Nostalgie de la bou', *October*, 56, p. 111–20.

Laderman, D. (2010) *Punk Slash! Musicals: Tracking Lip-Sync on Film*. Austin, TX: University of Texas Press.

Language, A. (1995) 'We Aim to Be Amateurs', in *Art and Politics*. Nottingham Contemporary Art & Language.

Lavin, M. (1990) 'Androgyny, Spectatorship, and the Weimar Photomontages of Hannah Höch', *New German Critique*, 51, pp. 63–86.

Lavin, M. (1993) *Cut with the Kitchen Knife: Weimar Photomontages of Hannah Hoch*. New Haven; London: Yale University Press.

LeFanu, M. (1997) 'Metaphysics of the "Long Take": Some Post-Bazinian Thoughts', *POV*, (4). Available at: http://pov.imv.au.dk/Issue_04/section_1/artc1A.html.

Leslie, E. (2002) 'Philistines and Art Vandals Get Upset', in Roberts, J. and Beech, D. (eds) *The Philistine Controversy*. London: Verso Books, pp. 201–27.

Leslie, E. (2014) *Derelicts: Thought Worms from the Wreckage*. Illustrated edition. London: Unkant Publishers.

Letts, D. (2005) 'iJamming.net » Punk: Attitude by Don Letts', *Punk: Attitude by Don Letts*, July. Available at: https://www.ijamming.net/punk-attitude-by-don-letts/ (Accessed: 15 July 2020).

Lippard, L. (1978) 'Making Something from Nothing (Towards a Definition of Women's "Hobby Art")', *Heresies*, (1), pp. 62–5.

Lippard, L. (1984) *Get the Message: A Decade of Art for Social Change*. London: EP Dutton.

Lippard, L. R. (1995) *The Pink Glass Swan: Feminist Essays on Art*. New York: The New Press.

Lippard, L. (2017) 'From the Archives: No Regrets', *ARTnews.com*, 16 March. Available at: https://www.artnews.com/art-in-america/features/from-the-archives-no-regrets-63252/ (Accessed: 18 October 2020).

Longworth, K. (2009) *Porn and Being Poor, Then & Now: Bette Gordon Interview, Tribeca 2009 | IndieWire*. Available at: https://www.indiewire.com/2009/04/porn-and-being-poor-then-now-bette-gordon-interview-tribeca-2009-227276/ (Accessed: 6 August 2020).

MacDonald, S. (1988) 'Carolee Schneemann', in *A Critical Cinema 1*. Berkeley, CA: University of California Press, 1988–2006, pp. 134–51.

MacDonald, Scott (1988) *A Critical Cinema: Interviews with Independent Film Makers*. Berkeley, CA: University of California Press.

MacDonald, S. (1983) 'Interview with Beth and Scott B', *October*, 24, pp. 3–36.

MacDonald, S. (2005) 'Abigail Child', in *A Critical Cinema 4*. Berkeley, CA: California University Press, pp. 196–228.

MacDonald, S. (2006) 'MFJ: Peggy Ahwesh Interview', in *A Critical Cinema 5*. Berkeley, CA: University of California Press, 1988–2006, pp. 111–42.

Marcus, G. (2001) *Lipstick Traces: A Secret History of the Twentieth Century*. London: Faber & Faber.

Marks, L. U. (2002) *Touch: Sensuous Theory and Multisensory Media*. First edition. Minneapolis: University Of Minnesota Press.

Marks, L. U. and Polan, D. (2000) *The Skin of the Film: Intercultural Cinema, Embodiment, and the Senses*. Illustrated Edition. Durham, NC: Duke University Press Books.

Marks, L.U. and Syms, M., Conversation, SFU Galleries, 27 June 2018 https://www.youtube.com/watch?v=IkQLbRMAFoY.

Marris, P. (1999) *Media Studies: A Reader*. 2nd revised edition. S. Thornham (ed.). Edinburgh: Edinburgh University Press.

Masters, M. (2007) *No Wave*. London: Black Dog.

Maziere, M., and Danino, N. (2014) 'Roundtable Discussion: London Film-makers' Co-Op – the Second Generation', *MIRAJ*, 3(2), pp. 236–47.

McLeod, K. (2018) *The Downtown Pop Underground: New York City and the Literary Punks, Renegade Artists, DIY Filmmakers, Mad Playwrights, and Rock 'n' Roll Glitter Queens Who Revolutionized Culture*. New York: Harry N. Abram.

McNay, A. (2016) *Margaret Harrison: 'You Have to Have a Strategy to Draw People into the Work'*. Available at: https://www.studiointernational.com/index.php/ margaret-harrison-interview-accumulations-middlesbrough-institute-of-modern-art (Accessed: 15 March 2021).

McRobbie, A. and Garber, J. (2006) 'Girls and Subcultures', in Hall, S. and Jefferson, T. (eds), *Resistance Through Rituals: Youth Subculture in Post-War Britain*. London: Routledge, pp. 209–23.

Mekas, J. (1960) 'Cinema of the New Generation', *Film Culture*, 19, pp. 2–12.

Mercer, K. (ed.) (1987) *Black Film British Cinema by Institute of Contemporary Arts*. London. Available at: https://issuu.com/icalondon/docs/blackfilmbritishcinema (Accessed: 11 April 2019).

Mercer, K. (1994) *Welcome to the Jungle: New Positions in Black Cultural Studies*. New York; London: Routledge.

Mercer, K. (1999) 'Ethnicity and Internationality: New British Art and Diaspora Based Blackness', *Third Text*, 48, pp. 51–2.

Mercer, K. (2002) 'Romare Bearden: African American Modernism and Mid-Century', in Holly, M. A. and Moxey, P. F. (eds) *Art History, Aesthetics, Visual Studies*, pp. 29–46.

Meskimmon, M. (2010) *Contemporary Art and the Cosmopolitan Imagination*. London: Routledge.

Meyer, M. and Schapiro, Winter (1977–78) 'Waste Not Want Not: An Inquiry into What Women Saved and Assembled- FEMMAGE', *Heresies*, 1(4), pp. 66–9.

Meyer, S. (2016) *Political Animals: The New Feminist Cinema*. London: I.B. Tauris.

Michelson, A. (1991) '"Where Is Your Rupture?": Mass Culture and the Gesamtkunstwerk', *October*, 56, pp. 42–63.

Milletti, C. (2004) 'Violent Acts, Volatile Words: Kathy Acker's Terrorist Aesthetic', *Studies in the Novel*, 36(3), pp. 352–73.

Modleski, T. (1984) 'Time and Desire', *Women's Film Cinema*, 23(3), pp. 19–30.

Mulvey, L. (2004) 'Looking at the Past from the Present: Rethinking Feminist Film Theory of the 1970s', *Signs*, 30(1), pp. 1286–92.

Mulvey, L. (2018) 'Afterword: Some Reflections on the Engagement of Feminism with Film from the 1970s to the present day', *MIRAJ*, 7(1).

Mulvey, L. (1975) 'Visual Pleasure and Narrative Cinema', *Screen*, 16(3), pp. 6–18.

Munder, H. (2006) *It's Time for Action*. Zurich: Jrp/Ringier Migros Museum.

Nava, M. (2007) *Visceral Cosmopolitanism: Gender, Culture and the Normalisation of Difference*. London: Bloomsbury.

Nichols, B. (Summer 2001) 'Documentary Film and the Modernist Avant Garde', *Critical Enquiry*, 27(4), pp. 580–610.

Nochlin, L. (1989) 'Why Have There Been No Great Women Artists? (1971)', in *Women Art and Power and Other Essays*. Icon, pp. 145–178.

Nochlin, L. (1995) *The Body in Pieces: The Fragment as a Metaphor of Modernity*. London: Thames and Hudson.

Nogués, R. (2015) '"I Am a Man": Performing Black Masculinity in Shirley Clarke's The Cool World', *MIRAJ*, 4(1,2), pp. 136–51.

Novaczek, unpublished interview with author, 2014.

Novaczek, R. (2015) *New Vernaculars and Feminine Ecriture; Twenty-First Century Avant-Garde Film*. unpublished PhD. University of Westminster.

Novaczek, R. et al. (2015) 'Roundtable Discussion: The Women of the London Film-Maker's Co-op', *MIRAJ*, 4(1&2), pp. 164–79.

O'Brien, L. (1999) 'The Woman Punk Made Me', in Sabin, R. (ed.) *Punk Rock So What? The Cultural Legacy of Punk*. London: Routledge, pp. 186–98.

Oliver, K. (1993) 'Julia Kristeva's Feminist Revolutions', *Hypatia*, 8(3), pp. 94–114.

Osborne, P. (2013) *Anywhere or Not at All: The Philosophy of Contemporary Art*. 1st edition. London; New York: Verso Books.

Osterweil, A. (2014) *Flesh Cinema: The Corporeal Turn in American Avant-garde Film*. Illustrated Edition. Manchester: Manchester University Press.

Osterweil, A. (2016) 'Carolee Schneemann's Cinematic Worlding the Frame', in Breitwieser, S. (ed.) *Carolee Schneemann: Kinetic Painting*. Munich: Prestel, pp. 146–51.

Payne, J. (2015) *Reel Rebels: The London Film-Makers' Co-Operative 1966 to 1996*. Bloomington, IN: AuthorHouse.

Pellegrini, A. (1997) 'Whiteface Performances; "Race," Gender, and Jewish Bodies', in A Boyarin, J. and Boyarin, D. (eds) *Jews and Other Differences: The New Jewish Cultural Studies*. Minneapolis; London: University of Minnesota Press.

Perry, C. (2016) *Into the Mainstream: Independent Film and Video Counterpublics and Television in Britain, 1974–1990*. unpublished PhD. University of the Arts.

Perry, C. (2017) 'History, Landscape, Nation: British Independent Film and Video in the 1970s and 1980s', MIRAJ, 6(1 & 2), pp. 25–37.

Petro, P. (1989) *Joyless Streets: Women and Melodramatic Representation in Weimar Germany*. Princeton, NJ; Guildford: Princeton University Press.

Piper, A. (2003) 'The Triple Negation of Coloured Women Artists', in Jones, A. (ed.) *The Feminism and Visual Culture Reader*. London: Routledge, pp. 239–46.

Piper, K. (2005) 'Wait, Did I Miss Something? Some Personal Musings on the 1980s and Beyond', in Baucom, I., Bailey, D., and Boyce, S. (eds) *Shades of Black: Assembling Black Arts in 1980s Britain*. Durham, NC: Duke University Press, pp. 35–40.

Pollock, G. (1977) 'What's Wrong with "Images of Women"?', *Screen Education*, (24), pp. 25–33.

Pollock, G. (2003) *Vision and Difference: Feminism, Femininity and Histories of Art*. 3rd edition. London: Routledge.

Pollock, G. and Parker, R. (1981) *Old Mistresses: Women Art and Ideology*. London: Bloomsbury.

Poynor, R. (2016) *The Art of Punk and the Punk Aesthetic, Design Observer*. Available at: http://designobserver.com/feature/the-art-of-punk-and-the-punk-aesthetic/36708 (Accessed: 3 December 2019).

'Pragmatics and Problematics: Art and the Philosophy of Error' (2013) *Create Innovation*, 28 June. Available at: http://createinnovation.org.uk/resources/conference-papers/pragmatics-and-problematics/ (Accessed: 19 September 2020).

Raaberg, G. (1998) 'Beyond Fragmentation: Collage as Feminist Strategy in Art', *Mosaic: An Interdisciplinary Critical Journal*, 31(3), pp. 153–71.

Rabinovitz, L. (1991) *Points of Resistance: Women, Power & Politics in the New York Avant-garde Cinema, 1943–71*. Urbana, IL: University of Illinois Press.

Rachel, D. (2016) *Walls Come Tumbling Down: The Music and Politics of Rock against Racism, 2 Tone and Red Wedge 1976–1992*. London: Picador.

Rancière, J. (1991) *The Ignorant Schoolmaster; 5 Lessons in Intellectual Emancipation*. Stanford, CA: Stanford University Press.

Reekie, D. (2007) *Subversion: The Definitive History of Underground Cinema*. London: Wallflower.

Renov, M. (2004) *The Subject of Documentary*. Minneapolis, MN; London: University of Minnesota Press.

Reynolds, S. (2006) *Rip It Up and Start Again: Postpunk 1978–1984*. London: Faber & Faber.

Rhodes, J. D. (2003) 'Ahwesh, Peggy – Senses of Cinema'. Available at: https://www.sensesofcinema.com/2003/great-directors/ahwesh/ (Accessed: 31 January 2021).

Rhodes, J. D. (2014) 'From Ruin to Ritual', *Screen*, 55(4), pp. 494–9.

Rhodes, L. (2014) *Whose History?* Available at: http://archive.org/details/pdfy-317gI-cEKOkSdKYY (Accessed: 19 October 2020).

Rich, B. R. (1998) *Chick Flicks: Theories and Memories of the Feminist Film Movement*. Durham: Duke University Press.

Roberts, J. (1998) *The Art of Interruption: Realism, Photography and the Everyday*. 1st edition. Manchester; New York: Manchester University Press.

Roberts, J. (2001) 'The Practice of Failure', *Cabinet*. Available at: http://cabinetmagazine.org/issues/5/roberts.php (Accessed: 8 August 2020).

Roberts, J. (2008) 'The Amateurs Retort', in Kook-Anderson, G. and Fitzsimmons, C. (eds) *Amateurs*. San Francisco, CA: CCA Wattis Institute, pp. 15–25.

Roberts, J. (2014) *Photography and Its Violations*. New York: Columbia University Press.

Robinson, H. (ed.) (1988) *Visibly Female: Feminism and Art Today*. London; Camden: St Martins Press.

Rodowick, D. N. (1987) 'The Last Things before the Last: Kracauer and History', *New German Critique*, 41, pp. 109–39.

Rodowick, D. N. (1994) *The Crisis of Political Modernism: Criticism and Ideology in Contemporary Film Theory*. 1st paperback edition. Berkeley, CA: University of California Press.

Rombes, N. (2005) *New Punk Film*. Edinburgh: Edinburgh University Press.

Rombes, N. (2009) *A Cultural Dictionary of Punk*. New York: Continuum.

Ross, A. (1989) *No Respect: Intellectuals and Popular Culture*. New York: Routledge.

Ross, A. (2004) *No Collar: The Humane Workforce and Its Hidden Costs*. Philadelphia, PA: Temple University Press.

Rowe, D. (1995) 'Desiring Berlin: Gender and modernity in Weimar Germany', in Meskimmon, M. and West, S. (eds) *Visions of the 'Nueue Frau' Women and the Visual Arts in Weimar Germany*. Manston, England: Scolar Press, pp. 143–64.

Rubin, G. (2011) *Deviations: A Gayle Rubin Reader*. Durham: Duke University Press.

Russell, C. (1999) *Experimental Ethnography: The Work of Film in the Age of Video*. Durham, NC: Duke University Press.

Russell, C. and Lewis, J. (1998) '"Culture as Fiction: The Ethnographic Impulse in the Films of Peggy Ahwesh, Su Friedrich, and Leslie Thornton', in J. Lewis (ed.) *The New American Cinema*. Durham, NC: Duke University Press, pp. 353–78.

Russell, L. (2020) *Glitch Feminism: A Manifesto*. London: Verso.

Sabin, R. (1999) '"I won't let that dago by": Rethinking Punk and Racism', in Sabin, R. (ed.) *Punk Rock So What? The Cultural Legacy of Punk*. London: Routledge, pp. 199–218.

Savage, J. 'Jon Savage – The Secret Public' (2008) *Indie Originals: The New Hormones Story*, 11 March. Available at: https://newhormonesinfo.com/2008/03/12/jon-savage-the-secret-public/ (Accessed: 20 February 2021).

Savage, M. (2016) 'The Fall and Rise of Class Analysis in British Sociology, 1950–2016', *Tempo Social*, 28(2), p. 57.

Schlüpmann, H. and Gaines, J. (1991) 'The Subject of Survival: On Kracauer's Theory of Film', *New German Critique*, 54, pp. 111–26.

Schneider, R. (1997) *The Explicit Body in Performance*. 1st edition. London; New York: Routledge.

Schrader, P. (1972) 'Notes on Film Noir', *Film Comment*, 8(1), pp. 8–13.

Sciolino, M. (1990) 'Kathy Acker and the Postmodern Subject of Feminism', *College English*, 52(4), pp. 437–45.

Sebestyen, A. (ed.) (1988) *'68, '78, '88: From Women's Liberation to Feminism*. Bridport: Prism Press.

Seitz, W. C. (1961) *The Art of Assemblage*. New York: Museum of Modern Art.

Shaviro, S. (1993) *Cinematic Bodies*. Minneapolis; London: University of Minnesota Press, pp. 201–40.

Sherwood, Y. (ed.) (2018) *The Bible and Feminism: Remapping the Field*. Oxford, NY: Oxford University Press.

Shukaitis, S. (2010) 'Variant Issue 37 | Overidentification and/or Bust?', *Variant*. Available at: http://www.variant.org.uk/37_38texts/10Overident.html (Accessed: 10 August 2020).

Siegel, K. (2020) 'My Own Lens and Skin: Betzy Bromberg on Personal Filmmaking', *Another Gaze*, 1(4), pp. 78–89.

Sitney, P. A. (2008) *Eyes Upside Down: Visionary Film Makers and the Heritage of Emerson*. Oxford: Oxford University Press.

Skelton, P. (1985) 'Women and Art Education', *Circa*, (26), Education Supplement 3, pp. 18–21.

Smaill, B. *Cinema against the Age: Feminism and Contemporary Documentary*. Available at: http://www.screeningthepast.com/2012/08/cinema-against-the-age-feminism-and-contemporary-documentary/ (Accessed: 20 October 2020).

Smith, E. (2011) 'Are the Kids United: The Communist Party of Great Britain, Rock against Racism and the Politics of Youth Culture', *Journal for the Study of Radicalism*, 5(2), pp. 85–117.

Sollors, W. (1986) *Beyond Ethnicity: Consent and Descent in American Culture*. New York: Oxford University Press.

Sosa, A. (2018) *Conversation | Martine Syms with Laura U. Marks*. Available at: https://www.youtube.com/watch?v=IkQLbRMAFoY&t=3097s (Accessed: 29 March 2021).

Spicer, F. G. (2009) *'Just What Was It That Made U.S. Art So Different, So Appealing?': Case Studies of the Critical Reception of American Avant-garde Painting in London, 1950–1964*. Ph.D. Case Western Reserve University. Available at: http://search. proquest.com/docview/304861559/abstract/C23FE199C148457DPQ/1 (Accessed: 31 December 2019).

Spout and Spout (2009) 'Porn and Being Poor, Then & Now: Bette Gordon Interview, Tribeca 2009', *IndieWire*, 29 April. Available at: https://www.indiewire. com/2009/04/porn-and-being-poor-then-now-bette-gordon-interview-tribeca-2009-227276/ (Accessed: 18 August 2020).

Sterling, L. and Bovier, L. (2006) *Linder: Works, 1976–2006*. Zurich: Jrp/Ringier.

Sterrit, D. (2015) 'In the Movie-Viewing Machine: Essential Cinema and the 1970s', in Hawkins, J. (ed.) *Downtown Film and TV Culture 1975–2001*. Bristol: Intellect, pp. 5–12.

Steyerl, H. (2012) *The Wretched of the Screen*. Berlin: Sternberg Press.

Steyn, J. (2000) *The Jew: Assumptions of Identity*. London: Routledge.

Sterling, Linder (2015) *Linder*. London: Ridinghouse.

Sterling, Linder: *Works 1976–2006 – Les presses du réel* (2006). Available at: https:// www. lespressesdureel.com/EN/ouvrage.php?id=781 (Accessed: 20 February 2021).

Stratton, J. (2000) *Coming Out Jewish*. London: Cassell.

Stratton, J. (2008) *Jewish Identity in Western Pop Culture: The Holocaust and Trauma through Modernity*. Basingstoke: Palgrave Macmillan.

Styrene, P. (2005) *Poly Styrene: Plastic Fantastic, Dazed*. Available at: https://www. dazeddigital.com/music/article/24454/1/poly-styrene-plastic-fantastic (Accessed: 31 August 2020).

Supanick, J. (Dec 2011–Jan 2012) *The Brooklyn Rail*. Available at: https://brooklynrail. org/2011/12/film/is-this-what-you-were-born-for.

Syms, M. (2011) *Implications and Distinctions: Format, Content and Context in Contemporary Race Film*. Future Plan and Program.

Syms, M. *Borrowed Lady – SFU Galleries – Simon Fraser University* (2016). Available at: https://www.sfu.ca/galleries/audain-gallery/past1/Martine-Syms.html (Accessed: 23 August 2020).

Syms, M. *Fact & Trouble* (2017). Available at: https://archive.ica.art/whats-on/ martine-syms-fact-trouble (Accessed: 23 August 2020).

Syms, M with Marks, L.U. (2018). San Francisco University Gallery. Available at: https://www.youtube.com/watch?v=IkQLbRMAFoY (Accessed: 17 August 2020).

Taubin, A. (2011) *Look Both Ways: Amy Taubin on Bette Gordom*. Available at: https://www.artforum.com/film/amy-taubin-on-bette-gordon-27984 (Accessed: 20 October 2020).

Taylor, B. (2004) *Collage: The Making of Modern Art*. London: Thames and Hudson.

Taylor, G. (1999) *Artists in the Audience: Cults, Camp and American Film Criticism*. Princeton, NJ: Princeton University Press.

Teitelbaum, M. (ed.) (1992) *Montage and Modern Life 1919–1942*. Cambridge, MA; London: MIT Press; Boston: Institute of Contemporary Art.

The Slits – In Conclusion. Available at: https://www.punk77.co.uk/groups/ slitstessapolittinterview.htm (Accessed: 1 March 2020).

Thornham, S. (ed.) (1999) *Feminist Film Theory: A Reader*. Edinburgh: Edinburgh University Press.

Throp, M. and Walsh, M. (eds) (2015) *Twenty Years of Make Magazine*. London: I.B. Tauris.

Tippins, S. (2014) *Inside the Dream Palace: The Life and Times of New York's Legendary Chelsea Hotel*. London: Simon & Schuster.

Turim, M. (2005) 'Germaine Dulac, Maya Deren, Yvonne Rainer, and Marina Abramovic: The Violence of Desire in the Avant Garde', in Petrolle, J. and Wright Wexman, V. (eds) *Women and Experimental Film Making*. Urbana and Chicago: Unviersity of Illinois, pp. 71–90.

Turim, M. (2007) 'Sounds, Intervals, and Startling Images in the Films of Abigail Child', in Blaetz, R. (ed.) *Women's Experimental Cinema Critical Frameworks*. Durham: Duke University Press, pp. 263–89.

Turner, V. (2002) 'The Factors Affecting Women's Success in Museum Careers: A Discussion of the Reasons More Women Do Not Reach the Top, and of Strategies to Promote Their Future Success', *Journal of Conservation and Museum Studies*, 8, pp. 6–10. DOI: http://doi.org/10.5334/jcms.8022.

Tyler, P. (1995) *Underground Film: A Critical History*. Boston, MA: Da Capo Press.

Vries, P. (2012) 'Why the West Rules – For Now: The Patterns of History and What They Reveal about the Future', *Journal of Global History*, 7(1), pp. 143–7.

Watney, S. (1982) 'Making Strange: The Shattered Mirror', in Burgin, V. (ed.), *Thinking Photography*. London: Macmillan, pp. 154–76.

Webber, M. (ed.) *Shoot Shoot Shoot: The First Decade of the London Film Makers' Co-Operative 1966–76*. London: LUX.

Wees, W. (2001) 'Carrying On, Leslie Thornton, Su Friedrich, Abigail Child and American Avant Garde of the 1980s', *Revue Canadienne*, 10(1), pp. 70–92.

Wees, W. (2005) 'Leslie Thornton, Su Friedrich and Abigail Child: No More Giants', in Petrolle, J. and Wexman, V. (eds) *Women and Experimental Film Making*. Urbana; Chicago: University of Illinois Press, pp. 22–44.

Wheeler, W. D. (1995) 'The Practice of Theory, the Theory of Practice: The Postcolonial Cinema of Maureen Blackwood and the Sankofa Collective', *New Film Theory, Film Criticism*, 20(1/2), pp. 131–43.

Whitman, L. (1981) 'Women and Popular Music', Spare Rib, June, pp. 6–9.

Whyman, T. (2019) 'The Ghosts of Our Lives', *The New Statesman*, 31 July. Available at: https://www.newstatesman.com/politics/uk/2019/07/ghosts-our-lives (Accessed: 19 October 2020).

Williams, L. (2004) 'Why I Did Not Want to Write This Essay', *Signs*, 30(1), pp. 1264–72.

Williams, R. (1961) *The Long Revolution*. Harmondsworth: Penguin Books.

Wilson, S. (2015) *Art Labor, Sex Politics*. Minneapolis: University of Minnesota Press.

Wittig, M. (1980) 'The Straight Mind', *Feminist Issues*, 1(1), pp. 103–11.

Wittig, M. (1991) *'The Straight Mind' and Other Essays*. Boston: Beacon Press.

Wittig, M. (2007) *Les Guérillères*. Champagne, IL: University of Illinois Press.

Wizisla, E. (2016) *Benjamin and Brecht: Story of a Friendship*. London: Verso Books.

Wollen, P. (1993) 'The Last New Wave: Modernism in the British Films of the Thatcher Era', in Friedman, L. (ed.) *British Cinema and Thatcherism*. Minneapolis, MN: University of Minnesota Press.

Women in Punk (2008). Available at: https://www.youtube.com/watch?v=NznmF9cyFpw (Accessed: 3 October 2020).

'Women Working in the Arts' (1992). Arts Council England.

Worley, M. (2013) 'Oi! Oi! Oi!: Class Locality and British Punk', *Twentieth Century British History*, 24(4), pp. 606–36.

Worley, M. and Copsey, N. (2016) 'The Far Right, Punk and British Youth Culture 1977–87', *JOMEC Journal*, (9), pp. 27–47.

Zupančič, A. (2008) *The Odd One In: On Comedy*. Cambridge, MA: MIT Press.

Index